THE SACRED COVENANT
OF DIVINE COMMUNION

A Guide To Trans-Cultural Spirituality and
The Practice of Loving Touch Therapy™

SRI AKHENATON

THE PORTAL PRESS®
Columbia, Maryland

First Printing
Library of Congress Catalog Card Number 96-72257
International Standard Book Number 0-9621839-8-9

To the aspirant,
the earnest seeker of Divine Truth,
and to the discovery of The Light
of The Living God Spirit
alive in the heart of man –

Sri Akhenaton

CONTENTS

Loving Touch

INTRODUCTION

In the conscious journey of Soul Evolution, each soul incarnate seeker of Spiritual Truth learns to transcend the obstacles to Spiritual Unfoldment by accepting responsibility for all aspects of personal self, and implementing The Divine Precepts of Universal Conscience. Additionally, each earnest seeker chooses to commit self, with the Conviction, Faith and Love of The Living God Spirit, to the task of addressing The Greater Good of All by conscionably serving the needs of Creation.

Many times, it might appear to others as though earnest seekers of Truth are beset by unusual hardships, austere disciplines and harsh realities that require dedication and personal sacrifice beyond that which would be deemed acceptable or possible for personal engagement by on-lookers. But the conditions and situations that require steadfast Conviction and unwavering Faith are viewed by the seeker as simply opportunities to further strengthen Faith and Conviction, instead of hardships designed to destroy the possibility of accessing Enlightened Consciousness.

As the earnest seeker of Spiritual Truth becomes more aware and more willing to Selflessly participate in the journey toward Enlightenment, so does the seeker realize that transforming the nature and importance of personal self, through Acknowledgement, Forgiveness, Blessing and Release, facilitates the opening of The Way - The opening of The Portal of Understanding for The Realization of God, of Self. It is then that true acts of service that attend the needs of Creation can begin through the seeker's evolved, Heart-centered Being, which is that aspect of Self which lives as One within The Heart of God.

Similarly, engaging in the practice of Loving Touch Therapy™ is not an endeavor in which the practitioner performs simple, superficial tasks. Rather, it is that practitioners of Loving Touch Therapy™ are called upon to make solemn commitments on both a conscious and an intuitive level to function as living tools for the transmission of Divine Light Energy. Further, as a result of committing self to serving mankind and the whole of Creation in The Light of The One Infinite Creator, Loving Touch Therapy™ practitioners find that their lives become guided and are impacted by the Spiritual implications inherent to attending the physical, mental, emotional and Spiritual needs of their clients. What this means is that when a child of God makes the conscious choice to serve Creation in such intimate, dynamic ways, it is soon to follow that the practitioner learns through graphic representations that he/she has come to enjoy closer communion with The Living God Spirit, as the very Presence of God lives in The Divine Energies of Love transmitted through touch and the resonance of the spoken word.

You see, it is for each practitioner of Loving Touch Therapy™, as well as each earnest seeker of Enlightenment, to integrate those aspects of consciousness that are known to be "good and right" through the functioning of an open, evolved Heart Chakra with those aspects of The Living God Spirit engaged and transmitted in Loving Touch Therapy™ sessions. It is equally as important that aspects of The Living God Spirit identified in daily activities and engagements with both mankind and with each of the other Kingdoms of Creation are integrated with elements of Knowingness deemed to be "good and right" throughout Universal Existence.

It is for each child of God to learn to embrace and apply the precepts of The Wisdom of One in conscionable, efficient ways that benevolently facilitate the unfoldment of each soul incarnate's journey of Conscious Existence with whom contact or communion is shared. Therefore, it is essential to learn how best to prepare self to render service to all things born of Creation with The Lightminded Ideals that are the mandates of Universal Law.

SHALOM

DEFINITIONS:
Language Of The Seeker

CHAPTER 1

In the journey of Spiritual Unfoldment, aspirants or seekers of Spiritual Truth encounter a myriad of terms and phrases that might well be seen as alien to mainstream western thought. Nonetheless, in order to understand the nature of the journey and to become a conscionable servant to the needs of Creation, each seeker will have need to fully comprehend the terms used to identify and describe the various aspects, conditions and dynamics of Spiritual Unfoldment. Even though many Spiritual/Metaphysical/New Age terms presently enjoy limited use and acceptance as idiomatic expressions or "buzz words" in trendy conversations, let us examine the deeper meanings of many terms that are vital for sound comprehension of the Spiritual Journey toward The Realization of God, of Self.

Let us begin by briefly defining terms that identify, describe and/or qualify the presence, nature and condition of God:

Allah is the name used in Islamic Tradition to identify The Supreme, Universal Being through Whom all Creation was conceived.

Angelic Presence or an **Angel** is a Disincarnate Soul Consciousness State of Third or Fourth Density Evolution that serves as a mes-

(Note: In most instances, terms beginning with a capital letter appear in this chapter in bold letters with a definition.)

15

senger of Divine Truth or as a guide to assist in the Conscious Evolution of mortal man. **Archangelic Presence** is the definitive energy state that represents a specific aspect of The Living God Spirit, and can be invoked to facilitate or to provide guidance in the execution of Earthly tasks. Archangelic Presence is the purest, most dynamic, most evolved vibration within the Angelic Order. Even though Archangelic Presence can be invoked by name, these are not personified energy states that are represented in human form. Contrary to religious myths, legends and some contemporary beliefs, Archangels are not seen as winged, benevolent beings. Rather, the presence of Archangelic Energy is seen in various color bands within the spectrum of Divine Light Vibration, and can be felt as warm, pulsating or tingling sensations that enrapture mortal consciousness. Communication with Archangelic Presence is intuitive, nonverbal or telepathic in nature.

Archangelic Presence, color designation, function and direction for Invocation are as follows: **Archangel Michael** - purple - The All-Knowing Presence of God that has dominion over all natures and states of discordant energies - invoked from the East; **Archangel Gabriel** - golden yellow - The Strength and Conviction of God - invoked from the West; **Archangel Raphael** - green - The Medicine of God that can facilitate physical, emotional, mental and spiritual well-being - invoked from the North; **Archangel Uriel** - lapis blue - The Light of God that illuminates The Path of Truth with The Wisdom Of One (The Wisdom of The Sage) - invoked from the South; **Archangel Barachiel** - white - The Blessing of God - invoked from Above; **Archangel Jehudial** - white - The Praise of God - invoked from below; **Archangel Salatiel** - white - The Prayer of God - invoked from Within.

Divine Light Vibrations are energies born of and directed by God-Realized Consciousness to affect The Greater Good of All Creation.

The **Hindu Pantheon** consists of: **Brahman** - The Supreme, Absolute, Eternal Soul of The Universe; **Vishnu** - The Preserver, whose incarnate forms were known as Rama and Krishna; **Shiva** - (Nataraj) The Lord in His form as the cosmic dancer - the destroyer of ignorance - the power of reproduction and restoration.

In the Mystical Tradition of the Hebrew Kabbalah, **Kether** is defined as The Infinite, Unknowable, Universal Supreme God-Head that is beyond the capability of mortal consciousness to comprehend. It is Kether that is perceived as The Source of All Universal Creation.

The Council of Twelve is The Etheric Group of Evolved Social Memory Complexes charged with the responsibility of overseeing the galactic plan for the Earth Colony. These are They who once sent representatives to Earth that were known as "The Oversouls" during the Lemurian and early Atlantean eras. As fully evolved, collective energy matrices, each member of The Council of Twelve has a unique, signature Resonance Rate, but all members of The Council chose to vibrate, communicate and exist at the same Divine Resonance to provide a stable, identifiable, harmonious presence of Divine Light Vibration. The Yahweh Entity is one member of The Council of Twelve, who define, represent and promulgate The Conscience and The Wisdom of One.

The Infinite Body of God is The Transcendent, Collective Phase of Consciousness and The Divine Condition of Being that allows for the greater expression of Self within the omnipresent dynamics of The Living God Spirit. This is the energy system and plane of awareness accessed through the realization of Absolute Truth in God-Conscious Being.

The Infinite One is The Absolute, Universal Source of All Creation. It is through The Divine Intelligence and Grace of The Infinite One (or **The One Infinite Creator**) that each and every element of Creation finds material and/or conscious realization.

The Legion of Light is The Etheric Group of Fourth, Fifth and Sixth Density Ascended Soul Initiates who acknowledge allegiance to The Yahweh Entity and The Council of Twelve. Familiar names such as Jesus, Buddha, Krishna, Mohammed, Enoch and Melchizedek are among the conscious energy states that exist as One within The Legion of Light.

The Living God Spirit is the pervasive, omnipresent energy of Creation, Life and Consciousness. The Living God Spirit can be represented as Angelic, Archangelic and other forms of "Spirit Presence" that can serve as guides, messengers or teachers of mortal man, and through which mankind can learn to access The Infinite Body of God.

The Yahweh Entity is the Creator of modern man that evolved to Realized Consciousness on what is called "The Dark Star" or Sirius "B." A fully Evolved, Seventh Density, Social Memory Complex, The Yahweh Entity came to Earth over 200,000 years ago to seed the consciousness of early man with the precepts of The Wisdom of One, so that mortal man could learn to comprehend and make unilateral application of Universal Law. Through telepathic reinforcement and selective breeding between homo sapiens sapiens and the incarnate form of The Yahweh Entity, modern man, homo sapiens, was subsequently created to embody the ideals of Universal Law, The Wisdom of One and to conscionably attend the other Kingdoms upon Mother Earth.

Wankan Tanka is the name given to the pervasive, Universal Spirit of God, The Great Spirit, The Universal Father, by The Lakota Nation of North America.

Next, let us examine some of the terms that describe aspects of states of consciousness and behaviors that lead to or are the result of Conscious Unfoldment:

An **Adept** is one who is fully versed in the teachings, practices and philosophies of a specific Spiritual Tradition.

An **Ascetic** is a seeker of Spiritual Truth who has forsaken the comforts of the material world. Typically, an Ascetic is a wonder-er, who through the experience of life and the acceptance of pover-ty deduces the meaning of incarnate purpose, the reality of God and the union of God and Man.

Bodhisattvas are evolved mortal beings who upon reaching the threshold of Nirvana chose to forego entry into this final state of Conscious Existence due to heightened senses of Compassion for the masses that remain locked in the Illusions of egocentric design. Instead of becoming fully Illuminated as The Buddha, Bodhisattvas remain in the realm of Third Dimension to assist in the Salvation and Illumination of mortal man. No longer bound by the physical limitations of mortal life, Bodhisattvas exist in an interdimensional realm through which he or she is able to offer guidance and/or Illuminate others with The Divine Perceptions of God-Conscious Evolution.

The **Brahmins** are the priest caste of India, identified as "The Knowers of God."

A **Conduit** is either a Soul Incarnate or a Soul Initiate who experiences a constant, conscious mind-link with an Etheric Being or with the aggregate energy consciousness of a group of Etheric Beings or with a Social Memory Complex.

Conscionable Behaviors are acts or patterns of behavior designed to translate Divine Truth and/or Divine Guidance into Third Dimension realities, conditions or processes of being that facilitate The Greater Good of All Creation.

Enlightenment is the ongoing process of Spiritual Unfoldment that leads the seeker of Spiritual Truth toward the assimilation of The Wisdom of One.

God-Realization is the evolved, Transcendent State or condition of being enjoyed by The Fully Sealed Initiate of The Light of One that embraces the continuum of Universal Existence through the Heart-centered expansion of Divine Love. God-Realization, in and of itself, is not the completion of a phase of evolution. Rather, God-Realization signals the beginning of the true application of Self to rendering conscionable service to the needs of Creation - needs that can only be perceived and met through Selfless expressions of Divine Love. God-Realization or **God-Realized consciousness** is clearly evidenced in acts of altruism designed to affect The Greater Good of All Creation, and the expressions of Self found in acts of service that reflect the engagement, comprehension and release of Self from the Illusions of Maya.

The **God-Self** is that aspect of mortal consciousness through which Intuitive Wisdom emerges to direct Conscionable Behavior.

It is the God-Self that houses the "Knowingness" of Intuitive Wisdom and Divine Truth, as it is the God-Self that is the refined, evolved essence of the Soul.

Heart-centered Consciousness or Behavior is the application of Patience, Compassion, Wisdom, Mercy, Serenity and Love in The Light of One to all things born of Creation. It is through Heart-centered Behavior that precepts of Divine Truth are given life within the plane of Third Dimension to nurture the Conscious Evolution of mankind.

Intuitive Wisdom is the inherent state or condition of "Knowingness" that is born of past incarnate association or experience.

Light-minded Behaviors are activities or patterns of behavior that are structured to attain and maintain Heart-centered Consciousness. By making conscious choices to release self from the importance of self and by identifying counterproductive behavior patterns that sustain egocentric attitudes, mortal consciousness willingly participates in the evolution of self toward Enlightened Consciousness and God-Realized Being.

A **Mystic** is a Soul Initiate who through past incarnate experience is Intuitively aware of and actively practices the principles of Ancient Spiritual Traditions.

A **Prophet** is a visionary messenger of Divine Truth.

The **Rishis** were the ancient Sages, Mystics and Seers who established the foundations of Religious and Spiritual Traditions of India.

A **Sadguru** is a Realized Soul and an Illuminated Teacher of Hindu Philosophy who leads aspirants toward Enlightened Consciousness, and is thought to be an "Anointed Guide" to the realization of Divine Truth.

A **Saint** is a practitioner of The Way of Selflessness, and is a Fully Sealed Soul Initiate who serves the needs of Creation with the deepest sense of Divine Commitment and Loving Kindness.

Selflessness is the Universal, unilateral application of Love and Compassion to all things born of Creation.

A **Soul Incarnate** is the physical entity of mortal man who exists in Third Dimension reality primarily through states of Ego-consciousness.

A **Soul Initiate** is an Evolved Soul Incarnate Being who understands and chooses to implement the designs of The Wisdom of One and Universal Law upon the Earth Plane.

Spiritual Attunement is the process of accessing the source of Divine Light Energy within mortal consciousness that is the "Soul-Link" to The Infinite Body of God.

Transcendence is the process and/or condition of being that facilitates evolved perceptions of reality by dispelling the Illusions of Duality and allowing the acceptance of Third Dimension existence as a continuum of learning experiences designed ultimately to affect The Greater Good. Through Transcendence, mankind learns that life is not a system of opposites or polar extremes; rather, that life on Earth, as well as Universal Existence, is a continuum of beginnings - not beginnings and endings or life and death - but birth and rebirth beyond the parameters of time.

Transcendence is a process of Ascension that frees mortal consciousness from the restrictions of Ego and self-serving design, thereby facilitating man's active bonding with The Infinite Body of God. Stages of Transcendence: Acknowledgement/Acceptance, Forgiveness, Blessing, Release.

Transformation is the process of birthing and rebirthing through life experience and through the release of Ego-consciousness that allows man to understand the changes in attitude and the subsequent changes in behavior that take place in various phases of Conscious Evolution.

Now, let us briefly examine a variety of additional terms and concepts that are central to the comprehension of Spiritual Unfoldment:

Absolute Truths are principles of Universal Law and Divine Will that hold true in application throughout the realm of Universal Existence.

Acknowledgement is the identification of the nature and dynamics of an event, condition, energy state or element of consciousness, without reactionary attitudes or emotions coloring the perception of the experience. Since there are no compelling motives, energies of fear, resentment, uncertainty, hostility or mistrust in operation, Acknowledgement leads to the **Acceptance** of Truth and the **Allowance** of all things to simply be.

Agnosticism is the doctrine that the concept of God is unknown and unknowable, thereby neither denying, nor affirming the existence of God. **Atheism**, on the other hand, is the committed belief that there is no God.

The **Akasha** is the elemental, sub-atomic material from which all physical reality is fashioned. It is said that the entirety of Universal Creation is the result of The Divine Creative Process issued by The Universal God-Head or The One Infinite Creator by directing the Akasha through the illusions of time and space into materialized form. Through states of Divine Illumination and through the higher levels of Meditation, some Soul Incarnates are able to access the living Akashic Memory of all thoughts, events and phenomena that have ever been conceived throughout the span of Galactic Existence.

Altered States of Consciousness are spontaneous episodes of interdimensional and intradimensional experience that reveal the implication and/or confirm the existence of realities outside of and beyond the experience of Third Dimension, while **Expanded States of Consciousness*** are purposefully induced episodes of interdimensional and intradimensional experience that illuminate and validate the existence of realities outside of and beyond the experience of Third Dimension. Altered States of Consciousness occur as a result of external stimuli or through outside intervention that man is not party to, but Expanded States of Consciousness occur as a direct result of man's conscious, willing intent to induce "other-worldly" or higher consciousness experiences through the use of sound, color, light, electro-magnetic devices, geomagnetic locations, Meditation and Prayer or specially designed, optical illustrations.

Atlantis was the populated continent that existed in the Atlantic Ocean between North America, South America and Africa. Famed for its abundance and splendor, Atlantis existed until about

*See **CRYSTAL COMMUNION: LOVELIGHT MEDITATIONS** by Sri Akhenaton, pages 38-71 for "Symbols and States of Expanded Consciousness."

15,000 years ago, and was the site upon which the first "Garden of Eden" stories were based. As the result of volcanic, seismic and devastating tidal wave activities, Atlantis was reclaimed by the ocean. The Islands of the Caribbean Ocean are all that remain of the land mass of this once magnificent parent culture.

Ayurveda is the body of Hindu Medical Treatises that outlines the use of botanicals in the treatment of physical, emotional, mental and Spiritual disease, drug therapy, surgical procedures such as Caesarean Sections and brain operations and techniques for combating the effects of poison gas.

Buddhism, established in the 6th Century B.C. by Guatama Siddartha, teaches that "right living," "right thinking" and "self-denial" will enable the Soul to reach Nirvana, a Divine State of Release from bodily pain and Third Dimension desires, compulsions and sorrows.

Chakras are energy centers through which the flow of vital life energy is regulated for the physical systems of the body. **Chakra Scanning** is the technique used to determine the nature of Chakra Orientation and the quality of vital life energy flowing through a given Chakra.

Channeling is the act or process of Intuitively, consciously and/or etherically accessing information outside of or beyond one's conscious awareness for use in problem-solving or for guidance in negotiating mortal life. The three forms of channeling are: **Conscious Channeling** - episodes in which one hears and repeats dialogue or information that is transmitted from a source outside of one's conscious awareness. **Intuitive Channeling** - episodes in which one hears and can repeat information accessed from one's own memory of past incarnate experience. **Trance Channeling** -

induced episodes in which one chooses to "vacate" his/her physical body to allow an outside entity consciousness to use one's body as a tool for verbal transmission in Third Dimension.

Chi (pronounced Chee) is a Chinese term for the life-force that is defined as a cohesive, bonding agent, which in its most elemental state forms the very fabric of the Universe.

Chiropractic is a method of treating disease that employs the manual manipulation of bodily joints, especially those of the spinal column.

Choice of Free Will is a Divine Precept that prescribes non-intervention upon the Karmic Destiny of any conscious being. Choice of Free Will stipulates that each Conscious Light/Life Energy State has the undeniable right to select those life-sequences that best fulfill Karmic Destiny, and that under no circumstances is it ever conscionable for one conscious being to manipulate, coerce or influence the Free Will of Choice of another conscious being.

Clairvoyance is the ability to perceive information that is beyond or unavailable to conventional modes of perception.

Co-Creation is the act or process of conscionably translating elements of Divine Truth and/or Divine Guidance into practical, Third Dimension realities that are designed to impact upon The Greater Good of All Creation. The act of Co-Creation is engaged by Soul Initiates through contact with and Illumination from Evolved, Etheric Consciousness States to help raise awareness of the many possible applications of Universal Law Dynamics and Ideals of Divine Will upon the Earth Mother.

Compassion is The Evolved, Etheric Precept of Divine Conscience that prescribes the rendering of Heart-centered Communion that facilitates another Soul Incarnate's journey through The Lessons of Existence.

Confucianism is the 6th Century B.C. Chinese Doctrine in which the directive of social morality was applied to the arts and to the activities of city/state government. Confucianism was chiefly concerned with the ethical and moral problems and issues that arose from man's relationships with his/her brethren. In the view of the Confucians, service to God was meaningless if service to man was neglected.

In Hindu philosophy, **Dharma** is the recognized system of socially viable thoughts and acceptable behaviors.

Dharshan is a time of public veneration during which the Sages, Gurus and Spiritual Leaders of India display The Radiant Presence of The Light of God alive in the heart of man.

Divination is an act of manifestation designed to foretell or explain future events, behaviors or life-conditions. Tools of Divination include Tarot Cards, Rune Stones, Ouija Boards, Crystal Balls, Animal Bones, Colored Stones, Sacred Sand and Bird Feathers to name a few.

The **Ego-self** is that aspect of mortal consciousness that is designed to maintain drives and states of survival, control of reality, pleasure and self-interest, and works diligently to suppress and otherwise thwart the evolution of the God-Self.

Ego Transformation is the process and the spontaneous acceptance of change in the nature, dynamics and function of Ego-consciousness, thereby facilitating the emergence of the God-Self.

Empowerment is the attempt to manifest or exercise the Illusion of control over elements of Conscious Existence that pose problematic situations to the function of Ego-self.

Esotericism is the practice of teaching secret Spiritual Doctrines only to the initiated few, as specific doctrines and information are not intended for the general body of disciples of a given Spiritual Tradition.

The **Essenes** were a Jewish Brotherhood of Ascetics and Mystics who lived in the desert of the Middle East from about 200 B.C. to about 200 A.D. These were They who lived by strict vows of abstinence and devotion, and were the Teachers of Jesus of Nazareth.

The **Etheric System** is the body of knowledge and Wisdom that comprises Spiritual Truth, while the **Phenomenal System** is the continuum of physical experience, and the **Auric System** comprises the planes of energy states by which and through which perceptions of reality occur.

Evocation is an act or process of manifestation that is a calling forth or a summoning of Spiritual Energies in ritual incantations for self-serving reasons and/or to satisfy ritual intent.

Existentialism is a philosophic approach to mortal life that teaches that mortal man exists as individual incarnate beings in a Universe without direction or purpose, and that man must resist and oppose his/her non-nurturing, hostile environment through the exercise and execution of Choice of Free Will.

Gnosticism is a system of Religious, Mystical and Philosophical Doctrines based in Christian, Greek and Eastern Traditions.

Gnostics were thought to have been keepers of "Higher Wisdom" with extensive knowledge of the mysteries of life and Spiritual Truth.

Harvest is the period at the end of each Karmic Cycle (approximately every 65,000 years) when the Evolved Soul Vibrations of mortal man are etherically prepared to pass from Third Density, Material Consciousness to Fourth Density, Heart-centered or Christ Consciousness.

Healing Facilitation is the act or process of assisting a Soul Incarnate in the release of counterproductive, debilitating energy states, and the realigning of both physical and auric energy matrices through the application and infusion of Divine Light Energy.

Hinduism, formally established over 3,000 years ago, is the religious and social system of India based upon Vedic Scripture that strives to bring every action of man into Harmony with Divine Law.

Homeopathy is the theory and system of curing disease through the use of very minute doses of medicine that in a healthy person and in larger doses would produce a condition similar to the condition being treated. In contrast, **Allopathy** is the method of medical practice that seeks to cure disease by the production of conditions in the body that are either different from or opposite to the conditions produced by the disease being treated.

Homeostatis is the dynamic state of balance or equilibrium that is sought by elements of a system.

Illumination or Cosmic Illumination are instances of Etheric Transmissions that may last a few seconds, minutes, hours or days, during which a Soul Initiate, seemingly suspended in time and space, telepathically receives information about the nature, dynamics, function and operation of Divine Order and Universal Existence.

Illusion is the product of conscious thought projection or wishful thinking, while **Delusion** is the state or condition one experiences when one chooses to believe elements of consciousness not in existence, instead of accepting reality in the manner of its true experience. The Ego employs a variety of devices to create Illusions of self that are deemed necessary for the establishment, maintenance and protection of self. The egocentric devices or **Defense Mechanisms** most often encountered are: **Rationalization** - a cognitive process of devising acceptable reasons or excuses to justify short-comings of dysfunctional behavior; **Repression** - the process of pushing undesirable ideas, impulses, acknowledgements, behaviors, life-conditions or images from the conscious mind into the realm of unconscious reality. Repressed energies most often find expression in physical reality through inappropriate, unconscious behaviors that arise at the most unexpected moments; **Suppression** - the conscious exclusion of undesirable behaviors, impressions or life-conditions from conscious acceptance in one's pattern of incarnate existence that can lead to withdrawal and detachment from aspects of physical reality. Frequently motivated by issues of fear, performance and self-worth, Suppression can stimulate severe emotional dysfunctions; **Intellectualization** - the process by which behaviors are identified by rational, pseudo-intellectual means, but in truth are indeed something else entirely. Through Intellectualization, reasons for short-comings and dysfunctional behaviors sound authoritative and based in scholastic merit, but indeed are unfounded and predicated upon bits and pieces of gathered information; **Sublimation** - the attempt to discharge undesirable urges or energies by focusing upon and redirecting energies toward socially acceptable activities, without ever addressing the nature of or motivation for undesirable urge.

Invocation is the act or process of calling upon Divine Presence and/or The Divine Light Energy of The Living God Spirit to assist man in acts or practices of Spirituality.

Islam is the monotheistic Moslem Religion founded by Mohammed in the 6th Century A.D. that prescribes submission and obedience to The Will of God.

Janism, founded about 500 B.C., is the doctrine of a Hindu Sect that adheres to the basic tenets that there are no absolutes, all activities are to be efficient, all behaviors are to be non-violent and the ultimate state of "passionlessness."

Judgement is an activity of the Ego-self that attempts to categorize thoughts, behaviors, experiences and life-conditions, which leads to **Reactions** or **Reactionary Behavior** that are acts and feelings directed by compelling thoughts or behaviors of emotion.

The **Kabbalah** is the ancient Hebrew system of Divination based upon mystical interpretations of the Scriptures.

Karma is The Law of Cause and Effect, action and reaction, as applied to the reincarnate journeys of Soul Evolution. It is The Law of Karma that dictates the lessons and life-sequences that each incarnate soul will engage in each life-cycle. The repetitive cycles of life-sequences are designed to assist mortal consciousness in resolving egocentric thoughts and behaviors so that mankind can ultimately fulfill the destiny of becoming true children of God.

Karmic Debt is the inevitable result of engaging in behaviors that one knows to be counterproductive, dysfunctional, self-serving, malevolent or destructive. When a Soul Incarnate makes the conscious choice to participate in behaviors that reflect a willful disregard for The Greater Good, then at some point during the reincarnate journey of the Soul, the Soul Incarnate will engage life-experiences designed to not only illustrate the same counterproductive attitudes and behaviors, but to offer the Soul Incarnate the opportunity to resolve the behaviors in question.

Karmic Resolution is the process of identifying and breaking the patterns of bias and conditioning that stimulate and perpetuate discordant, counterproductive behaviors. Through Karmic Resolution mankind also finds Conviction and Faith in the process of Spiritual Unfoldment.

A **Kindred Spirit** is a Soul Incarnate Being who exhibits similar patterns of knowledge and life-experience to one's own, and with whom one can identify concurrent and/or similar reincarnate journeys. Additionally, domesticated animals may well hold Karmic Ties with man and can also be called Kindred Spirits.

The **Koran** is The High Holy Text of the Moslems that contains the revelations received by Mohammed from Allah.

Kundalini is the primal energy force described in Hindu Tradition that when awakened allows mortal man to experience his/her cosmic connection to all things born of Creation. Kundalini typically lies dormant at the Base Chakra, but when activated comes to life as a swirling energy force that rises from the Base Chakra, penetrating and opening each Chakra en route to and including the Crown Chakra. Kundalini rising up the Chakra Cord and literally exploding through the Crown Chakra can be one of the most dynamic and euphoric moments that seekers of Higher Consciousness may experience.

Lemuria was the populated continent, also known as Mu, that existed in the Pacific Ocean between North America and Asia, and flourished until about 100,000 years ago when seismic activity reclaimed its major land mass, submerging Lemuria beneath the ocean. What remains of the continent Lemuria are Polynesian Islands of the Pacific.

Levels (Dimensions or Densities) of Consciousness are the states of Conscious Evolution through which Illusions and Realities are perceived, thoughts conceived and behaviors enacted.

Linear Thought is the logical, analytical, empirical, left-brain process of conscious thought patterns.

Love is The Evolved, Etheric Precept of Divine Conscience that prescribes the altruistic giving of Self in service to the needs of Creation. Love does not place limits on the kind, quality or amount of Selfless giving that may be required by various elements of Creation to affect conscionable, necessary resolutions. To the contrary, as it is Love that is the simplest, purest, most unfettered expression of Evolved Self in acts that render service to the needs of all things born of Creation, without expectation, desire for or interest in personal well-being.

Mana is the term used by the Melanesian Peoples of the Pacific to define and describe the Life-Force Energy that pervades matter.

Manifestation is the act or the attempt to influence or alter the natural order of existence for personal interests or the Illusion of well-being, and is a process that always leads to Karmic Debt.

Mantras are sacred syllables and/or words used particularly in Hindu and Eastern worship that invoke changes in energy, consciousness and being. Mantras are also used in Buddhism, African Spiritualism and other traditions that employ "Ritual Chanting."

Maya is the Cosmic Illusion of Duality that mortal man is charged to transcend in the journey toward God-Realization.

Meditation is the act or process of stilling or clearing the conscious mind of active, Linear Thought process to allow and foster communion with the internal Peace and guidance of the Intuitive Wisdom of the Soul. It is through Meditation that mortal man comes to know that The Voice of God speaks in the quietude of man's Intuitive, Heart-centered Soul.

Mercy is The Evolved, Etheric Precept of Divine Conscience that prescribes the implementation of Patience, Compassion and Wisdom in the rendering of comfort and support to all things born of Creation in times of confusion, anxiety, conflict and pain.

Nirvana is the state of total and final absorption in Divinity as described in Hindu Tradition.

Out of Body Experience can be either an Altered State of Consciousness, or an Expanded State of Consciousness in which man experiences a separation or state of detachment from the physical self, as if one were observing self engaged in various activities as an onlooker or experiencing Visions of self from an elevated vantage point. Out of Body Experience is a natural part of **Near Death Experience** in that man is consciously aware of his/her Soul Essence being distinctly separate from the still, vacant physical body. **Astral Projection** is another aspect of the Out of Body Experience, and is also an Expanded State of Consciousness. In Astral Projection, one consciously propels self out of and beyond the physical body to investigate perceived other-worldly realities, or to commune in some other physical place or Astral Plane. In Astral Projection, one can visit distant galactic worlds, commune with other types of intelligent life forms, discover answers to problematic life-situations on Earth and engage in activities that render service to All Creation.

Patience is The Evolved, Etheric Precept of Divine Conscience that prescribes the conscionable allowance of all things, all life-conditions, evolutionary transition states and conscious life forms to find their own moments of Peaceful Resolution. Patience is The Absolute Foundation upon which all states of Evolved Consciousness are built.

In Hindu philosophy, **Prana** is the Life-Force Energy System that pervades The Universe and is responsible for Creation.

Prayer is an act of supplication to beseech The Living God Spirit for guidance or assistance in negotiating problematic life-situations. The act of Prayer leads the consciousness of man toward recognizing and accepting The Presence of The Spirit of God alive in one's own evolving God-Self.

Pranayama is the Yogic practice of breath control for the production, regulation and control of vital life energy.

Precognition is an Intuitive Process or a condition of conscious awareness in which one accesses information or is privileged to knowledge about an event prior to the occurrence of that event.

A **Premonition** is a thought or feeling that forewarns of future hardships, injuries or setbacks, and frequently arises in the form of

Dreams or Visions.

Psychometry is the sensory ability that allows information to be gathered about a person, place or object simply by holding an object held or associated with a given person, place or object. Psychometry also encompasses the reading of energy states or transmissions and subsequent behavior traits of a person through the resonance and energy pattern of a person's name.

Resonance is the vibrational frequency or "pitch" at which or through which transmission and reception of thought pattern energy states are acknowledged, affected or produced.

Samadhi is a Sanskrit term that describes a prolonged, meditative trance or state of absorption and union with The God Spirit.

Serenity is The Evolved, Etheric Precept of Divine Conscience that prescribes the establishment of an Illuminated State of Contentment as a result of the experience of God-Realization. To be sure, Serenity is the birthright of all things born of Creation.

Shinto is a principal Religion of Japan, predating Buddhism, that emphasizes the Intuitive, direct experience of Divinity, rather than placing importance upon an intellectual approach or a cognitive understanding of the experience of The Divine. Shinto embraces the worship of nature as the vehicle for the experience of The Divine.

Sikhism is the devotional system and way of life founded by Guru Nanak in the early decades of the 16th Century A.D. Sikhism can be described as a Hindu Sect that propounds the belief in one God and the unilateral rejection of the caste system, yet is nonetheless deeply influenced by the structure of the Punjab society of Northern India.

Sirius is the star group from which all Galactic life in this quadrant of The Known Universe originated. It was **Sirius "B"** or what is called **"The Dark Star"** that was the birthplace of The Yahweh Entity. Sirius "B" has been virtually lifeless for eons, and exists as an imploded, super-dense satellite locked in a fixed, sixty year orbital path around **Sirius "A."** Some Aboriginal Peoples such as the Dogon of West Africa, have known about the existence of Sirius " B," displayed in pictographs, for thousands of years, even though modern technology did not discover Sirius "B" until 1954.

A **Social Memory Complex** is the Collective Consciousness Matrix in Divine Light Energy Form of an Evolved Civilization that no longer exists in physical form, but the Collective Incarnate Memory and Energy Matrix of which exists as one dynamic, resonant, homogeneous system of Conscious Existence.

The **Soul** is the storehouse of conscious memory, and is the essence of life-consciousness through which the God-Self is identified and accessed.

The **Subtle Body** is the aspect of conscious being through which energies of Life-Force are perceived, while the **Causal Body** is that aspect of physical being through which conscious thought is executed, and the **Gross Body** is that aspect of being through which physical reality is experienced.

Sufism is a system of Moslem Mysticism that embraces the belief and practice of Ecstatic Love for God and man, and through prescribed practices of Asceticism, man ultimately finds union with God.

Synergy is the cooperative action or force exerted that makes the resultant activity greater than the sum of its parts.

Tantricism is the Religion of the **Tantras,** which are dialogues between Lord Shiva and his **Shakti** or "power" of the "Great Goddess," his wife Parvati. Hindu Tantricism attempts to overcome the essential polarity in union, male/female energies, and attain Liberation from the material world. Tantricism, as it applies to opposites, can be seen and is used to describe aspects of other Religious Traditions as well.

Taoism is a Chinese system of Religion and Philosophy based on the 6th Century B.C. teachings of Lao-tse that advocates Simplicity, Selflessness and Oneness as the true Path of Conscience.

The **Tao Te Ching**, "The Way And Its Power," is the classic mythical text of Taoism by Lao-tse that addresses Harmony, Simplicity and Selflessness as the principles of Evolved Being.

Telepathy is the ability to communicate non-verbally through thought energy transmissions, and **Telekinesis** is the ability to influence or impact upon physical objects through thought energy transmissions.

The Greater Good is The Revelation, Grace and State of Conscious Being that embraces Universal Peace and Harmony in The Light of The One Infinite Creator.

The Lessons of Existence are the life-sequences or the reincarnate experiences of life that facilitate the assimilation of The Wisdom of One, and the acceptance and implementation of Universal Law upon the Earth Plane.

The Reality of Truth is that which is the subjective observation and identification of elements of Conscious Existence.

The Truth of Reality is that which is the objective observation and identification of elements of Conscious Existence.

The Wisdom of One (or The Conscience of One) is the acknowledgement and heart-felt application of the principle that all things born of Creation contain the same Life-Essence or Light/Life Consciousness, which entitles all things born of Creation to experience and be treated with Patience, Compassion, Wisdom, Mercy, Serenity and Love.

The **Torah** is the entire body of Jewish Religious Literature that includes The Scriptures and **The Talmud**, which is the collection of writings that constitute the body of Jewish Civil and Religious Law.

Trans-Cultural Spirituality is a belief system and way of Conscious Existence that acknowledges the commonality of Divine Truth found in major Religions and Spiritual Traditions throughout the world. Based in The Wisdom of One and Universal Law, Trans-Cultural Spirituality holds The Divine Precepts of Patience, Compassion, Wisdom, Mercy, Serenity and Love as the ideals by which the evolved consciousness of man expresses inherent connection to The Infinite Body of God. With emphasis placed upon the **Acceptance** and **Allowance** of mortal consciousness to conscionably embrace **The Lessons of Existence**, Trans-Cultural Spirituality applauds The Light of God alive in All Creation and sees mankind as brethren and kindreds of the other Kingdoms of The Universe. Through directives of simplicity and conscionable service to the needs of Creation, Trans-Cultural Spirituality affords mankind an avenue of Ascension - thereby consciously existing in The Heart of God.

Transmigration is the act or process of passing from one physical consciousness state to another. Transmigration is the evolutionary process by which the Soul Essence is allowed to pass from one physical vehicle of consciousness to another, as in the evolutionary journey of mortal consciousness through other Kingdoms and life-forms upon the Earth Mother.

Transmutation is the act or process of changing the nature of discordant energy states found to be problematic within mortal consciousness by releasing and/or dissolving hostile energies discovered with The Blessings of Love in The Light of One.

Universal Law is The Body of Higher Truth that each Soul Incarnate can access through his/her own open, evolved Heart Chakra that details the treatment and function of all life forms throughout The Universe. Universal Law acknowledges the conscionable application of Patience, Compassion, Wisdom, Mercy, Serenity and Love in The Light of The One Infinite Creator. Universal Law neither admonishes, nor restricts. Rather, Universal Law, through the implementation of Perseverance, Faith, Conviction and Courage, applauds and upholds the unilateral applications of Universal Conscience to all things born of Creation.

The **Upanishads** are the Vedic Metaphysical Treatises that describe man's relationship to The Universe, while describing the role of the Hindu Pantheon in Universal Order and Function.

The **Vedas** are the Sacred, Ancient Writings of Hinduism that are composed of four collections: The **Reg-Veda**, written between 1500 and 1200 B.C., is a collection of 1,028 hymns to the Vedic Deities, and is the oldest, living Religious Literature in the modern world; The **Sama-Veda** is a collection that isolates and delineates upon ceremonial chanting; The **Yajur-Veda** identifies and expounds upon manual operations that are required for ritual sacrifice; Unlike The Sama-Veda and The Vajur-Veda that both recount and explain aspects of The Reg-Veda, The **Artharva-Veda** contains rituals and incantations for medicinal purposes, success in battle and other aids to man in his/her quest for Realization of Self.

A **Vision** is an image revealed to one while awake that offers insights into problematic life-situations, past or future events and the connection between mankind and the Etheric Realm.

A **Vortex** is an area or land formation of heightened geomagnetic energy dynamics, where episodes of Channeling can be experienced with more clarity, processes of Healing Facilitation can be more comprehensive and effective and episodes of Etheric contact can be more pronounced or Illuminating. Aboriginal Peoples throughout the world identify Vortex Regions as Sacred Places, where man can talk to The Earth Mother and to The Heavens and hear The Voice of God.

Wisdom is The Evolved, Etheric Precept of Divine Conscience that prescribes the application of Heart-centered, Intuitive Knowingness to the experience of incarnate existence. It is through Wisdom that information is processed with the focus of Divine Truth to render the most Enlightened, purposeful, most benevolent expressions of conscience to facilitate Balance, Harmony, Peace and Contentment in the experience of mortal life, and in so doing, affect The Greater Good of All Creation.

Yoga, literally meaning "union," is the ancient Eastern Science of Meditation on God. A **Yogi** is an advanced practitioner of the disciplines of Yoga, while a **Guru**, literally meaning "dispeller of darkness," is an Evolved Spiritual Teacher who "Lights The Way" for students/seekers or aspirants who engage his/her counsel.

The **Zend-Avesta** is the Sacred Text of the Zorastrians that addresses the belief in an afterlife, and the continuous struggle between good and evil, with good ultimately prevailing.

Zoastrianism, still practiced in Iran and parts of India, was founded in Iran at about 500 B.C. The basic tenets of this Religion address the continuous struggle and conflict between Truth, represented by the aspects of God, and falsehood, represented by the spirits of evil, with Truth ultimately prevailing and the belief in an afterlife.

Even though we have only examined a sampling of terms and phrases that are central to understanding the journey of Spiritual Unfoldment, there should nonetheless be enough of a foundation now for identifying Principles of Conscience that will be elaborated upon later in this text. Let us move ahead and discuss the procedures of Spiritual Cleansing and Blessing that facilitate closer communion with The Infinite Body of God.

CLEANSING & BLESSING:
Practices Of Invocation And Communion With The Living God Spirit

CHAPTER 2

Practices of Spiritual Cleansing and Blessing are most certainly acts of ritual, and all earnest seekers of Enlightened Consciousness should understand and be aware that the use of a ritual, by its very nature, obligates the seeker to pledge allegiance to those Spiritual Entities or Energies that the seeker would entreat or enlist for guidance. To be sure, accepting communications and instructions from Etheric or Disembodied sources that one has not adequately identified can lead to very disquieting episodes in one's journey toward the assimilation of The Wisdom of One. Therefore, it is strongly suggested that The God Presence sought and/or invoked is called by name, and properly identified before any information or instructions received are implemented.

IDENTIFICATION OF SPIRIT PRESENCE

To identify the nature and purpose of Spirit Presence or Disembodied Entities, we recommend that three simple questions are asked at the beginning of contact:

1. By what name are you called?
2. By what authority do you commune with me?
3. Call The Name of God.

If the Disembodied Presence does not or can not satisfactorily answer these questions in a straight forward manner, then it is a fairly good chance that the Spirit Presence engaged is not benevolent in intent. Benevolent Spirits and Disincarnate Beings will respectfully and willingly answer any reasonable question that will validate their conscionable intent. On the other hand, hostile, self-serving Disincarnate Beings will tend to be evasive, illusive or argumentative in response to interrogation, and may transmit an air of arrogance or resentment, or resort to trickery to gain confidence.

Be advised that hostile Disincarnate Spirit Presence can be extremely clever and persistent in attempts to gain acceptance and entry into mortal consciousness. It is always best to trust the experience of "feeling" the nature of Spirit Presence through an open Heart Chakra, as to "feel" life-experiences is to "know" the true reality of that which is experienced.

SPIRITUAL CLEANSING & BLESSING

The practice of Spiritual Cleansing and Blessing is undertaken for several reasons:

1. Cleansing and Blessing is undertaken to purge self of discordant, counterproductive vibrations that could compromise one's effectiveness in attending the needs of Creation, as well as influence one's ability to conscionably engage hands-on Bodywork Sessions to facilitate the release of discordant energy from others. (Also, without the practice of Cleansing and Blessing, discordant energies engaged with one client can easily be transmitted to another, as the engagement of subtle energy fields opens the door for the possibility of transmission of hostile, discordant energy states by those practitioners who do

46

not respect the integrity or are unaware of the existence of subtle energy fields around and within the physical body.)

2. Cleansing is undertaken to purify the consciousness, thereby facilitating greater capacity to accept and transmit larger volumes of Divine Light Energy.

3. Cleansing is performed to provide an atmosphere conducive to the transmission and reception of Divine Light Vibrations.

4. Blessings are performed to enlist Divine Sanction and Guidance, and to proclaim Divine Allegiance.

5. Blessings are performed to raise consciousness levels, to access Heart-centered Behaviors and to assist in transmuting hostile, problematic, dissonant energy matrices.

In our practice of Trans-Cultural Spirituality and Loving Touch Therapy™, we rely heavily upon The LoveLight Invocation/Blessing and The 23rd Psalm to usher in states of Divine Consciousness, to proclaim Divine Allegiance, to assist in transmuting discordance and to stimulate an atmosphere that is conducive to Spiritual undertakings. We will discuss in detail The LoveLight Invocation/Blessing and The 23rd Psalm a little later, when we discuss The Invocation of Divine Guidance.

AROMATHERAPY

Incenses burned during Meditation and Prayer, Loving Touch Therapy™, Counseling, Bodywork or Facilitation Sessions can greatly contribute to setting a mood or atmosphere that lessens mental and emotional stress, assists in strengthening various aspects of consciousness, acts as a calming agent for agitated nerves, and can serve as an agent of Transformation that changes the nature of hostile, counterproductive energy states into more benevolent, constructive vibrations.

At present, available information explaining the principles of Aromatherapy, which is based in the Ayurvedic System of Fragrance use to stimulate conditions of physical, mental, emotional and spiritual well-being, is quite extensive. Therefore, a Meditation or Facilitation Area that is without incense and essential oils might be looked upon as incomplete, as both incense and essential oils have been proven to be most effective as tools in the facilitation of productive, Light-minded states of consciousness, as well as indispensable aids in transmuting hostile, discordant energies.

Some of the most effective resins, flowers, wood-powders, essential oils and fragrances used to dispel discordant, hostile energies in practices of Cleansing and Blessing are:

1   Agarwood - clears hostile/discordant energy systems from immediate environment
2. Cedar - provides purifying aromas that cleanse spiritual vibrations
3. Gum Benzoin - a resin used to cleanse environment and to invoke benevolent energies
4. Juniper - cleansing, fresh-scented agent used to dispel discordant energies from the environment
5   Sage - strong, earthy aroma that removes discordant vibrations from the environment
6   Sweet Grass - provides cleansing, uplifting aromas that invoke benevolent energies

(For complete Aromatherapy Charts, see Appendix I.)

INVOCATION OF DIVINE GUIDANCE

The LoveLight Invocation/Blessing and The 23rd Psalm are most effective in The Invocation of Divine Guidance and in the pledging of allegiance to The Yahweh Entity and The Council of Twelve. As The LoveLight Invocation/Blessing and The 23rd Psalm are recited, allow self to truly resonate with the words and the deepest meaning of the statements being affirmed. Allow self to vibrate as One with the Conviction and Faith inherent to both The LoveLight Invocation/Blessing and The 23rd Psalm. Use these Prayers as often as you can, as the more these words are silently recited, the deeper does the conscious bond grow between the seeker who uses them and The Conscience of The Living God Spirit.

(Additionally, the silent recitation of the words, "Attune, Balance, Integrate, Ground," in sets of three (3) acts as a mantra to activate Divine Light Energy along the Chakra Cord and within the Primary Chakra Centers. This silent recitation can be performed at any time of the day or night to strengthen personal connection to The Council of Twelve and The Infinite Body of God. The use of the abbreviated Prayer, "Almighty Yah, Great Spirit of Light, By The Spirits of Buddha, Krishna, Mohammed and Christ Jesus, In Thee do I Trust," is another excellent way of maintaining grounded focus within Light-minded Ideals.)

LOVELIGHT INVOCATION/BLESSING

Almighty Yah, Great Spirit of Light,
By The Spirits of Buddha, Krishna, Mohammed and Christ Jesus, in
Thee do I trust.
Protect me, Father;
Guide me, Father;
Strengthen me, Father;
Cleanse me, Father;
Heal me, Father;
Fill me with The Light of Thy Presence, Father.
Surround me, Father,
with Archangel Michael in the East,
Archangel Gabriel in the West,
Archangel Raphael in the North,
Archangel Uriel in the South,
and grant me communion, Father,
with Archangel Barachiel Above,
Archangel Jehudial Below,
Archangel Salathiel Within,
And surround me, Father, with Thy Legion of Light.
Almighty Yah, Great Spirit of Light,
By The Spirits of Buddha, Krishna, Mohammed and Christ Jesus, in
Thee do I trust.

THE 23RD PSALM

The Lord is my shepherd; I shall not want.
He maketh me to lie down in green pastures:
He leadeth me beside the still waters.
He restoreth my soul:
He leadeth me in the paths of righteousness for His name's sake.
Yea, though I walk through the valley of the shadow of death,
I will fear no evil:
for Thou art with me;
Thy rod and Thy staff they comfort me.
Thou preparest a table before me
in the presence of mine enemies:
Thou anointest my head with oil;
my cup runneth over.
Surely goodness and mercy shall follow me
all the days of my life:
and I will dwell in the house of The Lord forever.

The Invocation of specific Archangelic Presence* to assist in the day's work or for guidance can easily be accomplished in the following manner.

1. Seat self in a quiet, softly illuminated room and begin to center and focus self by silently and slowly repeating these words several times in sets of three, "Attune, Balance, Integrate, Ground." (The resonance produced by these words helps to raise mortal consciousness to Etheric Levels that facilitate acceptance of The Living God Spirit.)

2. Now, silently repeat to self, "In The Name of Yahweh, By The Spirits of Buddha, Krishna, Mohammed and Christ Jesus, I invoke the Presence of Archangel _____ (fill in the blank with the name of one or more Archangels whose energy presence would prove helpful in your day's work) to join with me in the Counseling and Facilitation of _____, _____ and _____" (fill in the name or names of scheduled clients for the day)

3. Silently repeat this statement three (3) times. Between clients, repeat the words, "Attune, Balance, Integrate, Ground," three (3) times to continually reaffirm and activate The Invocation of Archangelic Presence.

Another technique for The Invocation and maintenance of Divine Guidance uses Programmed Quartz Crystals** in grid patterns around the perimeter of the room used for Loving Touch Therapy™, Meditation or Facilitation/Counseling/Bodywork as follows:

*See **CRYSTAL COMMUNION: LOVELIGHT MEDITATIONS** by Sri Akhenaton, pages 277-284 for "Invocation of The Archangels."

See **CRYSTAL COMMUNION: LOVELIGHT MEDITATIONS by Sri Akhenaton, pages 247-257 for "Quartz Crystal Programming."

1. Select four (4) single terminated Clear Quartz Crystal Generators of equal size.

2. After programming the Crystals with the specific Archangelic Presence desired, place one of the Crystal Generators at the midpoints of each of the four (4) walls of the room, with the Crystal apexes pointed toward the center of the room.

3. When activated, the Crystals will transmit Divine Light Presence into the room for use as guidance or assistance in Spiritual Activities.

AFFIRMATIONS

Affirmations* are specific statements of Conviction and Faith designed to condition the conscious mind with Light-minded intent. In an attempt to establish and maintain conscionable behaviors and/or to extinguish counterproductive behavior patterns, Affirmations can be extremely effective in assisting the evolutionary process of Transformation, thereby resolving karmically oriented dysfunctional mind-sets and behaviors at odds with The Wisdom of One. Additionally, Affirmations offer a clear, definitive avenue by which the acknowledgment and implementation of God-Conscious motivations may be realized.

Additional techniques of Cleansing and Blessing, as well as techniques of Invocation and Communion with Divine Light Energies will be addressed in later chapters of this text.

*See **CRYSTAL COMMUNION: LOVELIGHT MEDITATIONS** by Sri Akhenaton pages 24, 35-37 for "Affirmations."

LIFE-FORCE ENERGIES:
Activating Prana, Opening The Heart Chakra And Raising Resonance Rates

CHAPTER 3

In many Religious and Spiritual Traditions around the world, the concept of "Life-Force" is addressed in great detail. Kundalini, Prana, Chi and Mana are just a few names that identify the dynamic energy presence known as Life-Force.

In Eastern Traditions, both Kundalini and Prana are terms used to identify aspects of The Life-Force. Kundalini is described as the golden serpent that lies dormant and coiled at the Base Chakra. When activated, "Kundalini Rise" feels like swirling, radiant energy that takes a serpentine path upward along the Chakra Cord. As the energy rises, penetrating and activating each Chakra, radiant, pulsing energy fills every cell of the body until the rising energy of Kundalini reaches and explodes through the Crown Chakra, producing euphoria, Altered States of Consciousness, Etheric or Cosmic Illumination and that which simply can be called "an uncompromised, unparalleled experience of Divine Bliss." From personal experience, we can attest that the rise of Kundalini allows for recognition and acceptance of Absolute Truth in a most intimate way that graphically demonstrates man's personal connection to The Infinite Body of God.

THE LIFE-FORCE - PRANA

Prana is said to be the Life-Force that is the energy system that pervades The Universe and is responsible for Creation. To access the flow of Prana within mortal conscious being, simply follow this procedure:

1. First, seat self in a comfortable, upright position with both hands resting in the lap, left hand resting in the right with both palms facing upward.

2. Next, begin a rhythmic breathing sequence by inhaling deeply through the nose and slowly exhaling from the mouth.

3. As you continue the rhythmic breathing sequence, silently repeat, "Almighty Yah, Great Spirit of Light, By The Spirits of Buddha, Krishna, Mohammed and Christ Jesus, In Thee Do I Trust."

4. Now, silently repeat these words several times, "Attune, Balance, Integrate, Ground." Allow self to relax.

5. Next, repeat the following statement three (3) times: "In The Name of Yahweh, By The Spirits of Buddha, Krishna, Mohammed and Christ Jesus, let me activate and access the Life-Force Energy within me."

6. Focus your concentration just below your navel, right above the point where your hands are resting in your lap.

7. Visualize a golden sphere of radiant energy swirling at the point just below your navel. Watch as the golden energy sphere first shows itself to be about the size of a golf ball, then

slowly begins to grow to the size of an orange and continues to expand until it reaches the size of a grapefruit. Feel the warm, pulsating, golden energy rising within you.

8. Slowly bring your hands upward from your lap to your Heart Chakra. As you lift your hands upward, watch as the golden sphere also moves upward along your Chakra Cord to your Heart Chakra.

9. When your hands reach the level of your Heart Chakra, turn your palms to face outward in front of you, and extend your arms straight out in front of you. Feel the radiant, golden Life-Force Energy of Prana that fills your torso, arms and hands.

10. Now, silently repeat to self, "In The Name of Yahweh, By The Spirits of Buddha, Krishna, Mohammed and Christ Jesus, All Things Are As One, All Things Are As One."

(See Illustrations 1 & 2)

When you are ready to end this exercise, simply breathe deeply through your nose and slowly exhale from your mouth. Slowly count backwards from ten to one. At the count of one, open your eyes and continue to breathe deeply. Do not be in a hurry to move about. Reflect upon your experience, and allow self to comprehend the dynamic nature of Life-Force Energy.

Illustration 1 : Prana Exercises

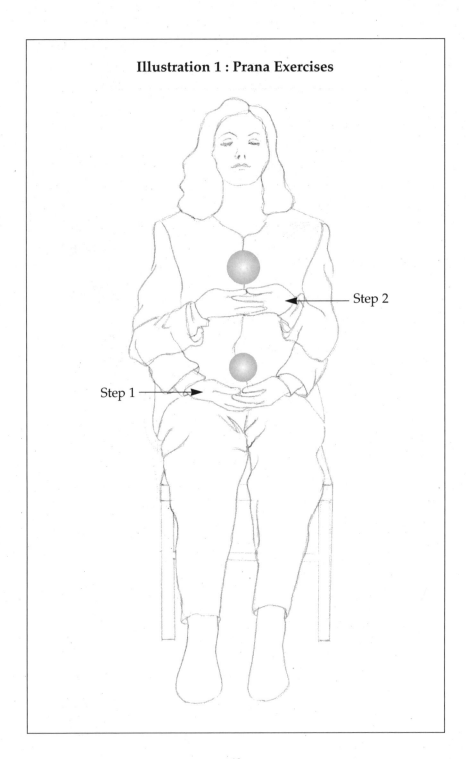

Step 2

Step 1

Illustration 2 : Prana Exercises

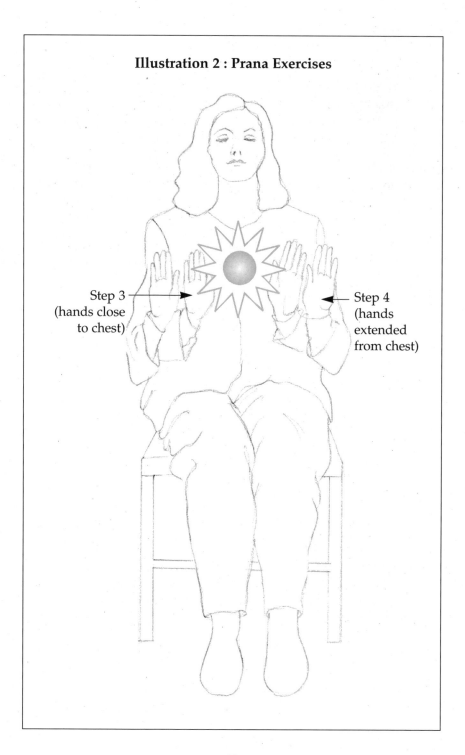

Step 3
(hands close
to chest)

Step 4
(hands
extended
from chest)

OPENING THE HEART CHAKRA

Frequently, in the course of spiritual pursuits, references are often made and conclusions are drawn about the impact and relationship between Heart Chakra Orientation and states of mortal consciousness. To be sure, we acknowledge that the relative state of evolution of Heart Chakra function bears direct correlation to levels of God-Conscious Being, or serve to signal the nature of egocentric design in operation within mortal consciousness.

For all seekers of Spiritual Truth and practitioners of Loving Touch Therapy™, Bodywork and Counseling, it is imperative that the Heart Chakra be oriented as an open, viable, receptive energy center, for only through evolved states of Heart Chakra function can true, accurate perceptions of reality be experienced. Only through evolved states of Heart Chakra function can one conscionably, Selflessly embrace The Soul of Creation.

One of the most effective visualization exercises we can recommend for opening and nurturing Heart Chakra functions is called "The Rosebud Visualization" and is shown in the sequence of Illustrations 3 - 6.

1. To begin The Rosebud Visualization, simply follow steps 1-4 of the Prana Exercise.

2. Now, begin to visualize the sequence depicted in Illustrations 3-6. Visualize self beneath the Golden/Yellow Rays of the noonday, summer Sun. Feel the warm, radiant energy of the Golden/Yellow Rays as they slowly and gently penetrate your Crown Chakra and send nurturing LoveLight Vibrations down the length of your Chakra Cord.

3. Now, visualize a pink rosebud at the center of your Heart Chakra. Watch as the Golden/Yellow Rays of the Sun caress the pink rosebud at your Heart Chakra, nurturing the delicate rosebud with The Benevolent Divine Light Energy of The Living God Spirit. Watch as the pink rosebud at your Heart Chakra slowly begins to open, revealing its brilliant pink blossom. Feel the comforting, inspiring energy presence that fills your Heart Chakra with The Presence of Love, and allow self to simply be.

4. After a short time, you will notice that the pink rose blossom begins to undergo a most wondrous Transformation. Watch as the Golden/Yellow Rays of the Sun bond with the pink rose blossom, and transform the pink rose blossom into a Golden/Yellow blossom filled with the pristine, radiant beauty of Divine Truth and Love Everlasting. Feel the absolute sense of Divine Knowingness, Truth and Love that now fill your Heart Chakra, and allow self to be a true child of The Living God.

When you are ready to end your Rosebud Visualization Exercise, simply begin to count backwards from ten to one. At the count of one, slowly open your eyes and breathe deeply, inhaling through the nose and slowly exhaling from the mouth. Remain seated. Allow self to reflect upon your experience, and feel the sense of openness and warmth that fill your Heart Chakra. Practicing this visualization exercise regularly can significantly enhance one's ability to facilitate Heart Chakra evolution, and in so doing become a more conscionable servant to the needs of All Creation.

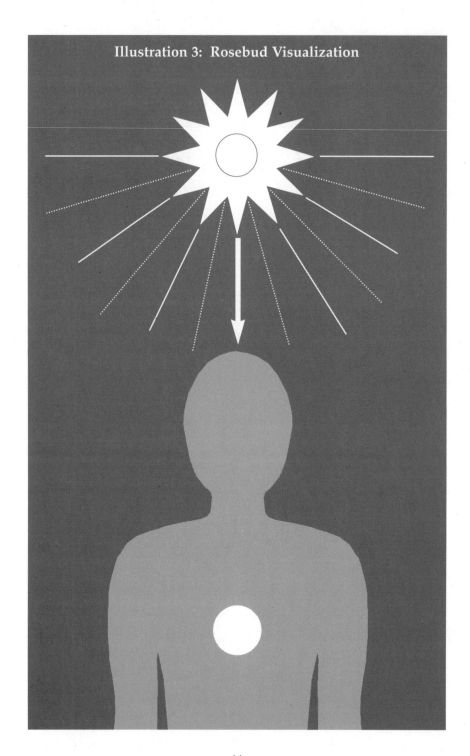

Illustration 3: Rosebud Visualization

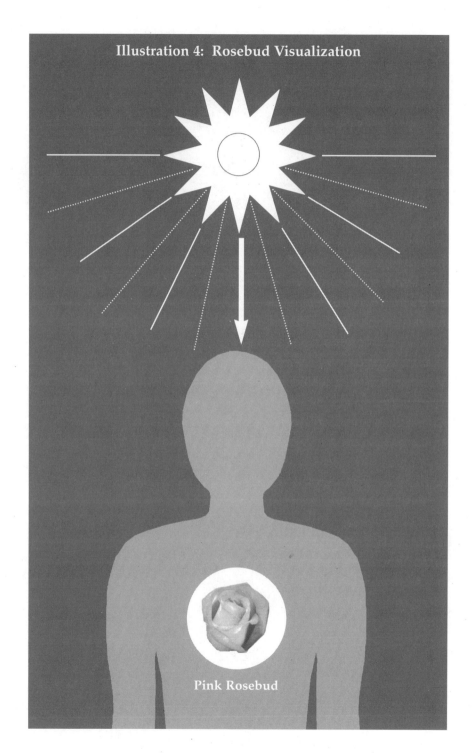

Illustration 4: Rosebud Visualization

Pink Rosebud

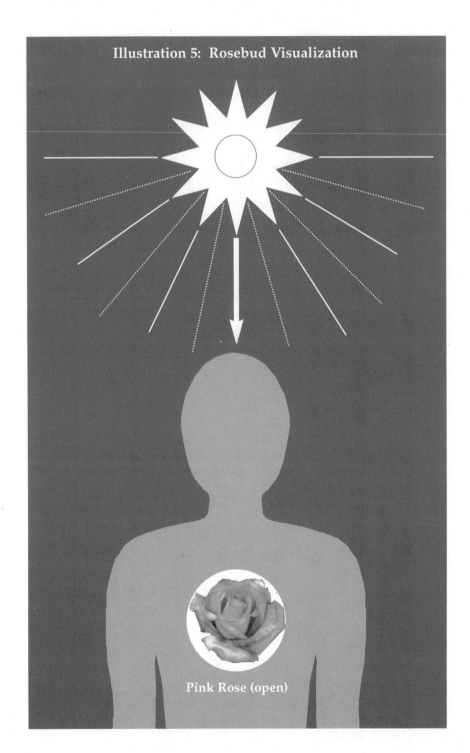

Illustration 5: Rosebud Visualization

Pink Rose (open)

Illustration 6: Rosebud Visualization

Golden Rose (open)

RAISING RESONANCE RATES

Resonance is defined as the frequency or vibrational "pitch" at which or through which thought energy transmissions are produced, transmitted or received. Raising the Resonance Rate simply means attuning one's vibrational frequency to more closely approximate the frequency of Divine Light Vibrations, which allows the seeker of Enlightened Consciousness to experience a closer, more dynamic state of communion with The Infinite Body of God. What this process accomplishes is the alignment of mortal consciousness with the true applications of Light-mindedness, and therefore facilitates mankind's ability to conscionably render service to Creation with efficiency, Benevolence and Grace. One technique we recommend for raising Resonance Rates we call "The Golden Stairway Meditation," and is shown in Illustration 7.

1. To begin The Golden Stairway Meditation, seat self in an upright, comfortable position in a softly illuminated, quiet room. Begin a rhythmic breathing sequence by deeply inhaling through the nose, holding the breath for three (3) seconds, then slowly exhaling from the mouth. As you inhale, visualize cleansing, radiant Golden/White Divine Light Vibrations entering your nose, traveling down your trachea, filling your lungs and Heart Center with glowing, vibrant LoveLight Sensations. As you exhale, visualize all tension and stress leaving your body in dark cloudy swirls of discordant energy that you expel from the mouth. Silently bless your energies of discordance in The Name of Yahweh, By The Spirits of Buddha, Krishna, Mohammed and Christ Jesus, as you embrace your energies of discordance with Love and cast them unto the bosom of Mother Earth for rebirthing and to find their own moments of Peace.

Illustration 7: Golden Stairway Meditation *(144 steps)*

2. Now, silently repeat the words, "Attune, Balance, Integrate, Ground." Repeat these words several times. Next, silently repeat this phrase slowly three (3) times, "Channel The Light Of Yahweh, Channel The Light Of One."

3. Now, visualize a Golden Stairway of 144 steps that lead upward toward a brilliantly glowing, Golden/Yellow noonday Sun. Visualize self ascending the Golden Stairway beginning at ground level at the first step of the stairway. Feel the growing sense of warmth, beauty and understanding that fills your body as you continue your ascent toward the final step.

4. When you reach the final step atop the Golden Stairway, look down and you will see that the final step is actually a Golden Platform with your name etched upon it. Stand upon the Golden Platform with your head, arms and eyes upraised to embrace the benevolent, Golden/Yellow Rays of the Sun, and silently repeat this phrase seven (7) times, "Almighty Yah, Great Spirit of Light, By The Spirits of Buddha, Krishna, Mohammed and Christ Jesus, In Thee Do I Trust. Amen."

To end The Golden Stairway Meditation, simply begin counting backwards from ten to one. At the count of one, slowly open your eyes and breathe deeply, inhaling through the nose and slowly exhaling from the mouth. Allow self to relax and reflect upon your Meditation experience. Do not be in a hurry to move about. Allow self ample time to fully reintegrate and ground in the reality of Third Dimension.

Regular practice of The Golden Stairway Meditation can lead to opening doors to Higher Consciousness States that once might have eluded the seeker of Spiritual Truth, and can facilitate mankind's Conscious Ascension into The Infinite Body of God.

Another visualization technique for raising Resonance Rates is as follows:

1. Prepare self by performing steps 1-4 of the Prana Exercise.

2. Now, visualize a dark brown sphere of energy at your Base Chakra that is about the size of an orange. Watch as the dark brown sphere of energy awakens and slowly begins to rise upward toward the Navel Chakra. As the dark brown energy sphere rises, it begins to change color, becoming lighter as it approaches the Navel Chakra.

3. As the brown sphere of energy reaches the Navel Chakra, it becomes a deep orange/brown in color and tingling, warm, pulsating sensations can be felt along your Chakra Cord.

4. As the orange/brown energy sphere continues to rise upward toward the Solar Plexus Chakra, it transforms into a golden/orange color as it comes to rest at the Solar Plexus Chakra.

5. Now, the golden/orange sphere of energy begins to move upward toward the Heart Chakra. As it enters the Heart Chakra, the golden/orange energy sphere becomes a brilliant Golden/Yellow color, and waves of pulsating, radiant Love-Light Energy are transmitted throughout your entire body. At the Heart Chakra, the Golden/Yellow sphere of energy begins to expand and intensify, growing larger and more radiant.

6. Now, watch as from the center of the Golden/Yellow sphere of energy at your Heart Chakra, Rays of Golden/White Energy are directed upward through the Throat and Third Eye Chakras and finally continue to penetrate the outer boundary and travel beyond the Crown Chakra.

7. Also, watch as the Golden/Yellow Rays from the center of the Golden/Yellow sphere at your Heart Chakra travel downward, filling and energizing the lower Chakra Triad. Feel the elevating, invigorating, transcendent, LoveLight Sensations that fill your entire body, and allow self to simply be.

When you are ready to end this visualization, slowly begin to count backwards from ten to one. At the count of one, slowly open your eyes, and breathe deeply, inhaling through the nose and exhaling from the mouth. Remain seated. Allow self ample time to reflect upon your experience before moving about.

Another technique we recommend for raising Resonance Rates, called "The Chakra System Energizer," is shown in Illustration 8. This is an excellent visualization exercise that not only energizes the entire Chakra System, but can also stimulate the experience of Kundalini Rise.

1. Prepare for the visualization procedure by performing steps 1-4 of the Prana Exercise.

2. Now, visualize the swirling Golden/White Light Matrix of Divine Conscience circling above your head. Begin the silent, continuous recitation of the mantra "Om" that you will maintain throughout this visualization exercise. Watch as the Golden/White Light Matrix integrates, becoming one brilliant Golden/White Light Ray that slowly orbits your Crown Chakra seven times, stimulating radiant, tingling sensations of warmth. Then watch as the Golden/White Light Ray slowly turns downward, penetrating your Crown Chakra and moves down your Chakra Cord toward your Third Eye Chakra to connect the Crown and Third Eye Chakras with the

Golden/White Light Ray.

3. As the Golden/White Light Ray slowly reaches the Third Eye Chakra, it turns to slowly orbit the Third Eye Chakra seven times with the glowing warmth and radiance of its Divine Golden/White Light Energy.

4. Watch, as now the Golden/White Light Ray slowly turns from the Third Eye Chakra, heading down the Chakra Cord to connect Crown and Third Eye Chakras with the Throat Chakra.

5. As the Golden/White Light Ray reaches the Throat Chakra, it orbits the Throat Chakra seven times with its Divine Golden/White Light Energy before slowly heading down the Chakra Cord toward the Heart Chakra.

6. Visualize each successive Chakra, down to and including the Base Chakra, being orbited seven times and connected to each of the other Primary Chakras by the continuous presence of the Golden/White Light Ray of Divine Conscience.

7. After the Base Chakra has been slowly orbited seven times by the Golden/White Light Vibration, watch as the Divine Ray slowly and gently penetrates the center of the Base Chakra and begins to travel upward along the Chakra Cord. Slowly, the Golden/White Light Ray travels up the Chakra Cord, tenderly embracing and gently penetrating each Chakra along the Chakra Cord en route to the Crown Chakra.

8. When the Golden/White Light Ray finally reaches the Crown Chakra, it gently passes through the Crown Chakra and is visualized as Twelve Golden/White Light Rays of Divine Energy radiating from the top of your head that stimulate

comforting, warm sensations of deep, "other-worldly" Knowingness, contented bliss, Conviction and Faith... And watch, as the Golden/White Light Rays leave the top of your head and are dispersed into The Ethers. Allow self to feel the radiant presence of Divine Conscience filling your Chakra Cord. Allow self to experience the blessed moment of communion with The Light of The Living God Spirit. Allow self to be as One with all things born of Universal Creation.

When you are ready to end The Chakra System Energizer Visualization, begin to slowly count backwards from ten to one. At the count of one, slowly open your eyes and breathe deeply, inhaling through your nose and slowly exhaling from the mouth. Remain seated. Allow self ample time to fully reintegrate into the reality of Third Dimension. (It may be helpful to have a Sheen Obsidian Egg to assist you in grounding.) Reflect upon your experience and allow self to simply be.

The exercises we have offered in this chapter can be performed with equal success in group settings or by the individual. Though some prefer the quietude of private Meditations, others benefit more from group settings with one person leading the group in the Meditation or exercise engaged. In any event, by following the guidelines we have offered, states of Higher Consciousness can easily be accessed to assist mortal man in rediscovering the true meaning of being a child of God.

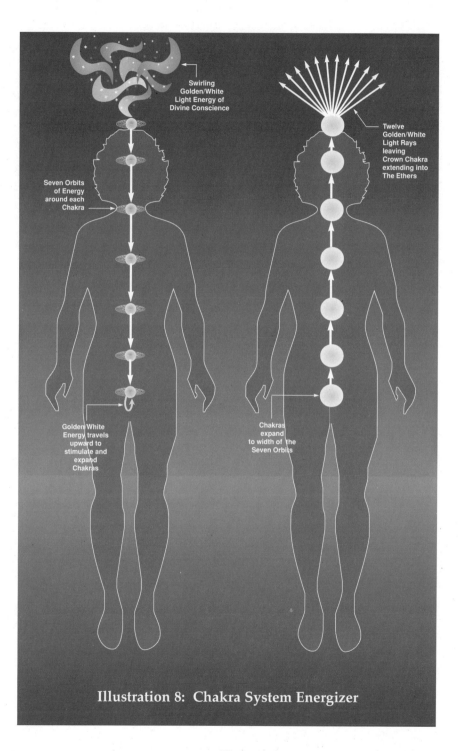

Swirling
Golden/White
Light Energy of
Divine Conscience

Twelve
Golden/White
Light Rays
leaving
Crown Chakra
extending into
The Ethers

Seven Orbits
of Energy
around each
Chakra

Golden/White
Energy travels
upward to
stimulate and
expand
Chakras

Chakras
expand
to width of the
Seven Orbits

Illustration 8: Chakra System Energizer

KARMIC TIES:
Accessing And Identifying Past Life Influences Upon Present Behavior Patterns

CHAPTER 4

We have defined Karma as The Law of Cause and Effect, which prescribes the repetition of discordant life-sequences until The Lessons of Existence or Higher Truth associated with the release of self from discordant life cycles is acknowledged, accepted and practiced. The Karma of dysfunctional attitudes and behaviors from ages past will always find expression in present incarnate phases unless and until mortal man willingly takes responsibility for everything that he/she thinks, feels and does, and makes the necessary adjustments or changes in ideology and practice to facilitate more conscionable, Light-minded Behavior.

PRE-INCARNATE CHOICE & SUBTLE ENERGY PLANES

Though it is difficult for the conscious mind and the ego-self to accept, all behaviors experienced in present incarnate phases were born on the subtle energy planes of past incarnations, and that through pre-incarnate choice, the soul and God-Self structure the nature of present incarnate life-sequences to facilitate Soul Evolution. The subtle energy planes of consciousness hold the memory of past incarnate attitudes and behaviors that the soul matrix calls upon to fashion the nature and purpose of subsequent incarnate phases and experience. Subtle energies of consciousness are then directed through the causal body or conscious thought process to impact upon and/or execute the reality that the gross body experiences. It is through the auric system that subtle energy states or "predisposed thought patterns" of pre-incarnate choice exist, and are transmitted to fashion the life-sequences of the phenomenal system of experience.

But let us not forget about the active influence of the ego, for it is the ego that would use the misdirected illusion of Choice of Free Will to justify resistance to accepting changes in the growth or dynamics of self. Further, the ego would diligently campaign against allowing or acknowledging the inevitable reality of Spiritual Unfoldment by stimulating and maintaining the thought that Spiritual Unfoldment was not a conscious choice of the soul incarnate; rather, that Choice of Free Will had been violated by thrusting the soul incarnate into a process of life-experience that the soul incarnate had not willingly or consciously agreed to engage. Clearly, the ego would resort to any means necessary to maintain and/or protect the illusions of self, even if it means distorting Truth, exploiting naiveté or declaring delusion to be reality.

It is a case of predestined Truth that mortal man will evolve in mind, body and spirit. It is yet another predestined Truth that mortal man will experience moments of readiness that will allow more evolved states of consciousness to unfold. It is both Truth and predestined reality that mortal man, the children of God, will in time assume Divine Responsibility within The Living God Spirit as dedicated servants to the needs of Creation.

It is simply one of the ego's functions to try to dissuade mortal man from seeking "The Way of Spirit," and instead focus upon issues of personal comfort, survival, control of reality and self-importance. This is simply the natural course of mortal evolution to be understood and accepted. But too it is for mankind to understand and accept that the time of readiness approaches when the collective soul of man will embrace the revelation of The Living God Spirit, and finally come to know that The Light of God has always lived in the heart and soul of mankind.

REGRESSION THERAPY

Influences of past incarnate attitudes and behaviors upon present incarnate states of consciousness can be accessed through techniques of Regression Therapy, as well as through the use of simple visualization exercises that illuminate the willing seeker by revealing episodes of past incarnate behavior that impact upon and give insights into present behavior patterns. On several occasions, we have found that sessions of Regression Therapy have raised more questions that could be resolved. In some cases, especially when a soul incarnate is so inclined, information accessed through Regression Therapy can contribute to sustaining illusions of past incarnate importance that overshadow the purpose of present incarnate experience.

When subjects are regressed, instances occur in which soul incarnates are so amazed, impressed or consumed by the knowledge of lofty, royal or powerful positions of status enjoyed in past incarnate phases that some soul incarnates develop an air of self-satisfaction and self-importance that on the surface would seem to obscure and defeat the very purpose of the therapeutic session. When regressed, it is the hope that the subject will discover past circumstances, thoughts and behaviors that will assist him/her in understanding present incarnate problems and dysfunctions, not instances by which the subject can justify the illusion of superiority or indulge self-serving interests.

It can be very easy for some soul incarnates to loose sight of the true purpose of Regression Therapy, as in some cases the ego will unconditionally seize any opportunity to create or sustain the illusions of self. So then, it is a significant responsibility that rests with each Regression Therapist to assist the subject by guiding him/her toward the realization of Truth - not that which the therapist "thinks" is Truth, but that which through Divine Guidance knows to be Truth - instead of sanctioning the subject's egocentric interpretations that serve to bolster the distorted illusion of self created by the ego. Therefore, we strongly suggest that only the most reputable facilitators of Regression be engaged, and that only those seekers of Spiritual Truth who fully understand the purpose and value of Regression Therapy expose self to these techniques.

ACCESSING PAST INCARNATE THOUGHTS & BEHAVIORS

One visualization technique that we recommend to access past incarnate thought and behavior patterns is represented in Figure 1. The Twelve Concentric Triangles shown in Figure 1 act as a portal that can lead to visual episodes of past incarnate activities. (Please note that even though full-color, three-dimensional, panoramic visionary representations of past incarnate sequences do occur, more often than not, visionary representations with this and many other techniques will be holographic in nature.)

1. To begin The Concentric Triangle Visualization, situate self in a comfortable, upright position in a quiet, softly illuminated room.

2. Allow self to relax and begin a rhythmic breathing sequence, inhaling through the nose, holding the breath for three (3) seconds, then slowly exhaling from the mouth.

3. Silently repeat the following phrase several times, "Attune,

Balance, Integrate, Ground."

4. Now, begin to gaze upon The Twelve Concentric Triangles. Allow self to travel deeply into the center of the triangles.

5. Hold your gaze and silently repeat the following phrase three (3) times, "In The Name of Yahweh, By The Spirits of Buddha, Krishna, Mohammed and Christ Jesus, let me see the reality of past incarnate behaviors."

6. Hold your gaze for as long as you can without blinking. After a time, you will feel as though you are being drawn into the center of The Concentric Triangles. Allow your consciousness to flow into the center of the concentric triangles without resistance. Simply allow self to travel into and through the center of the triangles.

7. Now, close your eyes and visualize The Twelve Concentric Triangles situated in the center of your Third Eye Chakra. Allow your consciousness to pass through the center triangle, and soon visual references to past incarnate thoughts and behaviors will appear as fleeting holographic impressions. At this time, there may also be the presence of sounds, aromas or emotional sensations associated with past incarnate activities that can give valuable insights into past behavior patterns and inferences into present attitudes and behaviors.

When you are ready to end your Concentric Triangle Visualization, simply begin counting backwards from ten to one. REMAIN SEATED. At the count of one, open your eyes and breathe deeply, inhaling through your nose and slowly exhaling from your mouth. REMAIN SEATED. Breathe deeply several times, and allow self to reintegrate into Third Dimension reality.

Reflect upon your visualization. (If you do not experience visual representations or physical sensations in your first attempt, please do not be discouraged. Continue your efforts diligently, and when you are ready to experience and accept the Truth of past incarnate existence, the visual references will most certainly appear.)

Reflect upon the sensations and images you experienced during this visualization exercise. Please DO NOT try to "Figure Out" the meaning of the references given. Allow self to accept any and all representations given, without judgment, expectation or concern. Simply allow self the moment of experience, and in due course, the meaning of the references give in your visualization will become self-evident. Please remember that there is never need to push or press for answers, for such compelling attitudes and drives can only be those of ego-self and not the higher design of Divine Truth.

Allow self to identify and accept the existence of discordant behavior patterns in one's present incarnate phase that were represented in the visualization exercise. Allow self to transcend the fear of seeing the true reality of self in The Light of Divine Truth. Embrace all aspects of self with Love, Compassion and Understanding, and allow self to truly be a conscionable child of God in The Light of The One Infinite Creator.

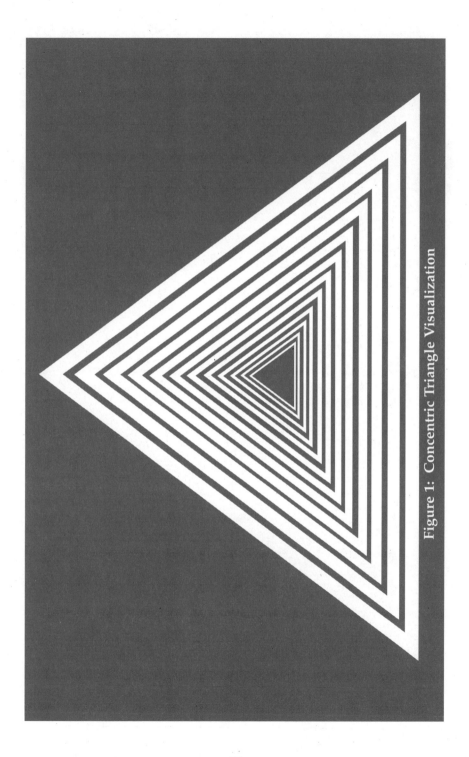

Figure 1: Concentric Triangle Visualization

INTUITIVE WISDOM:
Accessing The Voice Of The God-Self

CHAPTER 5

As mortal man engages the journey of Soul Evolution, the most profound and dramatic changes that occur in states of consciousness involve man's perceptions of reality. Slowly, mortal consciousness evolves to accept incarnate existence as a wondrous adventure filled with untold possibilities, instead of a troubling, obstacle-strewn, chaotic survival experience designed to drain life from the soul of man. Slowly, man's perceptions of life-sequences undergo radical shifts that allow man to view incarnate reality through eyes of Liberation, much the same as viewing a water glass as being half-full of water, instead of half-empty. With liberated perceptions, man's interests become directed toward harmonies coexistence with the other Kingdoms of Mother Earth, instead of allowing compelling, single-minded drives of self-interest, curiosity, fear and the illusion of need motivate behaviors. As mankind learns to allow Heart-centered, Intuitive Guidance to become man's primary tool for the engagement of and participation in life-experiences, too will mankind come to appreciate more evolved states of Liberation and the clarity of perception inherent to conditions of God-Conscious Being.

TRANSFORMATION OF PERCEPTION - TRANSCENDENCE

Man's understanding of lower density perceptions and one's

ability to implement more evolved perception states lie in man's willingness to acknowledge and transform linear, judgmental, reactionary thought and behavior patterns. When mankind reaches the point in evolution that demonstrates willingness to Acknowledge, Forgive, Bless and Release those aspects of conditioned, counterproductive, dysfunctional behaviors that impede Light-minded Behaviors, then man will not only be ready to accept responsibility for all that he/she thinks, feels and does, but man will also be ready to perceive the reality of life-experience in Third Dimension from a perspective of Transcendence. This is to say that mortal man will have released self from the importance of self, and will have allowed Evolved Self to consciously Ascend and bond with The Infinite Body of God.

The level of evolved perception we define as Transcendence is the state of Conscious Existence that allows a soul incarnate being the opportunity to clearly see, comprehend and assimilate The Lessons of Existence and The Precepts of Universal Law that underlie every life-condition, scenario and experience of mortal life. The understanding of life-conditions experienced facilitates acceptance of that which had been one's personal reality, thereby making it unnecessary to judge, react or to feel personally damaged by any life-condition one might experience. Though this does not mean that one becomes impervious to emotional pain or no longer cares about or empathizes with the misfortunes and suffering of mankind, it does mean that one can transcend misplaced emotional feelings of responsibility or overwhelming desires to right the wrongs that frequently are clearly the result of another's Karmic Choice and/or Karmic Debt.

The evolution of perception states facilitates Divine Understanding that in turn facilitates mankind's conscionable application of Universal Law. So then, it is man's willingness to accept his/her place of responsibility and function within Divine Order that further allows man to understand the reality of Divine Truth, Co-Creation and the Etheric LoveLight Vibration that is The Oneness of Creation. Accordingly, acknowledging the need for Heart-centered Behavior in the treatment of all things born of Creation allows mankind to surrender the compelling drives and the single-minded intent of ego-consciousness to The Greater Universal Will of The One Infinite Creator, which then allows man to become a truly conscionable servant to the needs of Creation.

When mankind evolves to The Transcendent Perception States of Divine Consciousness, there will be no reactionary, judgmental thoughts or behaviors to compromise the expression of Divine Love. This then will allow mankind to express those aspects of God-Realization that facilitate Universal Evolution by benevolently impacting upon The Greater Good of All Creation.

INTUITIVE WISDOM - THE OPEN HEART CHAKRA & GOD-SELF

The discovery and utilization of Intuitive Wisdom signals the beginning of the acknowledgment and the acceptance of the God-Self as a viable, functional aspect of mortal consciousness. Each soul incarnate being in his/her journey toward the assimilation of The Wisdom of One will learn to access and accept the guidance of his/her own Intuitive Wisdom.

Intuitive Wisdom lies dormant within the energy matrix of each mortal being, awaiting the moment of discovery through the functioning of an open, evolved Heart Chakra. It is inevitable that at some point in the process of Soul Evolution that each mortal incarnate will reach the moment of readiness to accept the reality of Intuitive Wisdom generated by the God-Self, which is the evolved, conscious energy matrix of the Heart Chakra.

Through the process of opening and transmuting the emotional wounds of the Heart Chakra, mortal man is given the first glimpse of Patience, Compassion, Wisdom, Mercy, Serenity and Altruistic Love. For it is through the open, evolved Heart Chakra that mankind learns of his/her true inter-connected relationship with all things born of Creation, and in so doing, mankind learns of man's shared, personal connection to The Infinite Body of God.

You see, it is for each seeker of Spiritual Truth to accept the reality of Intuitive Wisdom and realize that Heart-centered Behavior is the only true course of behavior that will facilitate the conscious acknowledgment of man's place and responsibility in The God's Divine Order. Each soul incarnate being will experience his/her moment of readiness to resolve Karmic Debts and to transform counterproductive, conditioned behaviors, making it possible for man to transmute the memory systems and energy of emotional wounds that would compromise the flow of benevolent, Heart Chakra Energy - the very vehicle by which the recognition and the implementation of Intuitive Wisdom is achieved.

Intuitive Wisdom frequently surfaces through symbolic references in dreams, visions, during Meditation and Prayer and during the process of Intuitive Channeling. Only when one has consciously chosen to transmute the wounds and fears of the Heart Chakra and is willing to break the bonds of bias and societal conditioning can one learn to fully access the Absolute Truth and simplistic beauty of one's own Intuitive Wisdom.

CASE STUDIES

To illustrate the nature of the symbolic references offered through Intuitive Wisdom, let us examine several cases of Dreams, Visions and Meditations. (Appendix II lists Trans-Cultural Symbols of Intuitive Wisdom.)

CASE 1. MEDITATION SEQUENCE:

A young woman visualizes a familiar woodland setting, and enters a cave that she has visited many times before during her Meditations. Much to her surprise, the interior of the cave was drastically different - no longer was the cave a cozy, friendly sanctuary. Now the cave was lined from top to bottom in thick layers of impenetrable ice. The scene abruptly changes and the young woman begins to visualize three items: 1. a very large, very old key; 2. a clamp like the kind used to hold two pieces of wood together while glue sets; 3. a hammer. The Meditation Sequence ends.

One interpretation of the symbolic references of this Meditation Sequence is that the young woman is experiencing some kind of personal or emotional conflict that has caused her to "freeze" her innermost feelings or shut down that part of self that could be invaded by or injured as a result of emotional engagement. Her safe haven, her innermost feelings and illusions of self are represented by the comfort and quietude offered by the cave, but when she discovers that the cave has been transformed into a lifeless, inhospitable place, she is being told that she has closed her Heart Chakra in anticipation of the possibility of being injured through emotional encounter. The young woman is being told that she is responsible for changing the nature of her once safe haven in reaction to perceived potentials for damage to her illusions of self.

93

The abrupt change in visual references shifts the focus from the illusions of self to the constructive engagement of elements of self to resolve dysfunctional attitudes and rebuild the essence of self by facing long standing issues of fear and uncertainty. The very old key represents an answer to unlock a very old dysfunction, or resolve a very old illusion of self that has been available to the young woman for some time. The clamp indicates a condition or state of mind held together by outside, artificial means, and the hammer implies that the young woman has the tools or necessary equipment to effect needed changes in perceptions and rebuild the true reality of self.

Visual references like those given in this Meditation can offer the seeker of Conscience the impetus to release self from the illusions of self, and accept the Truth of Reality wherever it is found.

CASE 2. DREAM SEQUENCE:

A young man sees himself holding a golden-brown wing feather from a large bird of prey. Suddenly, the young man sees himself in midair, flying, soaring over places he once lived, schools he had attended and places he once worked. Slowly, while in midair, the young man begins to visualize the faces of many people he had once known, and a sense of anxiety begins to grow within him. He sees family members, teachers, old girl friends, neighborhood pals and bullies, church ministers, athletic coaches, former employers and his ex-wife. The young man's sense of anxiety escalates and overtakes him, causing him to lose confidence in his ability to fly. The young man begins to falter in midair. Then he starts to fall to Earth at an ever increasing speed – spiraling downward, down, down, down... A few seconds before he crashes into the ground, he awakens from the dream soaked with perspiration, gasping for breath and terrified.

The symbolic references contained in this Dream Sequence indicate that this young man has apparently been traumatized by the effects of attempting to live up to the expectations of others, the kind of performance anxiety that literally destroys self-esteem and the ability to execute the simplest of life tasks without wondering what others will think of one's performance. The wing feather from the bird of prey, probably a golden eagle, represents the young man's desire to "fly free" and purge self of the crippling illusions of self and performance anxieties that haunt him. Seeing people and places from his past from an elevated position of flight fails to reassure the young man that he can or will transcend the haunting pressures and threats of failure that follow him. And as his fears and lack of confidence overtake him, he begins to plummet back into the very reality that he fears the most - that indeed he is a failure in life and must live with the humiliation and pain of his gaping imperfections for the rest of his life.

Dream Sequences of this type can be invaluable diagnostic tools in the assessment and subsequent facilitation of dysfunctional energies, attitudes and behaviors. Care and caution should be employed, however, as hasty decisions about the behavior traits of soul incarnates who experience disruptive sleep episodes, frightening Dream Sequences or who exhibit compulsive, anxious, reactionary, or self-abasing attitudes require considerable observation, empathy and understanding to effectively and conscionably assist them through the dynamics of their own Karmic Choices.

CASE 3. MEDITATION SEQUENCE:

A woman sees a beautiful white swan swimming around the perimeter of what appears to be an abandoned lake. Soon the sky darkens, and it begins to rain, first in gentle droplets then in more pronounced, heavier droplets. Before long, it begins to rain harder and harder until it becomes a severe downpour. The swan continues to swim slowly around the lake. After a time the rain subsides, and the sun begins to peer through the clouds. The swan swims to the center of the lake, and as the rays of the sun gently warm its body, the swan nestles its head against its wing feathers.

We can interpret the references in this Meditation Sequence as being indicative of the illusion of times of abandonment, disruption, hardship and dysfunction that pass like a summer storm to reveal the Truth of a radiant sky. The swan swimming around the abandoned lake is symbolic of a woman who has been left alone to fend for herself, be it the disruptive dissolution of a marriage or relationship, or children leaving home to engage the adult world, the feeling or the illusion of being alone to face an uncertain future is implied. Through the turmoil of the heavy downpour of life's trials and tribulations, the swan continues to swim, which indicates that the woman will not give up or give in to the feelings or illusion of being unable to cope with life on her own. And finally, when the rain or the discordant illusions of life dissipate and subside, the swan, the woman, is left knowing that there is comfort and Conviction in her own strength of being - her own ability to weather the storms of life and stand in The Light of God.

CASE 4. DREAM SEQUENCE:

A woman goes to meet three of her family members (mother, father and sister) at a restaurant for a meal. When she arrives at the restaurant, her family is already inside and seated. Her sister beckons to the woman to come inside and join them. The woman tries to enter the restaurant to go where her family is seated, but finds obstacle after obstacle impeding her path, making it impossible to join her family at the table. The woman decides to seek another entrance to the restaurant so that she can join her family.

She finds what appears to be another outside door to the restaurant and opens it only to find a red brick wall, instead of an entrance-way into the restaurant. The scene shifts and now the woman is standing with her mother, father and sister outside of the restaurant. The woman's sister asks, "Why didn't you join us at the table?" The woman replies, "I tried, but I couldn't get through." The Dream Sequence ends.

In this Dream Sequence, the woman is attempting to make contact, commune or communicate with family members who represent consolidated resistance to that which the woman is, wishes to communicate or hopes to resolve. Even though the woman's sister signals her to join them, neither the woman's sister, nor her parents make any effort to come to her. The woman is left to seek other avenues of entry to join her family group, but is met with obstacle after obstacle that denies her the opportunity to functionally engage her family. Then the final obstacle, a red brick wall that shouts, "Stop!" is placed before the woman, which represents the woman's family's unwillingness to hear or to accept that which the woman wishes to offer. The last scene of the Dream Sequence represents the woman's acknowledgment to self that she has not and can not penetrate her family's resistance and unyielding attitudes against that which she is, wished to communicate or would have hoped to resolve. This then leaves the woman with the clear impression that further attempts to engage her family about issues that they choose not to acknowledge will prove to be fruitless and possibly counterproductive.

CASE 5. DREAM SEQUENCE:

A woman sees a face begin to materialize out of the dark in front of her. At first, she thinks she sees a kind of animal-like, humanoid creature beginning to appear, then she sees that it is the face of a handsome young man she once knew. The woman begins to reminisce about the time she shared with this young man many years ago. The darkness surrounding the face of the young man begins to transform into a scene that depicts a beautiful, spring-time meadow with honeysuckle and clover filling the air, and the woman and her young man are seated by the edge of a crystal clear stream. The young man stands up, turns away from the woman and without a sound walks into the stream, the water becomes deeper and deeper, until the young man is totally sub-merged beneath the surface of the water. Everything becomes very quiet and still. The scene slowly fades into black. The woman awakens from the Dream Sequence.

The woman having this dream has in all likelihood kept the illusion alive that she shared a wonderful romantic interlude with a handsome young man who cared deeply for her. In truth, how-ever, the symbolic references in the Dream Sequence reveal that the handsome young man was indeed not what he appeared to be. Initially, the woman thinks that she is observing a kind of non-human creature that eventually becomes the face of her young friend. Then due to the woman's sense of wish fulfillment, she finds herself in a romantic setting with her handsome young man, but he leaves her without a word of explanation and is cleansed of his deceit in the crystal waters of the stream. It is also implied here that it is time for the woman to release the illusion she has carried about this young man and herself - release him and release herself from the folly of delusion.

CASE 6. OUT OF BODY EXPERIENCE/ALTERED STATE OF
        CONSCIOUSNESS SEQUENCE:

A man awakens from what he believes to be a natural state of sleep to find that he is flying over land masses that he intuitively knows to be North America. The man seems to be flying at an incalculable rate of speed, back and forth, one coast to the other, East to West and North to South. Even though the man seems to be traveling faster than the speed of light, he has no difficulty recognizing many things below him: 1. he sees a mother bear and her two cubs frolicking and fishing in a clear mountain stream for salmon; 2. he sees two mountain lions side-by-side, perched atop a hill, watching a small group of deer; 3. he sees seven bald eagles in synchronized flight soaring beneath him; 4. he sees a Giant Redwood Forest with dozens of small children joyously hugging the trunks of the trees; 5. he sees a rattle snake guarding the entrance to a pathway that leads to an Earthen Mound Temple high in the mountains. The Visionary Sequences end and the man slowly begins to reintegrate into his physical body. He feels chilled and a bit disoriented, but reflects upon his experience to comprehend what has happened to him.

In this Out-of-Body Sequence, the man is given many clues about his life and the course it will follow. The initial flying sequence illustrates the kind of freedom, the unfettered, unencumbered existence the man can and will experience in his journey of Self-Realization, and in his rendering of service to the whole of Creation. It is also given that the man will traverse North America many times in his quest for God-Realization, and in his giving of Self for The Greater Good of Creation. This point is represented in the man's complete flight over North America: "...back and forth, one coast to the other, East to West and North to South." The five sets of visual references hold particular symbolic meaning for this man. The mother bear and her two cubs represent the seriousness of introspection, while simultaneously not taking self seriously in the discovery of Self. The two mountain lions represent strength and Conviction poised to make a definitive statement of purpose and intent at the opportune moment. The seven bald eagles in synchronized flight are the symbolic representation of The Sealed Initiate of The Light of One existing in The Grace of God-Realized Consciousness. The Giant Redwood Forest and the small children represent the steadfast Patience, Compassion, Wisdom and Love of Grandfather embracing the innocence and exuberance of the children of Creation. The rattle snake guarding the path that leads to an Earthen Mound Temple high in the mountains is the symbolic rite of passage of Ascension into The Infinite Body of God. Here the snake is the guardian or the Earth Energy of life-experience that must be engaged and understood before initiation can occur. As the aspirant travels up the mountain, or ascends to the Temple, the Etheric Initiations begin. This then allows The Fully Sealed Initiate of The Light of One to enter The House of God. So, as we stipulated earlier, the man was given graphic representations about the nature of his life, the journey he would encounter in his evolution of Self and the areas of consciousness that he would uncover in his discovery of The Greater Truth.

PRACTICE EXERCISES

The cases that follow are examples for the reader to analyze for symbolic references of Intuitive Wisdom.

EXAMPLE 1. DREAM SEQUENCE:

A man is driving a brand new, red, two-door sedan down a deserted, somewhat familiar city street. It is about 6:00 AM and he is driving far in excess of the speed limit, but somehow he knows that all the traffic lights will turn green as he approaches each successive intersection. The man has no thought or fear that the police might suddenly appear and arrest him or that he might have an accident. He just seems to know that the way he is driving is acceptable. The Dream Sequence abruptly ends.

EXAMPLE 2. MEDITATION SEQUENCE:

A woman begins her daily Meditation period, and quickly enters a deep meditative state. For a time it seems as though she is drifting, without direction or purpose. Out of the mists and swirls of darting energy that fill the field of her third eye vision, images begin to appear: 1. she sees a pair of woman's hands, reaching out as if in need of something; 2. she sees a stained glass window colored predominately in shades of blue with a bit of purple and a little red; 3. she sees a weather-beaten, barren tree with an eagle's nest perched at the top. Slowly the images begin to fade, and the woman begins to reintegrate from her Meditation, reflecting upon the images she has seen.

EXAMPLE 3. DREAM SEQUENCE:

A man finds himself in the midst of a tropical jungle. The thick vegetation makes passage extremely difficult and slow. The man pauses a moment to catch his breath and to get his bearings. He looks down at his feet and sees a dark colored snake. The snake raises its head and body, and at that point the man notices the snake's hooded neck that identifies the snake as a cobra. The man continues his journey, and in the distance he sees a silhouetted human figure that seems somewhat familiar to him. The figure motions to him in a manner that seems to say, "Follow me, this is the way." The man glances at the cobra and sees that its eyes have turned a fiery, blood red. Suddenly, the man awakens from the dream.

EXAMPLE 4. MEDITATION SEQUENCE:

A woman visualizes a young Native American man with a large bird of prey perched on his arm. The bird has a long leather cord attached to its leg. The woman notices that the crown of the bird is a golden brown color, and that its body is a medium shade of dark brown. The woman is drawn to climb onto the back of the bird, but has difficulty positioning herself on the bird's back. As the bird leaps into flight, the woman reaches up and grasps the bird's talons so that she too can take flight. The woman flies with the bird for a time. She looks down upon the land and feels secure. Suddenly, the bird is unable to fly any higher. The woman and the bird are suspended in midair, unable to move in any direction. Now, the scene changes to show the woman dressed in a flowing white gown, standing upon the deck of a sailboat. The water is calm and the gentle wind softly caresses her gown, causing the gown to sway ever so gently back and forth. The Meditation Sequence ends.

Frequently, one's memory of Dream Sequences is fragmented, with only bits and pieces of feelings and images that linger upon awakening. And many times, the unsuccessful attempts to remember the details of dreams can prove to be frustrating or dis-courage one from considering dreams as useful tools in the Transformation of lower self. But what will have been overlooked is that the true "road-signs" given are those elements of Dream Sequences that are remembered, the references to life-experiences, thought and behavior patterns that are in common, recurring theme in several dreams.

Accurate interpretation of Dream Symbolism is the result of acknowledging the significance of the dream elements remem-bered and the contextual references that most dramatically impact upon the senses. The dream elements remembered are the "road-signs" that point to the areas of one's Conscious Existence that the Dream addressed. Simply put, one remembers the elements or symbols in dreams that one needs to remember in order to facilitate positive changes in attitudes and behaviors. One remembers what one needs to remember, not what one wants to remember, as it is the Intuitive Self that is responsible for generating the "road-signs" that lead to Conscious Evolution - not the ego that would demand and expect immediate understanding.

Allowing self to interpret and comprehend the symbolic references found in Dreams, Meditations and Visions allows one to actively embrace the "road-signs" given through Intuitive Wisdom. When mortal consciousness evolves to the state of awareness in which mankind collectively acknowledges Intuitive Wisdom as Divine Guidance, then too will mortal man have learned to accept and utilize one of the most dynamic tools possible for the successful, conscionable engagement of life upon the Earth Mother.

Though care and consideration are to be exercised in the assessment and interpretation of symbolic references given in Dreams, Visions and Meditations, it should also be noted that the context in which a specific symbol or reference is given must be granted special consideration in the determination of its meaning. Contextual differences and embellishing factors can subtly or dramatically change the meaning of a symbol from one instance of occurrence to another. It is also true that personal background and experience can lend additional evidence to support the interpretation of symbolic references encountered, especially when one is in the midst of turmoil, transition or problematic life-experience. And most importantly, the extent to which one is successful or accurate in deciphering the meanings of symbols or "road-signs" is largely determined by one's willingness to openly and Selflessly embrace the reality of experience, as the most evolved perceptions of reality occur as the direct result of engaging incarnate experience through an open Heart Chakra. It is then that every child of God can clearly see The Path of Truth that lies ahead, and through Intuitive Wisdom comprehend the insights offered each step along the way.

TRANSFORMING THE SEEKER:
Accepting And Nurturing The Light Of God

CHAPTER 6

It is vitally important for each seeker of Spiritual Unfoldment who feels called to engage in the practice of Loving Touch Therapy™ and Healing Facilitation to seek the highest, most evolved Heart Chakra states possible, for it is through the Heart Chakra that the facilitator is able to glean insights into the factors and subtle energy states responsible for precipitating the dysfunctions encountered in clients. It follows then that if a facilitator chooses to Shield his/her Heart Chakra from possible injury, or denies or suppresses personal emotional traumas, or has not taken the time or interest to address discordant emotional energies known to reside within his/her own Heart Chakra, then it is also the case that the facilitator can not function at optimum resonance, and is at risk of misreading clients' energy states and/or transmitting personal discordance (emotional energy) to each client engaged.

EGO TRANSFORMATION

In order to accept and nurture The Light of The Living God Spirit in one's heart, one must choose to engage a conscious process of Ego Transformation, in which the wounds of the Heart Chakra and the illusions of ego-self are Acknowledged, Forgiven, Blessed and Released with Love in The Light of One. But first, let us address the nature and function of the ego. The ego functions to attain and maintain successful survival drives that feed the physical consciousness or gross body with that which the conscious mind or causal body has been conditioned to believe are necessary emotional considerations and valuable material comforts. In short, the ego functions to feed self-serving drives that seek to actualize states of survival, pleasure, conquest, possession and control. When seekers of enlightened consciousness make the conscious choice to release self from the drives and illusions of ego, and to serve the needs of Creation, then each aspirant finds that the ego begins to undergo an interesting process of Transformation.

Frequently, at best it is a difficult task for some aspirants to truly see the nature of self and identify the compulsions and the veils of illusions of self created by the ego. Indeed, it can most certainly be a difficult task to unravel the illusions of self and decipher the intricate, egocentric devices that have allowed a soul incarnate to enjoy reasonable success in negotiating mortal experience. But under no circumstances does this mean that it is ever impossible for a soul incarnate being to effectively identify and understand the ego-facilitating devices that have been used to maintain the illusions of self. There are, of course, occasions and circumstances that present more of a challenge than others to accurately identify the illusions and devices of ego-self, but the dedicated seeker of Spiritual Truth will discover that which is needed in the journey of Unfoldment through the execution of Patience, Conviction and Faith in The Wisdom of The Universal Will of The One Infinite Creator.

ILLUSIONS & MECHANISMS OF EGO DEFENSE

As discussed in Chapter 1, the egocentric devices or Defense

Mechanisms employed by the ego to create and maintain the illusions of self are:

1. Rationalization - the process of devising superficially plausible reasons or excuses for behaviors, desires or beliefs, usually without being aware that the reasons given are not the true motives.

2. Intellectualization - the process of endowing superficial elements of consciousness with intellectual significance.

3. Repression - the unconscious process of forcing ideas, impulses, beliefs or feelings that are painful to the conscious mind into the unconscious mind, where the energy of the ideas, impulses or beliefs nonetheless remain active and influence behavior.

4. Suppression - the active process of deliberately excluding an idea, desire or feeling from conscious thought or behavior, which frequently leads to a state of denial and/or withdrawal.

5. Sublimation - the process of expressing socially unacceptable thoughts, behaviors or biological drives in more constructive, socially acceptable forms.

6. Denial - the blatant disregard for and detachment from an aspect of reality that threatens or holds the potential of danger or injury to the illusions of ego-self.

Each of these egocentric devices begins as a simple conscious or unconscious desire to control the illusions of self or as an attempt to conform to attitudes and behaviors thought to be appropriate, but in time, the devices become second-nature and are engaged with little or no conscious thought. The seemingly "natural" response patterns that subsequently develop are anything but natural, for the soul incarnate will have followed a deliberate course of action specifically designed to avoid the Truth of Reality, instead of engaging Truth for The Greater Good of All. You see, it is the soul incarnate who indulges self with elaborate plans of ego defense that quickly learns to generalize responses to perceived danger, and more often than not, judges and quickly reacts to potential situations thought to be damaging to the illusions of self before actual dangers really develop.

At this stage, it is very difficult for some soul incarnates to identify or to accept that behavior patterns engaged have been counterproductive or are impeding the development of God-Conscious Being. In fact, it is not uncommon to hear a soul incarnate speak of his/her proficiency in protecting self from "feeling" or from "being damaged" by unpleasant aspects of life by creating mind-sets designed to rationalize, repress, suppress or completely deny the reality of harsh life-situations. Maintaining attitudes of this nature is not in keeping with the Conscious Evolution of God-Realized Being, but nonetheless may be required by some soul incarnates to assist self in ultimately breaking free from the designs and illusions of the ego.

WARRIOR/PROPHET/SAGE CONSCIOUSNESS

The time of Transformation during which the ego-self is re-oriented we describe as the periods of The Warrior/Prophet/Sage Consciousness. As an evolving being of consciousness, the Warrior seeks to find instances of injustice and inequity, and willingly, eagerly rushes to champion the cause of the weak or down-trodden in the name of righteousness. It is the Warrior, however, who takes pleasure in engaging and defeating any adversary that he/she deems to be behaving in unconscionable, malevolent ways.

110

It too is the Warrior or more aptly termed "The Spiritual War-rior/Protector of Righteousness" who is an illusion of self and is compelled by states of ego to defend those precepts that he/she sees as the only avenue of access to The Wisdom of One and The Living God Spirit.

Gradually, as the result of Meditation, Prayer and Contempla-tion, the consciousness of the Warrior begins to transform into the more refined conscious being of the Prophet. The Prophet is not compelled to wage war against the injustices perpetrated against humanity and the Earth Mother. Rather, the Prophet is the evolv-ing Soul Initiate who preaches the philosophy of Spiritual Unfoldment in The Light of The One Infinite Creator. It is the Prophet who seeks to find opportunities to deliver explanations and guidance from his/her understanding of The Wisdom of One. (It should be noted here that there are many intermediate stages of consciousness between the orientation of the Warrior and the fully realized Prophet.) It too is the Prophet who enjoys being center-stage and having a working understanding of the journey of Soul Evolution. Therefore, the Prophet is also directed by aspects of ego, but it is a state of ego-consciousness that is loosing its fear of personal injury and its predilection for instant gratification - as the Prophet is at constant risk of ridicule, castigation and rebuke.

Slowly, the Prophet begins to evolve into the Enlightened Consciousness of the Sage. There are many stages of Conscious Evolution required to transform the Prophet into the Selfless, Benevolent Knowingness of the Sage. The Sage is The Conscience and The Wisdom of The Universe existing in mortal form. The Sage has neither need, nor compulsion to fight for or preach about that which he/she knows to be the Truth of Reality. Rather, the Sage is content to simply be, to simply know, to simply allow, without desire or motivation to prove Self to anyone or anything.

The Sage simply makes Self available to answer questions and offer guidance concerning the nature of Conscious Existence, the Spiritual Journey and The Universal One to those earnest seekers of Truth who would seek his/her counsel. The Sage is The Conscience and The Wisdom of The Living God Spirit alive in the body of man.

LEVELS OF CONSCIOUSNESS

As we discuss Ego-Transformation and man's ability to accept and nurture The Light of The Living God Spirit, it is also appropriate to discuss the Levels of Consciousness or the Dimensions or Densities of Conscious Existence that man traverses in the Transformation of ego, and in the realization of Self. Chart 1 details the first Seven Levels of Consciousness, and shows associated Chakra States.

The First Level of Consciousness is defined as Time. Time is the illusion of existence within a given period or moment of reality that exerts a compelling influence and urgency regarding issues of survival, personal safety and need. The First Level or Density of Consciousness stimulates the least refined aspects of ego that can be represented in stubborn, argumentative, self-aggrandizing attitudes and behaviors. These are the most difficult attitudes to evolve beyond, because self-interest and personal well-being tend to be deeply conditioned in the conscious mind and behavior of mankind. Yet, as the opportunity and choice to seek more Light-minded Behaviors eventuate, so does man find that the struggle between the elements of self becomes less pronounced, and the understanding of Divine Purpose begins to develop.

The Second Density or Level of Consciousness is described as Space, which is the illusion of existence within a given area or

Chart 1 :
Levels of Consciousness (*Dimensions*)

1st Dimension - Time
    Focus: Lower Base Chakra Activity
    Issues: Immediacy of Personal Survival; Obsessive Desire for
           Order; Urgent Drives of Self-service

2nd Dimension - Space
    Focus: Lower Navel Chakra Activity
    Issues: Drives to Manipulate and Control Physical Reality

3rd Dimension - Form
    Focus: Lower Solar Plexus Chakra Activity
    Issues: Emotional Drives of Personal Will; Illusions of
           Self-worth and the Importance of Material Reality

4th Dimension - Thought
    Focus: Upper Heart Chakra Activity
    Issues: Acknowledgement of The God-Self; Acknowledgement
           of The Presence of God Alive in All Creation

5th Dimension - God-Realization
    Focus: Upper Throat Chakra Activity
    Issues: Conscionable Verbalization of Divine Truth

6th Dimension - Light-Being
    Focus: Upper Third Eye Chakra Activity
    Issues: Evolved Perceptions of Reality Through States of
           Liberation

7th Dimension - Unified God-Conscious Being
    Focus: Upper Crown Chakra Activity
    Issues: Conceptual Realization and Actualization of Divine
           Truth in the Engagement of All Creation

within the finite parameters of an energy state. The Second Density of Consciousness is responsible for stimulating attitudes and behaviors designed to control the elements of physical reality. So strong can the urge for control and acquisition of physical or material reality become that man can easily loose sight of other lower density drives that require attending. When Second Density Consciousness is man's primary focus, then man cares neither for the concept of Oneness, nor does man intend to relinquish the single-minded drive for the embellishment of self through the control and acquisition of property and physical reality.

The Third Dimension or Level of Consciousness is defined as Form. Form is the illusion of existence within the physical parameters of substance or the identifiable properties ascribed to a materialized energy state or finite state of being. The Third Dimension of Consciousness impacts upon the dynamics of personal will and influences man's choice of behaviors where issues of sacrifice and personal involvement in acts of service appear to lead to problematic situations for self. Third Density Consciousness places the ego at the crossroads of evolution, for the ego must now find an acceptable way to embrace its own self-interest, while engaging a process that will ultimately mean the release of self-importance all together. Clearly, Third Dimension Consciousness places the ego in an untenable position that requires the ego to utilize all of its devices and tricks to convince the conscious mind to maintain control and focus upon the prime directives for maintenance of self. Even though the ego works diligently and ruthlessly to maintain control of personal will and the directives to embellish self, it is through natural evolution that the existence of the God-Self is realized. No matter what the ego does, or how deeply entrenched in linear processes one might be, the time will arrive when the dynamics of the God-Self can no longer be denied.

The Fourth Level of Consciousness is that of Thought. Thought is defined as the illusion of existence that describes the state of Transcendence from material significance into the state of Divine Being through Light-minded, Heart-centered Consciousness. It is the Fourth Level of Consciousness that exerts the most profound influence upon the process of Ego-Transformation, for in the transition to and the existence in Fourth Density, the ego looses all of its energy of self-importance, and releases the conscious mind to bond with and work for the God-Self. Fourth Density Consciousness is the state in which the soul incarnate becomes the Soul Initiate, and chooses to actualize his/her existence within The Infinite Body of God. It is then that the Divine Mind of Universal Conscience becomes mankind's expression of Self. It is then that the true expressions of the God-Self can be made through an open, willing Heart Chakra. It is then that mankind will have evolved to accept his/her place within The God's Divine Order.

The Fifth Density of Consciousness is God-Realization. God-Realization is The State of Existence that utilizes Divine Thought to motivate behavior, and employs the unilateral implementation of Universal Law Dynamics throughout the realm of Conscious Being, thereby complimenting Divine Being with Divine Actions. The state of God-Realization acknowledges the use of both physical form and Divine Light Transmissions for the expression of Evolved Self. It is in the Fifth Density of Consciousness that Evolved Beings exist within "The Word of God," and through the Consciousness of Fifth Density, Evolved Beings transmit "The Word of God." At this Level of Consciousness, the self-serving ego simply does not exist, as it has undergone dramatic changes in orientation and has been absorbed in part by The Conscience of The Sage. The ego is now reshaped to function as a tool of discrimination, one that assists the God-Self in identifying elements of Conscious Existence. What this means is that the ego no longer functions to maintain survival drives or states of physical well-being. Rather, the ego's purpose is to assist the God-Self by identifying avenues by which The Greater Good can be served, and directing energies and efforts toward assisting the evolutionary function of all things born of Creation.

It is in the Fifth Dimension that the energies of the Prophet are finally transformed into the initial stages of the consciousness of the Sage. As the Sage becomes more integrated in Fifth Dimension reality, the greater expression of Self becomes evident in the energies of Patience, Compassion, Wisdom, Mercy, Serenity and Altruistic Love for all things within the realm of Universal Creation. It is now that the journey of Spiritual Truth begins in earnest, as the Sage awaits the seekers with whom he/she will share The Wisdom of The Ages.

The Sixth Level of Consciousness is described as Light-Being. Light-Being is The State of Existence in which all states of Conscious Being are accessed through and reside within the Evolved, Etheric Body, which is the completed energy matrix of the Soul Essence. The completed energy matrix of the Soul Essence is the state of Absolute Assimilation of The Lessons of Existence that is complimented by The Absolute Understanding of The Dynamics of Universal Will. In this Density, Karma, Karmic Debt and Karmic Resolution have no meaning, for all thought and behavior is processed through The Universal Will of The One Infinite Creator. This Level of Consciousness finds physical form for the expression of Self to be impractical and unnecessary. In the Sixth Density, perception modes reach the highest state of evolution, and the consciousness of the Sage finds even more dynamic expression as Thought Energy Transmissions.

The Seventh Dimension of Consciousness is the condition of Unified God-Conscious Being. Unified God-Conscious Being describes The State of Existence in which the evolved energy matrix of consciousness enjoys complete and Absolute Communion with The Living God Spirit, thereby facilitating the functional existence of The Living God Spirit in the physical plane as an Illuminated, Fully Sealed Initiate of The Light of One. This is the most dramatic expression of Realized Self that can touch and impact upon each of the other Six Densities of Consciousness. Seventh Dimension Consciousness is the full realization of The Wisdom and Compassion of The Sage, the state of Conscious Existence that requires nothing for the generation, existence and benevolent sharing of Love and Peace with all things born of Universal Creation. Seventh Density Consciousness engages Universal Existence without the need of physical form by means of Divine Light Transmission, yet within the lower planes, Seventh Dimension Consciousness is expressed in the most efficient manner possible, be it form, Divine Light Transmission or otherwise that will announce the existence of The Living God Spirit within any Density of Consciousness.

The first four Dimensions of Consciousness are described as "illusions of existence," because each state exists solely in transient, temporal terms, which can be identified through the experience of Conscious Evolution. Dimensions Five through Seven, however, exist regardless of mortal considerations, and though mortal consciousness can on occasion access these Higher Evolved, Etheric States, only through the process of surrendering the egocentric designs of mortal consciousness to The Greater Universal Will of The One Infinite Creator, and through Conscious Ascension into The Infinite Body of God, can mortal consciousness be transformed into Unified God-Conscious Being.

CASE STUDY

To help clarify the concepts of ego-facilitating devices and Levels of Consciousness, let us analyze the following example for the purpose of identifying the operative states of Defense Mechanisms, and to observe behaviors associated with the different Levels or Dimensions of Consciousness.

EXAMPLE:

John is extremely punctual and is an exacting person who expects everyone around him to live up to his standards of performance. In fact, John's preoccupation with deadlines, schedules, matters of punctuality and efficiency has on many occasions triggered frustration, resentment and hostile judgments about co-workers, friends and family who did not live up to John's standards. In many cases, John judged others to be unworthy of his consideration, especially when others proved themselves to be incapable of keeping scheduled appointments or were unable to complete a given task by the deadline set for its completion. John sees himself as a man incapable of making a serious error in judgment or performance, yet after 15 years with the same company, he has not advanced beyond the lower management level. John reasons that he has not advanced because the company needs strong managers like he is "down in the trenches" to stabilize the foundation of the company.

ANALYSIS:

John's attitudes and behaviors can be identified as both controlling and compulsive, as his predilection with punctuality and efficiency illustrate John's attempt to maintain order within the illusion of existence, which is an illusion of existence within a finite moment of reality or his primal, First Density State of Consciousness. John's compulsive preoccupation with interests of time and performance is the primary driving force in his life.

John's judgmental attitudes about the behaviors of others help to maintain his inflated illusions of superiority and self-worth, and stimulate John's ability to use Rationalization and Suppression as tools for the defense of his illusions of self. Indeed John would reason that if he could not justify and discard his feelings about the ineptitude of co-workers, friends and family, in all likelihood, his sense of frustration and resentment might well cause inappropriate outbursts and counterproductive displays of emotion. Even John's deepest sense of betrayal and disappointment in being overlooked for job advancement is Rationalized and Suppressed so that he is not injured by his true emotional feelings.

John's behavior is quite predictable and will most likely follow the pattern of control and desire to protect the illusion of self-worth at all costs. John can reasonably be expected to be a soul incarnate who would seek to find fault and expose the shortcomings of others, and would use his findings, be they real or conjured, to validate his illusion of personal superiority. At virtually any time, John could be expected to attempt to exert control over any aspect of life or consciousness that would substantiate and offer continued validation in his eyes that he is in charge and most of all, that he is right.

CHAKRA SYSTEM FUNCTIONS:
Identifying The Orientations Of Energy States Within The Physical Body

CHAPTER 7

The Chakra System is responsible for regulating and directing the flow of vital life energy through the physical body. Primary Chakras are located within the swirling energy matrix of the Chakra Cord that exists as a sheath of energy covering the length of the spinal column. Secondary or Meridian Chakras are located along the outer line of the body from shoulders to wrists and from hips to ankles. Chart III shows the placement of Primary and Meridian Chakras.

CHAKRA GAZING & CHAKRA SCANNING

Chakras or the individual energy centers responsible for the flow of vital life energy to a specific part of the body can be observed to exist in a variety of orientations or operative states of function. The process of Chakra Scanning and Chakra Gazing are used as tools to help the facilitator identify which of the Seven Chakra Orientations or combination of orientations are in evidence at any given moment within any specific Chakra. Illustrations 9 & 10 show Chakra Scanning Techniques.

Chakra Scanning is performed in the following manner:

1. After focusing, balancing and grounding self and after The

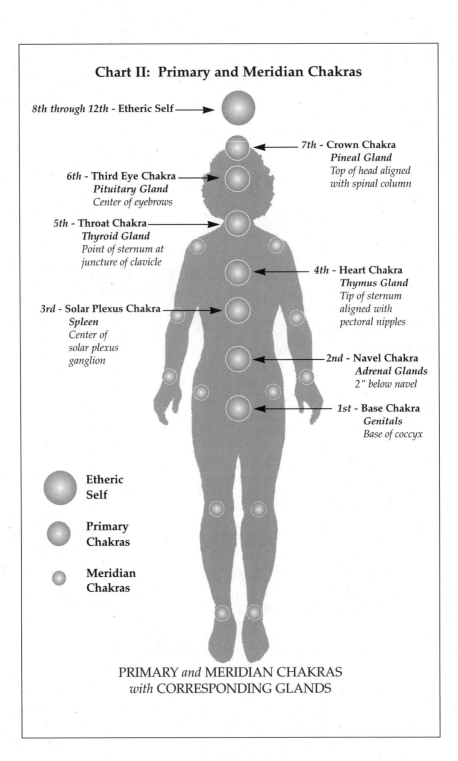

Chart II: Primary and Meridian Chakras

8th through 12th - Etheric Self ——▶

7th - Crown Chakra
Pineal Gland
Top of head aligned
with spinal column

6th - Third Eye Chakra ——▶
Pituitary Gland
Center of eyebrows

5th - Throat Chakra ——
Thyroid Gland
Point of sternum at
juncture of clavicle

4th - Heart Chakra
Thymus Gland
Tip of sternum
aligned with
pectoral nipples

3rd - Solar Plexus Chakra ——
Spleen
Center of
solar plexus
ganglion

2nd - Navel Chakra
Adrenal Glands
2" below navel

1st - Base Chakra
Genitals
Base of coccyx

Etheric
Self

Primary
Chakras

Meridian
Chakras

PRIMARY *and* MERIDIAN CHAKRAS
with CORRESPONDING GLANDS

Invocation of Divine Guidance, the facilitator asks the subject for permission to scan his/her Chakras before facilitation activities begin.

2. Beginning at the Crown Chakra, the facilitator, using the left hand with the palm open and facing the subject, moves from left to right in front of each Chakra. (If the subject is reclining, as in Illustration 10, scanning is performed from top to bottom, beginning at the Crown Chakra.) At the end of each pass in front of the Chakras, the hand is closed to disconnect from the energies transmitted by the subject. The hand is reopened when the next pass begins.

3. The facilitator is now allowing self to not only feel the energies in residence within the subject's Chakras, but also the facilitator is allowing self to feel the reality of the subject's experience within the facilitator's own Heart Chakra. This Intuitive aspect of Chakra Scanning is vital, as it is through the facilitator's willingness to acknowledge and accept the reality of the subject's Chakra conditions that accurate determination of Chakra Orientation is made.

Chakra Gazing is the Intuitive and cognitive process of identifying the nature of Chakra Orientation by literally "looking into" a Chakra. This process is accomplished by focusing a steady gaze upon one specific Chakra for an extended time. The facilitator allows self to move beyond Third Dimension reality to see and feel the true nature of the Chakra Orientation. The focused gaze is maintained for as long as is required to begin to feel Expanded States of Consciousness* starting to occur. Usually, within a few

* See **CRYSTAL COMMUNION: LOVELIGHT MEDITATIONS** by Sri Akhenaton, pages 38-91 for "Symbols and States of Expanded Consciousness."

Illustration 9: Chakra Scanning Techniques (*Subject Seated Upright*)

(Left hand moves across each Chakra from left to right.)

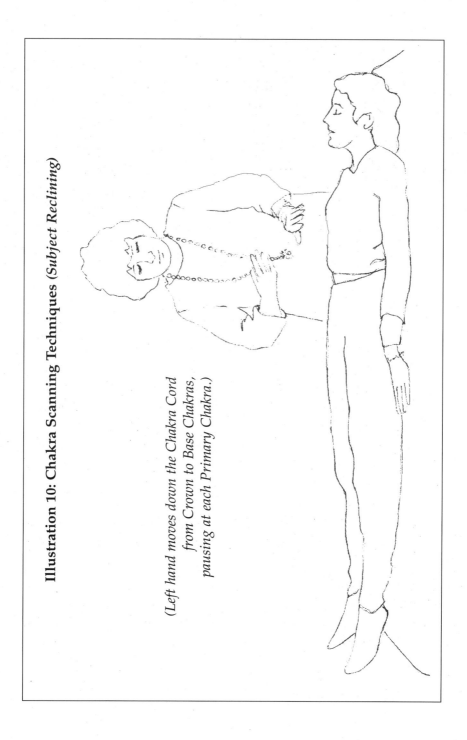

Illustration 10: Chakra Scanning Techniques (*Subject Reclining*)

(Left hand moves down the Chakra Cord from Crown to Base Chakras, pausing at each Primary Chakra.)

short moments, one's visual field seems to expand to reveal holographic images that depict the nature of Chakra Orientations. It is then that the facilitator will be able to ascertain, both Intuitively and cognitively, the true orientation of the Chakra being scanned. Begin Chakra Gazing at the Crown Chakra and repeat the same procedure at each successive Chakra en route to and including the Base Chakra.

CHAKRA ORIENTATIONS

Chakras can be observed operating in any one of several different states or combination of states based upon seven distinct Chakra Orientations:

1. An **Open Chakra** is a Chakra that facilitates the optimum free-flow of vital life energy to a particular area of the physical body. When scanned, an Open Chakra transmits sensations of comforting warmth and heat or tingling sensations that are registered by the facilitator as the Chakra's willing, productive, nonpretentious orientation and commitment to accessing Higher Evolved States of Consciousness. Open Chakras indicate that emotional memories and Karmic Debt have been Acknowledged, Transformed and Released, and that the soul incarnate will have consciously chosen to engage behaviors that impact upon The Greater Good of All Creation.

2. A **Partially Open Chakra** transmits a much smaller volume of vital life energy than does an Open Chakra. The reason for the reduced amount of vital life energy transmitted is due to one or more Blockages or obstructions that are essentially dysfunctional energy states and/or memory matrices of fear, anxiety, resentment, frustration, hostility or confusion that restrict

the volume of vital life energy that can flow through a Chakra classified as Partially Open. Nonetheless, sensations of hopefulness and a willingness to embrace elements of Truth can be Intuitively detected by a facilitator.

3. A **Closed Chakra** is a Chakra that when scanned offers the appearance of little or no detectable vital life energy flow. This is a Chakra that actually seems to feel cold and transmits sensations of lifelessness. (Technically, a Chakra can never actually be "closed," as there is always the presence of vital life energy flow through all Primary Chakras during incarnate life, no matter how infinitesimal the amount or how difficult it might be to detect.) Closed Chakra Orientations indicate that serious states of dysfunction exist within the energy matrix of a soul incarnate being, a state of emotional and/or physical arrest that must be conscionably engaged in order to affect conditions of well-being and Conscious Evolution. More often than not, a Closed Chakra will have one or more instances of emotionally arrested energy associated with Blockages that will have caused a soul incarnate to turn away from the acceptance of Truth represented in the conscionable, evolved behavior patterns affected through activities associated with a given Chakra. In short, a Closed Chakra indicates that a soul incarnate being has chosen to ignore, deny or effectively not address a troubling aspect of Conscious, Spiritual and/or Evolutionary Being, and upon closer investigation will most certainly have either a systemic/organic dysfunction or an emotionally induced physical dysfunction found to be centered in the region of the Closed Chakra.

4. Upon scanning, a **Partially Closed Chakra** can be observed to display a small amount of energy movement through its matrix, which indicates that less than an optimum flow of vital

life energy is being transmitted to a specific region of the body. The restricted flow of energy through a Partially Closed Chakra is usually the result of energy Blockages caused by unresolved conflicts: issues of self-worth, performance, security, anxiety, fear and basic perceptions and/or illusions of reality. There is always a distinct sense of trepidation, unwillingness or suspicion that the facilitator Intuitively registers when engaging a Partially Closed Chakra. Corresponding body regions to Partially Closed Chakras are usually sites of chronic physical dysfunctions that impact upon organ systems and general states of well-being.

5.   A dysfunctional energy matrix or **Blockage** may occur in Closed, Partially Closed and Partially Open Chakras to compromise or restrict the natural or optimum flow of vital life energy to a particular body region. The energy matrix of each instance of unresolved emotional conflict experienced by a soul incarnate is deposited as a Blockage in the Chakra area that corresponds to a given behavioral/emotional state or tendency. (See Charts IV & V for Chakra/Behavior Associations.) After a time, the accumulation of deposits of unresolved energy conflicts begin to adversely impact upon one's ability to clearly perceive elements of reality, and further hinder the effective engagement of life-situations that hold the potential for or represent the energy matrix of the unresolved energy dynamics of emotion and/or behavioral dysfunctions. In fact, the unpleasant life-experiences that mortal man thinks have been effectively dealt with or "put out of his/her mind," more often than not, have instead been Rationalized, Suppressed or Intellectualized and remain alive, unknown and unaddressed within mortal consciousness as dysfunctional memory patterns or discordant energy matrices. In any case, the existence of Blockages within the Chakra System identify specific needs

Chart III:
Chakra States & Associated Behaviors
Lower, Egocentric Phase

1st (Base) Chakra: Establishment and Maintenance of Personal Survival Drives and Personal Embellishments

2nd (Navel) Chakra: Control of Physical Reality through Conquest, Manipulation, Acquisition, Accomplishment, Dominance, Self-importance

3rd (Solar Plexus) Chakra: Execution of Personal Will and Impact of Emotional Matrix upon Attitudes and Behaviors

4th (Heart) Chakra: Behaviors Motivated by Drives of Self-worth and Need for Protection of Illusions of Ego-self

5th (Throat) Chakra: Repression of Personal Reality of Truth

6th (Third Eye) Chakra: Analysis, Speculation and Logical Progressions of Linear Thought Process; Rationalization and Justification for Self-serving Behaviors

7th (Crown) Chakra: Rejection of Spiritual Path as Viable or Practical Life-plan

Chart IV:
Chakra States & Associated Behaviors
Higher, God-Conscious Phase

1st (Base) Chakra: Cooperation

2nd (Navel) Chakra: Implementation of Godliness in
                                           Daily Behavior

3rd (Solar Plexus) Chakra: Selflessness

4th (Heart) Chakra: Expressions of God-self

5th (Throat) Chakra: Verbalizations of Divine Truth

6th (Third Eye) Chakra: Evolved Perceptions of Reality;
                                           Perceptions of Truth in The Light
                                           of One

7th (Crown) Chakra: Realization of Divine
                                           Consciousness

8th through 12th Chakras: Elements of Higher Self
                                           (Etheric Consciousness States that
                                           seek to integrate with the conscious
                                           thought process to develop Light-
                                           minded behavior)

for mortal man to Acknowledge, Forgive, Bless and Release energies of emotion, fears, anxieties, frustrations and any other counterproductive states of consciousness that impede the journey toward the realization of man's personal, undeniable relationship to The Infinite Body of God.

6. Occasionally, during Chakra Scanning and Chakra Gazing, there will appear to be a cellophane-like covering over a Chakra. The fleeting appearance or the Intuitive discernment of this phenomena is the discovery of a **Chakra Shield**. Chakra Shields occur as the result of a soul incarnate's desire to protect self from emotional realities that he/she fears will be unmanageable, potentially harmful or discrediting to the illusion of self. The relative age of a Chakra Shield can be determined by the thickness of its walls or outer edge, the newer Shield having a thin wall and the older Shield wall being significantly thicker. Typically, Chakra Shields occur in Closed or Partially Closed Chakras, but can occur in Partially Open Chakras as well.

The purpose of Chakra Shields is to create the illusion that the external world of emotion can not enter and upset the consciousness of the soul incarnate being who is Shielding self, but in truth the act of Shielding actually locks within one's energy matrix the very energy presence the soul incarnate had hoped to avoid. The very nature and presence of the emotional energy that was thought to be so threatening is now held within the energy matrix of the soul incarnate by the Chakra Shield. As a result, the soul incarnate tends to react and overreact to situations that appear to have the potential of generating the emotional energy that the soul incarnate fears engaging. Consequently, given the reactionary tendency and the growing fear and anxiety surrounding the engagement of the emotional energy in question, the soul incarnate loses his/her ability to clearly discern which life-situations actually lead to the unwanted emotional confrontations and those life-experiences that are only similar in appearance to those that promise the feared emotional energy. Interestingly enough though, the generalized pattern of reaction and the emotional turmoil created by the Shielding is typically unknown to the soul incarnate, but until the soul incarnate makes the conscious choice to engage the feared emotional confrontation, effectively dissolving his/her Shield(s), the soul incarnate will tend to remain in a constant state of alert, prepared to react to even the most innocent of images or instances seen by the soul incarnate to conjure the illusion of emotional conflict or engagement.

After a time, the degree of paranoia experienced by a soul incarnate can be overwhelming, causing him/her to completely withdraw from the reality of many life-situations, and in some cases, withdrawing entirely from the reality of Third Dimension life.

7. The final Chakra Orientation to be discussed is the most evolved state a Chakra can display in any single incarnate cycle. **Chakra Seals** or **Chakra Sealing** is the process of opening, clearing and elevating resonance rates that signals the evolution from soul incarnate to Soul Initiate. Chakra Sealing is an Etheric Process that acknowledges that a soul incarnate has effectively begun to learn The Lessons of Existence, and is moving toward a more dynamic assimilation of and a more proficient ability to unilaterally apply the precepts of Universal Law. Even though Fully Sealed Initiates of The Light of One engage in the practice of Sealing one or more Chakras, it is performed under the direct sanction and guidance of The Council of Twelve.

When scanned, an activated Chakra Seal can appear as a golden/white lotus blossom, a golden/white circle or a golden/white wheel with twelve spokes. Chakra Seals enable Soul Initiates to demonstrate higher, more refined perceptual abilities, greater comprehension of the nature of Conscious Existence and more dynamic and closer states of communion with The Infinite Body of God. On occasion, Fully Sealed Initiates will allow Self to be seen, and display the swirling, Golden/White Light Matrix of the Sealed Chakra Cord, with the radiance of each Primary Chakra pulsing, radiating in Harmony with The Very Heartbeat of God.

To assist in the development of proficiency in identifying Chakra Orientations, it is suggested that each soul incarnate interested in performing techniques of Loving Tough Therapy™ avail self of every opportunity to practice Chakra Scanning and Gazing. Ask permission to practice reading the Chakra States of friends and family as often as is possible. Take note of conditions under which Chakra States are read, and record any existing physical dysfunction at the time of reading. Observe behavior tendencies and the corresponding nature of the Chakra System. Practice as often and with as many different soul incarnates as possible to help broaden the experience of the various orientations and combinations of orientations Chakras can present.

Only through diligent practice and observation, along with a willing, open and evolved Heart Chakra, can the neophyte facilitator learn to access the Intuitive Guidance necessary to transform the process of Chakra Scanning, which at first glance might appear to be a complicated, laborious process, into one of the simplest, most natural procedures imaginable. Only by allowing self to fully participate in the process of discovery in service to the needs of Creation can one realize how simple, unfettered and liberating the experiences of life can be. Only by allowing self to be a conscionable servant to the needs of Creation can one participate in Loving Touch Therapy™ and acts of Healing Facilitation that ultimately impact upon The Greater Good of all things within the realm of Universal Existence.

HEALING FACILITATION
AND ENERGY TRANSMUTATION:
Fundamentals Of Loving Touch Therapy™

CHAPTER 8

Loving Touch Therapy™ is a dynamic process of Healing Facilitation in which Selfless Conviction and Love combine with Divine Guidance to inspire man to willingly embrace the pain and suffering of his/her brethren for the purpose of assisting another soul incarnate being in resolving dysfunctional energies of thought, emotion or behavior that adversely impact upon man's system of conscious well-being. It is the direct result of man's willingness to give of self without reservation to assist another in pain or to assist one's brethren trapped in the web of illusion, reaction and disharmony that stimulates the process of Transformation in Conscious Being - which is the very purpose of Loving Touch Therapy™. It is through Loving Touch Therapy™ and Healing Facilitation that a Soul Initiate assists another incarnate being in uncovering the motives for dysfunctional thoughts and behaviors. Subsequently through Loving Touch Therapy™, man learns to Acknowledge, Forgive, Bless and Release the counterproductive aspects of self that impede Light-minded Behaviors. Through Loving Touch Therapy™, mortal man is allowed to embrace all aspects of self with The Divine Presence of Love, and in so doing, come one step closer toward Divine Communion with The Living God Spirit.

LOVING TOUCH THERAPY™ & HEALING FACILITATION

The practice of Loving Touch Therapy™ requires the facilitator to become a willing vessel for the transmission of Divine Light Vibrations, as well as a willing receptacle for aspects of Karmic Energy and/or discordance engaged by the soul incarnate to be facilitated. Since mortal man does not "Heal," but is merely one component of the complex, Universal Process of Healing, it is important for man to understand and accept that man's role is that of a Divine Tool through which the Facilitation of Healing can be accomplished. It is vitally important that mortal man not take self seriously or think of self as an important person by virtue of the choice made to engage in acts of Healing Facilitation. Rather, it is for man to acknowledge self as a humble, willing servant to the needs of an incalculably dynamic process of Universal Being. So, the facilitator of Healing recognizes and accepts self as nothing more than a conscionable servant to a Divine Process of Unfoldment and Conscious Evolution.

Healing Facilitation and Energy Transmutation differ significantly from one another in the engagement of discordant vibrations, and in the establishment of states of conscious well-being. The primary difference between Healing Facilitation and Energy Transmutation is that the process of Healing Facilitation seeks to permanently transform the nature of dysfunctional thought, emotion and behavior by assisting mortal man in understanding the nature and function of behavior patterns that produce counterproductive energy states, whereas Energy Transmutation seeks to produce an immediate and often temporary change in the nature of discordant energy states.

As a facilitator of Healing, one seeks to uncover core motivations for thoughts, feelings and behaviors that demonstrate or lead to unwanted physical, mental, emotional and spiritual states of being. In the process of facilitating conditions of wellness, the facilitator is called upon to address the specific nature and underlying reasons for those behaviors and/or dysfunctions that are identified as problematic. This process of engagement allows the soul incarnate who is facilitated to understand the operations of ego-consciousness and the dynamics of hostile, subversive energies designed to thwart the acceptance of God-Realized Being. With an understanding of how specific thought and behavior patterns are established, an evolving soul incarnate being can choose to transform aspects of self, releasing self from the cycle of dysfunctional, reactionary behaviors that will have impeded the enjoyment of conscious well-being. Additionally, through the process of Healing Facilitation, the Transformation of elements of self finds states of completion, thereby making it unnecessary to repeat painful lessons of Third Dimension existence.

ENERGY TRANSMUTATION

Energy Transmutation is an act of facilitation designed to change the nature or form of an energy state from one experiential existence to another for the purpose of lessening the pain or burden of Third Dimension states of being. Energy Transmutation does not involve the recipient's understanding the process, form or nature of dysfunctional processes, energies or behaviors. Rather, Energy Transmutation has as its directive the immediate, short-term release of dysfunctional, discordant energy states that adversely impact upon the consciousness of man. Therein lies the major difference between Healing Facilitation and Energy Transmutation. Healing Facilitation engages a process that is designed to permanently resolve dysfunctional states of conscious being, while Energy Transmutation is concerned with the immediate, short-term relief from painful, problematic energies of life-experience.

You see, when discordant energies are engaged and simply transmuted, a memory matrix or energy framework from which the discordant energy was released remains within the energy system of the facilitated soul incarnate. When one does not understand the mechanics that perpetuate dysfunctional energies, then the soul incarnate will repeat the same behaviors that led to the development of the initial conditions of discordance. If there is no conscious understanding, then there is no conscionable directive to change behavior patterns, and the soul incarnate will simply find self in similar life-experiences that will stimulate similar conditions of discordance to those energies that were transmuted.

Though there can be many instances in which Energy Transmutation can be helpful or necessary to assist in the overall process of Healing Facilitation, it should be clearly understood that Energy Transmutation is at best a symptomatic, cosmetic treatment for a deeper, more complex condition. And it should also be noted that many times acts of Energy Transmutation inadvertently serve the counterproductive end of obscuring the deeper nature of dysfunctional energy systems. When one engages in acts of Energy Transmutation and allows the subject to believe that he/she is "cured," then the subject will feel as if the problem has been corrected without any conscious effort from the subject for resolution of issues, attitudes or behaviors that stimulated the dysfunctional condition. This then makes subsequent identification of similar energies of discordance very difficult, because the subject will be laboring under the assumption that "the problem had been solved." It is therefore very important to distinguish between acts of Energy Transmutation that are designed to bring instant relief from disturbing energy states and the process of Healing Facilitation that is designed to transform dysfunctional energies and change dissonant thought and behavior patterns into Light-minded Behaviors of Conscience.

SUBJECT'S READINESS TO
ACKNOWLEDGE & RELEASE DISCORDANCE

In Loving Touch Therapy™, when a facilitator engages a soul incarnate to render service, it is the facilitator's solemn responsibility to identify the subject's readiness to acknowledge and release the energies of discordance uncovered. Many times, a soul incarnate being will schedule a session for Loving Touch Therapy™ thinking that he/she is ready to release hostile, discordant energy states that have been identified, or in some cases, the energy state may not as yet have been fully revealed. In any event, the subject simply wants the facilitator to "get rid of the unpleasant energy." Typically, when a soul incarnate "thinks" that he/she is ready to release a discordant energy system, the odds are that the subject merely "wants" to release the discordance instead, and has not yet learned the lesson associated with that particular energy system of discordance. To transmute such an energy system will prove to be an unconscionable act on the part of the facilitator that ultimately creates a more obstacle laden path for the subject to negotiate.

You see, for one to "think" is for one to operate through the conscious mind and is therefore a function of a drive, either seen or unseen, of the ego - not a directive from the Intuitive Wisdom of the God-Self. If the ego is leading the way, then the higher purpose of evolved Self can not be the motivation for behavior. Therefore, the purpose of engaging in a Facilitation Session would be to strengthen an aspect of ego, instead of seeking to embrace Divine Communion. This kind of delusion is quite common, and each facilitator will experience occasions when the subject has to be told that he/she is not yet ready to release the energy system that the subject might be most eager to rid self of, as it will have been a system of discordance that will have proven to be the source of suffering, pain and disruption in life.

Nonetheless, it is the task of the facilitator to access the true, soul-level motives of the subject by gazing deeply into the subject's eyes and communing with the subject's soul consciousness, for in so doing, the facilitator can Intuitively ascertain that which the subject really needs at any given time. Since it is not uncommon for a soul incarnate being to say one thing, yet through the eyes, body language or tone of voice imply or transmit something entirely different, it is the responsibility of the facilitator to know that which is "good and right" through the functioning of an open, evolved Heart Chakra, and accurately "feel" the true reality of the subject. Then it is the task of the facilitator to tactfully assist the subject in unfolding the true feelings heretofore unidentified or embraced, thereby ultimately assisting the subject in the engagement and permanent release of dysfunctional energies and the Transformation of self.

RESPONSIBILITIES OF
THE LOVING TOUCH THERAPY™ PRACTITIONER

In the practice of Loving Touch Therapy™, the facilitator is charged with not only identifying and tactfully discussing the nature of the energies discovered, but most importantly, the facilitator must clearly understand which areas of consciousness the client is and is not ready or willing to engage. In short, the facilitator must not lead a client into an area of discussion or toward moments of self-discovery that the client has not been prepared or is not ready to conscionably engage, for to do so is to complicate the nature of the client's incarnate journey and to encroach upon Choice of Free Will. This point can not be over emphasized.

The facilitator of Loving Touch Therapy™ is charged with

knowing the limits within which each subject can comfortably engage aspects of self for conscionable resolution of dysfunctional energies. The facilitator can only know that which is good and right through the Intuitive Guidance of his/her own God-Self, and must be willing to simply allow the process of Facilitation to take place. What this means is that the facilitator can not be encumbered by preconceived notions about that which is or is not appropriate for a given client. Rather, the facilitator must be willing to accept the nature of any or all energy states that the client offers, and participate in the Facilitation Process as a humble servant to the needs of Creation. So then, as each client is presented for Facilitation, the practitioner of Loving Touch Therapy™ does not speculate about the outcome of a session, or set arbitrary goals to achieve, or guide the client toward realizations that the facilitator "believes to be in the best interest of the client." The facilitator knows that the only course of therapy that will not compromise the client's Choice of Free Will, or complicate the client's journey toward the assimilation of The Wisdom of One, or create Karmic Debt for all parties concerned is the path of Selfless Service that facilitates the needs of each soul incarnate being in the order and manner that is good and right, and in accord with The Precepts of Divine Will.

When clients schedule sessions for Loving Touch Therapy™, each soul incarnate being who seeks assistance from a facilitator is literally putting his/her life and consciousness in the hands of the facilitator. Each time a facilitator engages the energy matrix of a subject, the facilitator becomes a Divine Tool through which The Light of The Living God Spirit is Channeled. Clearly, responsibility for the engagement of the vital life energies of another soul incarnate being rests equally upon both the facilitator and the subject, but here we focus our attention upon the responsibilities of the facilitator.

The facilitator of Loving Touch Therapy™ is charged with educating each subject regarding the nature and dynamics of the relationship between and the specific responsibilities of both the subject and facilitator. It is for each facilitator to understand the parameters of his/her responsibilities to each subject and to the whole of Universal Creation. It is for each facilitator to understand how to conscionably communicate the respective areas of responsibility to each subject encountered, without expecting that subjects will automatically appreciate and respect areas of mutual and/or exclusive responsibility. It is for each facilitator to commune with each subject in The Light of Truth and Love, and in so doing assist in the Transformation of dysfunctional attitudes, behaviors and energies into states of conscious well-being.

It should be pointed out here that one of the primary responsibilities of a practitioner of Loving Touch Therapy™ is to respect the integrity of every client's energy matrix. What this statement means is that it is a matter of conscious commitment and diligent practice on the part of the facilitator to clearly define and execute that which is good and right in the performance of Energy Transmutation, Spiritual Counseling, Healing Facilitation and in the infusion of mortal consciousness with Divine Light Vibrations. Special care and consideration is to be acknowledged and implemented when confronted by obstacles that might hamper the successful completion of any stage of Loving Touch Therapy™.

On occasion, Loving Touch Therapy™ practitioners can encounter Chakra Shields or the fear and unwillingness of a client to constructively engage or resolve a dysfunctional energy state uncovered. It is for the facilitator to understand and accept the client's choice to Shield self or simply not engage dysfunctional energies discovered by the facilitator. Further, it is for the facilitator to clearly identify and acknowledge the existence of Chakra

Shields, and offer the client the opportunity to dissolve the Shields before the therapy session continues.

Under no circumstances is it conscionable for a facilitator to violate the integrity of a Chakra Shield by "pulling" discordant energies from a client. To do so is a direct violation of the client's Choice of Free Will, and establishes both Karmic Debt for the facil-itator and complicates the client's ability to find true resolution for the dysfunctional energy/behavior states at the time the client is ready to embrace the true elements of self. Additionally, tactics of this nature produce tears in the auric field, thereafter predisposing the client to additional levels of similar discordant energies. It is vitally important that facilitators of Loving Touch Therapy™ and other modalities as well clearly understand the parameters of con-scionable service and behavior, as upon the facilitator's shoulders can rest significant influence upon the Karmic Destiny of many soul incarnate beings.

PROCEDURES OF LOVING TOUCH THERAPY™

The commencement of Loving Touch Therapy™ begins with the facilitator's Invocation of Divine Guidance to assist in the acts of service scheduled for the day. After clients arrive for sessions and are allowed to relax, the facilitator then asks the client for per-mission to begin the session with a series of Chakra Scans. Now, the facilitator offers a Silent Prayer for guidance, then begins to identify areas of discordance by Chakra Scanning and Chakra Gazing. The facilitator simply allows his/her Intuitive Wisdom to focus upon those areas of the Chakra System that literally "call out" for assistance.

At this point, it is the facilitator's task to identify the nature of emotional energies in operation within dysfunctional Chakras.

Through empathy with the subject, the facilitator reflects upon the nature of the dysfunctional energies in residence within the subject, and "feels" the subject's true reality in his/her own Heart Chakra. Now, it is for the facilitator to tactfully inform the subject about the nature of the energies, dysfunctional behavior patterns and physical dysfunctions discovered. When both the facilitator and the subject are satisfied that the energies in residence within the subject have been accurately identified, then the facilitator can ask the subject if the subject would like to further investigate the nature of the energies uncovered and transmute the dysfunctions.

TRANSMUTATION OF DISCORDANT ENERGIES

To transmute discordant energies by touch, simply engage the procedures that follow:

1. Offer a Prayer for Blessing in The Name of Yahweh, By The Spirits of Buddha, Krishna, Mohammed and Christ Jesus, for the release of the discordant energy states. The use of The LoveLight Invocation/Blessing is appropriate.

2. Now, place the index and second finger of your left hand at the Chakra Point where discordance is discovered. Raise your right hand toward the sky, or in the case of "lower vibrations" to be released, point your right hand toward Mother Earth.

3. With Conviction, yet with Compassion and Love, recite the following Prayer: "In The Name of Yahweh, By The Spirits of Buddha, Krishna, Mohammed and Christ Jesus, let the discordant energy within this child of God be released, lifted with Love and Light, and returned to the place of its primordial birth to find its own moments of Peace. Go now, release this

child of God, and find thine own Peace. Shalom, Adonai, Shalom. Release...Release...Release..."

4. Now, visualize your left hand as being the suction tube of a vacuum. Watch as the discordant energy leaves the client and enters your left hand, travels up your left arm, enters your left shoulder, travels across your chest and enters your Heart Chakra, where you cleanse and bathe the discordance with Love, Compassion, Wisdom and Mercy. Now watch as the discordant presence leaves your Heart Chakra and travels into your right shoulder and down your right arm, into your right hand and finally is released from the fingertips of your right hand.

5. At this point, simply repeat: "Go now, and find thine own Peace. Shalom." (See Illustration 11.)

Another technique for transmuting discordant energy systems is as follows:

1. After identifying the site of discordant energy states, focus a gaze upon the Chakra that holds the discordance. Bless the client, the discordance and the Transmutation Process in The Name of Yahweh, By The Spirits of Buddha, Krishna, Mohammed and Christ Jesus and direct the discordance to leave the client and return to its own place of birth to find Peace.

2. Now, place your open left hand with the palm facing the client about 2-6 inches in front of the dysfunctional Chakra site. Ask the discordant energy to release the client by saying: "In The Name of Yahweh, By The Spirits of Buddha, Krishna, Mohammed and Christ Jesus, go now and find thine own Peace. Shalom."

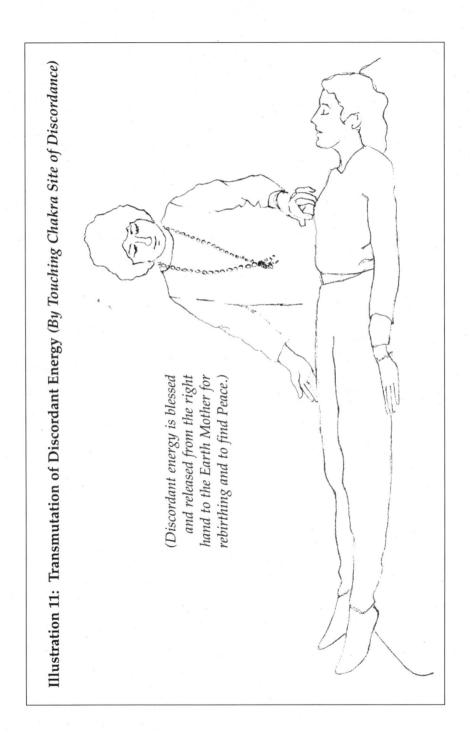

Illustration 11: Transmutation of Discordant Energy (By Touching Chakra Site of Discordance)

(Discordant energy is blessed and released from the right hand to the Earth Mother for rebirthing and to find Peace.)

1. Maintain your gaze upon the Chakra area and soon you will see what appears to be the head of a dark, snake-like creature, or a dark, oozing, amoebic energy mass begin to protrude from the Chakra area. (Image of the discordant energy state will appear in holographic form.) When the tip or head of the discordant energy presence is fully exposed, quickly close your left hand, grasping the head of this energy presence, and slowly, gently assist the discordant energy state from the client' s body. When you sense or see what appears to be the tail or end of the discordance coming to the surface, offer another Blessing of Love and Peace to encourage the discordance to completely release the client.

4. Now, with the discordant presence in your left hand, gently toss it toward The Ethers or direct it toward the Earth Mother, as the case may be, to find its own Peace. Bless the released energy and bid it parting farewell by saying, "Shalom." (See Illustration 12.)

After energies of discordance have been transmuted, it is then for the facilitator to counsel the client about the nature and dynamics of the energies released. It is through the client's comprehension of the energy state released, the attitudes and behaviors that sustain dysfunctional energy states and the nature of the subtle energy fields that allow discordant thoughts and impulses to exist that facilitates the Transformation of dysfunctional conditions - as now the client has sufficient input to warrant the resolution of counterproductive mind-sets and embrace behaviors that are Light-minded in nature. It is then that the process of Healing Facilitation takes its first steps toward completion.

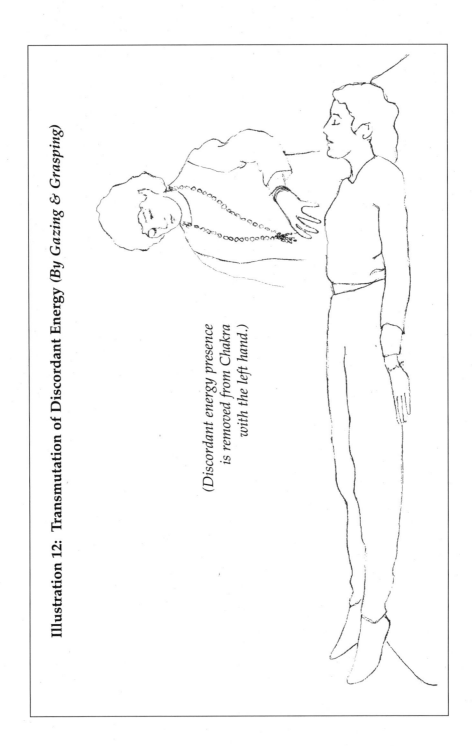

Illustration 12: Transmutation of Discordant Energy (*By Gazing & Grasping*)

(Discordant energy presence is removed from Chakra with the left hand.)

PERSONIFICATION OF DISCORDANT ENERGY STATES

Discordant energy states discovered in residence within human energy systems can frequently be seen as holographic images through Intuitive Vision by the evolved facilitator. Represented by a wide variety of unpleasant, animated creatures or personified two-dimensional states, discordant energies can present the illusion of being: serpents, dragon-like creatures, gnomes or gargoyles, hideous little creatures with ravenous mouths and razor-sharp teeth, crab-like or spider-like creatures clinging to the Chakra Cord, cunning, predatory animals like panthers, lions, tigers, wolves, hyenas, vultures or distorted, "possessed" domestic animals like dogs or cats - visual representations that would all seem to strike accord with mortal fears. Discordant, hostile energy states held within human energy matrices may also appear as dark, heavy veils of smoke or mists, or as thick, dark slimy ooze. These are but a few of the visual images that a facilitator may experience during the Transmutation Process that can help identify the true nature, purpose and dynamics of the energy system being transmuted.

RELEASE OF RESIDUAL ENERGIES FROM FACILITATOR

When Transmutation Procedures have been completed, it is necessary for the facilitator to release any residual energies of discordance that he/she might have retained as a result of the process. This is an extremely important step, as energies of discordance can not only impair the facilitator's perceptions, but can also be transmitted to subsequent clients. The facilitator is responsible for respecting this significant reality, and doing that which is conscionable to prevent the transference of discordant energies to other mortal beings. It is also the case that many facilitators simply "burn-out" as a direct result of the accumulation of residual energies of discordance received from clients during bodywork, massage and therapeutic counseling sessions.

By following the Transmutation Procedures below, a facilitator can successfully release residual energies of discordance received from clients:

1. Offer a Silent Prayer for Guidance and Blessing.
    (The LoveLight Invocation/Blessing is advised here.)

2. Place your left hand over your Heart Chakra. Allow self to visualize any discordant residual energies in your Heart Chakra as a dark energy mass.

3. Now, direct the dark energy mass from your Heart Chakra into your left hand, and watch as it moves up your left arm, into your left shoulder, across your chest, into your right shoulder, down your right arm and into your right hand.

4. Point your right hand either toward The Ethers or toward Mother Earth as required, and watch as the dark energy of discordance leaves you through your finger-tips. Again Bless the discordance energy in The Name of Yahweh, By The Spirits of Buddha, Krishna, Mohammed and Christ Jesus as you release it to find its own Peace. (See Illustration 13.)

SPIRAL BALANCING

An integral part of Loving Touch Therapy™, Spiral Balancing is designed to realign and integrate Chakra Energies, as well as raise Resonance Rate Potential. Through Spiral Balancing, subtle energy fields are stimulated to interact with the dynamics of the electrical impulses that impact upon the physical systems of the

ILLUSTRATION 13:
Release of Residual Discordant Energy

Left hand over Heart Chakra - right hand upward or downward

body, thereby aligning the energy matrix of the body with the more refined aspects of Conscious Being. What is achieved through Spiral Balancing is the acceleration of human energy systems toward Conscious Evolution, which enhances clarity of perception, stimulates Transformation of egocentric drives and validates the acceptance of God-Realized Consciousness. One of the oldest and most efficient Facilitation Techniques given to contemporary man from "The Rainbow Temple" of Lemuria, Spiral Balancing can assist each and every mortal being in accessing and maintaining states of Enlightened conscious well-being.

To perform Spiral Balancing:

1. With the client relaxed and reclined as shown in Illustration 14, offer a Silent Prayer for Guidance and Blessing. (A simple Prayer such as, "Almighty Yah, Great Spirit of Light, By The Spirits of Buddha, Krishna, Mohammed and Christ Jesus, In Thee Do I Trust," is effective but the entire LoveLight Invocation/Blessing is advised.)

2. Having received verbal confirmation from the client that he/she agrees to allow the procedure to commence, begin at the Crown Chakra. With the left hand, palm facing downward, make small circular, clockwise patterns about 6-8 inches above the client's body. Now with the right hand make counterclockwise circles in an alternating pattern above the circles made by your left hand. Silently, repeat this phrase continuously for the duration of this procedure, "Channel The Light Of Yahweh, Channel The Light Of One."

3. As you begin to feel Crown Chakra energies start to rise to meet your hands circling above, slowly begin to move down the Chakra Cord toward the Third Eye Chakra.

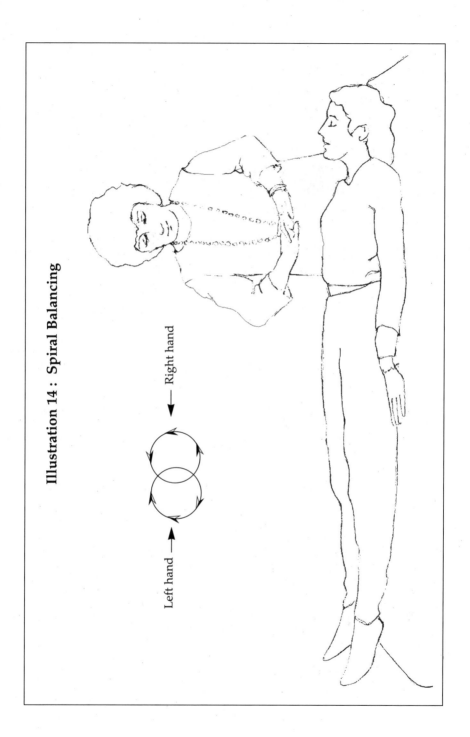

Illustration 14 : Spiral Balancing

Right hand

Left hand

Continue the circling pattern, as you move downward along the Chakra Cord. When you reach the Third Eye Chakra, pause and focus the circling pattern directly above the Third Eye Chakra. Once again, when you feel the energies begin to rise from the Third Eye Chakra, (after about 7-12 completed circular patterns), slowly move downward along the Chakra Cord toward the Throat Chakra. (Remember to continue to silently repeat the phrase, "Channel The Light Of Yahweh, Channel The Light Of One," over and over again.)

4. Pause at the Throat Chakra and focus the circular pattern directly above the Throat Chakra. When you feel Throat Chakra energy begin to rise, slowly move downward along the Chakra Cord never breaking the rhythm of the circular pattern for the duration of the procedure.

5. When you reach the Heart Chakra, focus the circular pattern directly above the Heart Chakra and follow the procedures for each successive Chakra as has been described earlier: Heart, Solar Plexus, Naval and Base Chakras.

6. When you reach the Base Chakra and complete the circular patterns, simply discontinue the motion and disengage the client by bringing both hands to your side.

7. Stand back, observe and gaze upon the client's Chakras, then move to the Crown Chakra to repeat the sequence. For the most effective results, the Spiral Balancing Procedure should be performed at least three (3) times with a maximum of seven (7) times in any one session.

Before attempting the technique of Spiral Balancing just described, it is best to develop the skill of Spiral Balancing by practicing the positions of the hands, wrists and arms using the flat surface of a table-top in the following manner:

1. While standing in front of a table, place both hands palm side down with fingers closed about twelve (12) inches apart on the surface of the table-top.

2. Begin making clockwise circles of twelve (12) inches in diameter on the surface of the table-top with the left hand.

3. Now, with the right hand, begin making counterclockwise circles of twelve (12) inches in diameter in an alternating pattern with the left hand. This motion will create a pattern of interlocking circles about sixteen (16) to eighteen (18) inches in width.

4. Now, while maintaining the circular motion, slowly lift both hands from the surface of the table-top. Be sure that the fingers are closed and straight and the wrists are locked in position, so that the angle made by the hands and arms remains at about 130°.

By practicing the steps given, proficiency in the technique of Spiral Balancing can be reached in a short period of time, and as one's confidence grows in the application of Spiral Balancing and other techniques of Loving Touch Therapy™, so the day approaches that the seeker of Spiritual Truth emerges as a conscionable facilitator of Loving Kindness in The Light of One.

INFUSION OF DIVINE LIGHT VIBRATIONS

We define Divine Light Vibrations as Energies born of and directed by God-Realized Consciousness to affect The Greater

Good of All Creation. These are Energy States that exist within the Golden/White Light Ray of The Divine Light Spectrum, and can stimulate states of conscious well-being, transmute energies of discordance and facilitate the Conscious Evolution of man. By accessing The Higher States of Conscious Being, a Soul Initiate can assist in the facilitation process by channeling the vibratory frequency of Divine Light Energy, and infusing human energy systems with the Golden/White Light Ray of Divine Conscience, thereby aiding in processes of Transformation that ultimately affect the Conscious Evolution of all things born of Creation.

The technique for infusing human energy systems with Divine Light Vibrations, shown in Illustration 15, is a direct, dynamic process by which mortal consciousness can be stimulated and assisted in accessing more evolved, higher resolved states of perception and conscious well-being.

To initiate the procedure for infusing mortal consciousness with Divine Light Vibrations, simply adhere to the following:

1. The facilitator must be focused and fully integrated and grounded in Divine Consciousness. This is accomplished through the Invocation of Divine Guidance with The LoveLight Invocation/Blessing, the silent recitation of the words, "Attune, Balance, Integrate, Ground," and by allowing self to release any and all notions of personal interest, thereby engaging a state of "Selfless Service" to assist in the client's evolutionary process of unfoldment. This is very important, because any personal thoughts or feelings about the task to be undertaken or expectations about its outcome will compromise the integrity of the operation. It is of paramount importance that the facilitator be conscionably aware of his/her role in the procedure and not confuse personal issues with the act of facilitation or

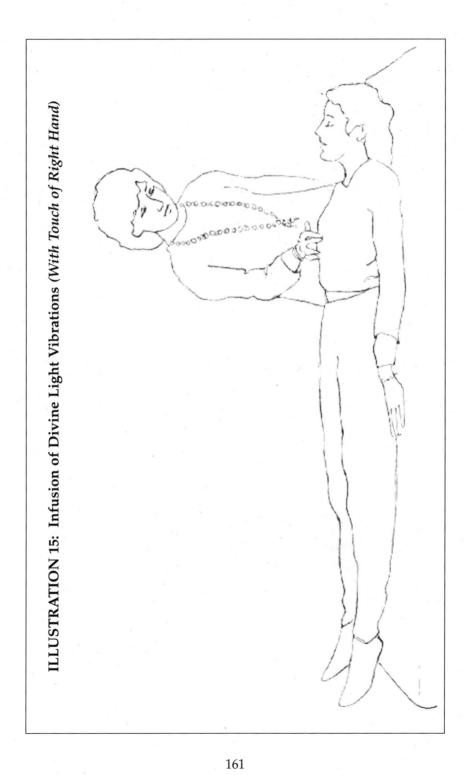

ILLUSTRATION 15: Infusion of Divine Light Vibrations (*With Touch of Right Hand*)

allow personal desires for a specific outcome to hamper one's ability to serve as a Divine Tool for The Infusion of Divine Light Vibrations into human energy systems.

2. Now, using the index and second finger of your right hand, touch the Chakra into which the infusion is to be made. (In the case of a full-body infusion, the facilitator will begin at the Third Eye Chakra and touch each successive Chakra en route to and including the Base Chakra, then return to the Crown Chakra to activate the entire Chakra Cord.) Silently repeat, "Channel The Light Of Yahweh, Channel The Light Of One," over and over again, and continue the silent recitation throughout the infusion.

3. The facilitator must now consciously open his/her Crown Chakra to receive The Light of One in a Golden/White Light Ray of Divine Energy. As the facilitator visualizes the Golden/White Light Ray entering his/her Crown Chakra, the silent recitation of, "Channel The Light Of Yahweh, Channel The Light Of One," becomes wonderfully resonant, sending Divine Light pulsing along the facilitator's Chakra Cord.

4. The facilitator now watches as the Golden/White Light Ray travels down his/her Chakra Cord to the Heart Chakra, whereupon the Golden/White Light Ray fills the Heart Chakra with radiant, glowing LoveLight Sensations, before moving across the facilitator's chest into his/her right shoulder, down the right arm, into the right hand and is released from the fingertips to enter the client's body. At this point, the facilitator and client experience a moment of Divine Communion, as the Golden/White Light Ray of Divine Consciousness enraptures them simultaneously in Divine Embrace. It is not uncommon for the experience of this euphoric moment to produce a lasting

conscious bond between facilitator and client.

A Consecrated Clear Quartz Crystal Generator that amplifies Divine Light Vibrations can also be used as an infusion tool to transmit Divine Light Energy into mortal consciousness in similar fashion as the preceding technique. As shown in Illustration 16, the Consecrated Quartz Crystal Generator is held in the right hand between the thumb, first and second fingers approximately six (6) to twelve (12) inches above and directly over one the Primary Chakras. The same procedure is followed as given in the preceding technique for The Infusion of Divine Light Vibrations. In Chapter 9, we will fully address the use of Consecrated Crystals & Minerals in the practice of Loving Touch Therapy™.

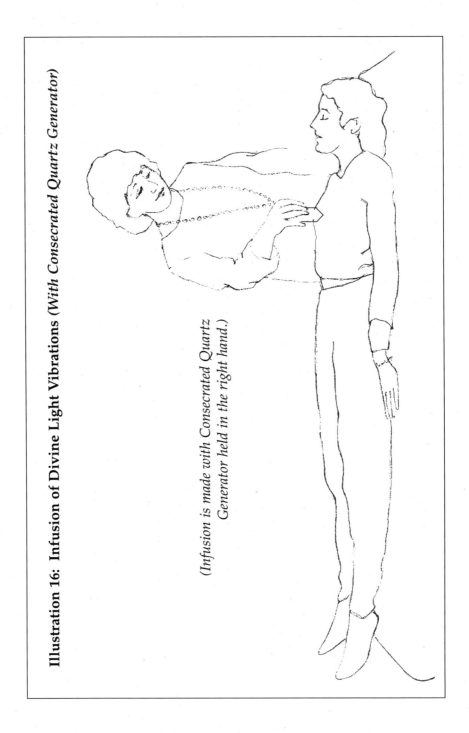

Illustration 16: Infusion of Divine Light Vibrations *(With Consecrated Quartz Generator)*

(Infusion is made with Consecrated Quartz Generator held in the right hand.)

QUARTZ CRYSTALS & MINERALS:
Tools Of Loving Touch Therapy™

CHAPTER 9

Crystals and Minerals used as tools to facilitate states of well-being predates recorded history by many thousands of years, but contemporary archeological evidence indicates that cultures in Asia, the Middle East, Africa, India and North America used Quartz Crystals, Jade, Lapis Lazuli, Malachite, Carnelian and Turquoise (to name a few) more than 8,500 years ago in practices of Healing Facilitation and to stimulate states of Conscious Evolution. Present day understanding of the use of Quartz Crystals and Minerals in practices of Healing Facilitation and in accessing evolved states of Spiritual Attunement is based upon information known by the ancients and through Etheric Channels, Conduits and Intuitive Wisdom of past incarnate associations with practices of Healing Facilitation.

The discussions and descriptions of the Crystal Lay-outs presented in this text are the result of many years of study, and through countless, successful applications on subjects at Portal have been shown to be safe and effective tools for facilitating mental, physical and emotional well-being. Additionally, the Crystal Lay-outs that follow have consistently proven to be dependable tools to assist earnest seekers in stimulating and accessing progressive states of Higher Consciousness. With practice, diligent observation and contemplation of the effects produced by various

Crystals, Minerals and Crystal/Mineral combinations upon human energy systems, the practitioner of Loving Touch Therapy™ can quickly develop a deep sense of understanding about the Crystals and Minerals that will truly assist him/her in becoming a dutiful, conscionable servant to the needs of Creation. In very short order, a Loving Touch Therapy™ practitioner can become quite proficient in the use of Crystals and Minerals, and have a profound impact upon the evolving consciousness of mortal man.

Crystals and Minerals used in Loving Touch Therapy™ sessions should be specifically prepared and programmed* to amplify the highest resonance rates possible, and used for the sole purpose of facilitating states of conscious well-being. Since Crystals acquired from different sources will be imprinted with a wide variety of energy states that reflect the manner in which the Crystals were collected, handled and treated in general, it is strongly recommended that Crystals and Minerals used in practices of Loving Touch Therapy™ are acquired from qualified sources that offer "Consecrated" Tools for Healing Facilitation. It should also be noted that Crystals and Minerals used in the practice of Loving Touch Therapy™ should regularly be cleansed by washing in mild soap and water, while simultaneously repeating the silent Prayer/Mantra, "In The Name of Yahweh, By The Spirits of Buddha, Krishna, Mohammed and Christ Jesus, Be Ye Cleansed and Blessed in The Vibrations of The One."

*See CRYSTAL COMMUNION: LOVELIGHT MEDITATIONS
pages 247-257 for "Quartz Crystal Programming."

LAY-OUTS OF CONSECRATED CRYSTALS AND MINERALS

A wide variety of Consecrated Crystals and Minerals can be used as tools to facilitate states of conscious well-being, and when Consecrated Crystals and Minerals are used in specific combinations and precise patterns of lay-outs, the most wondrous states of unfoldment can be realized. Though we are not advocating the sole use of Crystals and Minerals in the treatment of illness and disease, we are advocating the incorporation of Crystals and Minerals in the wholistic treatment of physical, mental, emotional and spiritual conditions that heretofore have remained in the realm of "speculative dysfunctions" by medical practitioners. What this means is that we have observed countless applications of Consecrated Crystals and Minerals to subjects who were either misdiagnosed or were beyond the diagnostic and treatment ability of medical science, who after a short course of Loving Touch Therapy™ showed marked improvements and/or complete recovery or remission from physical, mental and emotional dysfunctions that years of medical treatment were unable to effectively resolve.

The most dramatic results of the Consecrated Crystal/Mineral Lay-outs used in Loving Touch Therapy™ have been seen in the resolution of emotional and mental conflicts that precipitate physical dysfunctions. In many cases, after the first session, the subject registered immediate, consciousness altering energies that filled the subject with a new sense of purpose and reason for living. Many times, we observed depressed, troubled children of God with little or no self-esteem leave the treatment room with a sense of self and a willingness to engage life that had never before been known or understood. Indeed, in most instances, it is true that the apparent rapid turn-about was due to the fact that the subject had reached his/her "moment of readiness" to release Karmic Debt and accept responsibility for all aspects of personal self that will have allowed the facilitation session to have been so dramatically successful. Yet, without Divine Guidance and the uncompromised willingness to accept The Lessons of Existence, troubled souls who will have endured years of mental and/or emotional dysfunctions would be unable to assimilate the subtle, Divine Light Energies by which Loving Touch Therapy™ is effected, and the physical dysfunctions born on the subtle energy planes that are transferred to the physical body through dysfunctional mental and emotional patterns would at best find temporary relief in Transmutation - not the evolved resolution of Transformation.

The number of Loving Touch Therapy™ sessions and the variety of Consecrated Crystal/Mineral Lay-outs required to effect states of conscious well-being varies considerably from one soul incarnate being to another, but as a general rule, no less than nine (9) sessions, one session per week over nine (9) weeks, will be necessary to stimulate evolved states of Transformation. In most cases, however, a twelve (12) week period is required with one session each week before soul incarnates experience significant shifts in consciousness and experience heightened states of well-being. (Let us emphasize that the number of Loving Touch Therapy™ sessions, number of Consecrated Crystal/Mineral Lay-outs and treatment results experienced by subjects varies in accordance with the nature of the dysfunction, the subject's readiness to accept The Lessons of Existence and the subject's willingness to accept Higher Consciousness States.)

(Note: Before performing any of the Consecrated Crystal/ Mineral Lay-outs outlined in this text, be sure that the subject is fully aware of and comfortable with the process of Loving Touch Therapy™. Begin the use of Loving Touch Therapy™ slowly and with the utmost respect for each soul incarnate being upon whom

Loving Touch Therapy™ is practiced. Under no circumstances should a subject be hurried, coerced, tricked or manipulated into accepting treatments of Loving Touch Therapy™.)

Begin the introduction to Loving Touch Therapy™ by discussing potential benefits and the high degree of efficiency with which Loving Touch Therapy™ techniques effect states of conscious well-being. Only when and if the subject shows genuine interest and is consciously willing to engage in Loving Touch Therapy™ should the procedures be initiated. It is vitally important that the subject be a willing participant in the process, as without the subject's willing, conscious participation in the process, Loving Touch Therapy™ can not be utilized in keeping with The Precepts of Divine Conscience. It is also important to remember that the first Crystal Lay-out to be used on any subject should be the Foundation Consecrated Rose Quartz Crystal Lay-out.

The vast majority of Crystals and Minerals used in Loving Touch Therapy™ Lay-outs are cut and polished in oval cabochons of specific sizes to facilitate uniform energy transmissions from The Spectrum of Divine Light into the Chakras and along the Chakra Cord. Circular cabochons, free-form polished shapes and natural Crystal/Mineral formations are also used, but with the exception of free-form Rainbow Obsidian pieces and Sheen Obsidian eggs used as grounding agents, and clear polished Quartz Crystal Generators, shapes other than oval cabochons are used infrequently.

FOUNDATION LAY-OUTS

The Crystal and Mineral Lay-outs that follow are used to amplify and transmit Divine Light Energy into human energy systems to effect Conscious Evolution. It is advised that strict attention and adherence to the precise Crystal/Mineral placement and Lay-out order given is observed, as each Crystal/Mineral Lay-out has a specific purpose and a specific inter-related function to aid in stimulating the unfoldment of conscious well-being. Each Consecrated Lay-out is designed to compliment and supplement each preceding and/or each succeeding Consecrated Lay-out presented, and therefore should be deemed to be a part of a treatment process instead of an isolated Crystal/Mineral application. With Conviction, diligence and the commitment to conscionably impact upon The Greater Good of All Creation, the practitioner of Loving Touch Therapy™ can utilize the Consecrated Crystal/Mineral Lay-outs that follow to serve the growing needs of mortal consciousness in The Light of One.

CONSECRATED ROSE QUARTZ
FOUNDATION LAY-OUT #1 (See Diagram 1)

Rose Quartz is one of the most versatile facilitation tools available. Though it has been thought to be a Quartz Formation primarily associated with Heart Chakra function, the Pink Ray of Divine Light Energy amplified through Rose Quartz can be an effective, gentle facilitator of dysfunctional energy states discovered in association with any of the seven Primary Chakras. (As will be demonstrated shortly, the versatility of Rose Quartz and many other primary Quartz Formations by far exceed previously known applications.)

After the Invocation of Divine Guidance and asking the subject's permission to begin the Loving Touch Therapy™ session, simply follow these steps:

1. Perform a series of Chakra Scans to determine the subject's Chakra Orientations. Relax, breathe slowly, gently inhaling

DIAGRAM 1

Consecrated Rose Quartz - Foundation Lay-out #1

ORDER OF PLACEMENT

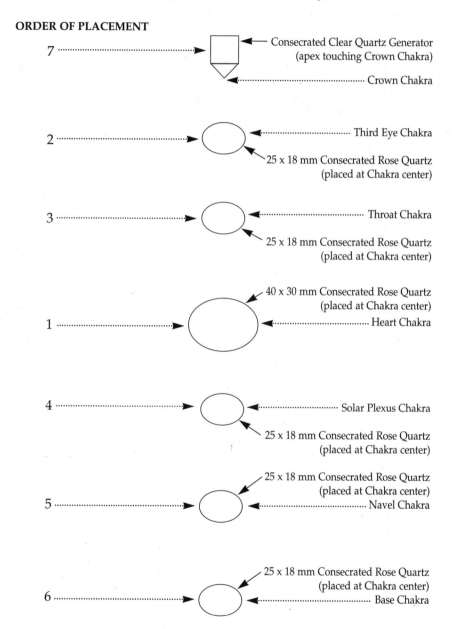

7 ....► ◄— Consecrated Clear Quartz Generator
(apex touching Crown Chakra)

◄.. Crown Chakra

2 ....► ◄.. Third Eye Chakra

↖ 25 x 18 mm Consecrated Rose Quartz
(placed at Chakra center)

3 ....► ◄.. Throat Chakra

↖ 25 x 18 mm Consecrated Rose Quartz
(placed at Chakra center)

↙ 40 x 30 mm Consecrated Rose Quartz
(placed at Chakra center)

1 ....► ◄.. Heart Chakra

4 ....► ◄.. Solar Plexus Chakra

↖ 25 x 18 mm Consecrated Rose Quartz
(placed at Chakra center)

↙ 25 x 18 mm Consecrated Rose Quartz
(placed at Chakra center)

5 ....► ◄.. Navel Chakra

↙ 25 x 18 mm Consecrated Rose Quartz
(placed at Chakra center)

6 ....► ◄.. Base Chakra

Remove in reverse order: 7, 6, 5, 4, 3, 2, 1

through the nose, and slowly exhaling from the mouth. Begin scanning the Primary Chakras. Relax. Allow self to feel and/or see the nature of the subject's Chakra energies.

2. Intuitively and consciously record the impressions received from the subject. Remain silent and continue to relax with steady, gentle breathing, slowly inhaling through the nose and exhaling from the mouth.

3. When the Primary Chakras have been scanned, step back from the table and begin gazing upon each Primary Chakra starting at the Crown Chakra and working down the Chakra Cord to the Base Chakra. Hold your gaze at each Primary Chakra for about ten (10) seconds. Relax and breathe.

4. Now, beginning at the center of the Heart Chakra, place a 40x30mm Consecrated Rose Quartz cabochon at the center of the Heart Chakra. Spiral Balance over the Heart Chakra, then Spiral Balance from the Crown Chakra to the Base Chakra. When complete, step back from the table and focus your gaze upon the Consecrated Rose Quartz cabochon at the Heart Chakra. As you gaze, continue the silent recitation of the words, "Channel The Light Of Yahweh, Channel The Light Of One." (Don't forget that whenever you Spiral Balance, the silent recitation, "Channel The Light Of Yahweh, Channel The Light Of One," is absolutely vital, as these words not only acknowledge your allegiance to The God Spirit but also invoke The Universal Energies of Divine Love that are the Foundation and Conscience of Loving Touch Therapy™.)

5. After several seconds of gazing upon the 40x30mm Consecrated Rose Quartz cabochon at the Heart Chakra, return to the subject and place 25x18mm Consecrated Rose Quartz cabo-

chons at the center of each Primary Chakra from the Third Eye Chakra to the Base Chakra (of course excluding the Heart Chakra where a 40x30mm Consecrated Rose Quartz cabochon has already been placed). Next, place a small polished Clear Quartz Crystal Generator (measuring 1 1/2-2" in length x 1-1 1/2" in width at the base) at the Crown Chakra with the apex pointed toward the subject.

6. Now, perform several Spiral Balancing passes along the Chakra Cord from the Crown Chakra to the Base Chakra. Allow self to feel The Divine Light Energies rising from the subject to meet your hands, as releases of emotional energy and memory matrices of discordance are lifted from the subject. Observe facial expressions, bodily movements and sounds and the degree to which the subject has relaxed and allowed self to experience the facilitation. (Frequently, observations made during the course of a facilitation session can lend significant insights into the nature of a subject's dysfunctions.)

7. When Spiral Balancing has been completed, stand back from the subject. Beginning at the Crown Chakra, focus your gaze upon the Clear Quartz Crystal Generator for about ten (10) to fifteen (15) seconds before slowly moving your gaze down the Chakra Cord, pausing a few seconds and focusing your gaze upon each successive Consecrated Rose Quartz cabochon placed upon the Chakras en route to and including the Base Chakra. Continue the silent recitation, "Channel The Light Of Yahweh, Channel The Light Of One." When complete, be seated nearby for up to five (5) minutes. Now, return to the subject and place a Consecrated Sheen Obsidian egg in each of the subject's hands.

8.   Begin removing the Consecrated Crystals from the subject's body in the reverse order from which the Consecrated Crystals were placed on the subject's body: the Consecrated Clear Quartz Generator is removed first, then the Consecrated Rose Quartz cabochons at the Base Chakra, Navel Chakra, Solar Plexus Chakra, Throat Chakra, Third Eye Chakra, and finally the Heart Chakra (Sheen Obsidian eggs are left in subject's hands to assist subject in reintegrating and grounding in the reality of Third Dimension).

9.   Now, while speaking in soft tones, gently encourage the subject to open his/her eyes. Gently stroke the subject's arm and shoulder to help stimulate Third Dimension recognition. Speak softly in reassuring tones to assist the subject in assimilating the experience of Loving Touch Therapy™. It is important for the facilitator not to rush the subject to sit up or allow the subject to leave the facilitation area too quickly. The facilitator must be sure to allow the subject ample time to gather and ground self in the reality of Third Dimension.

When the subject has regained a sense of Third Dimension balance, the sensations experienced by both facilitator and subject can be discussed. It is for the facilitator to remember that the perceptions of the facilitation experience held by facilitator and subject may be quite different. In most cases, the facilitator will be aware of energy states, emotional conflicts or behavioral tendencies revealed during the facilitation session that the subject will not be willing or ready to face. Therefore, it is mandatory that the facilitator exercise behaviors of Evolved Conscience (Patience, Compassion, Wisdom, Mercy, Serenity, Love) in discussing the observations of Chakra Orientations and energy matrices discovered during Loving Touch Therapy™ sessions, for the disclosure of information that the subject is not ready to receive or engage will inevitably compromise future moments of awakening in the process of Soul Evolution. Additionally, it is the facilitator's responsibility not to attempt to force the subject to see aspects of personal self that the facilitator "thinks" will be in the best interest of the subject, as if the facilitator is processing the facilitation experience in a linear fashion or "thinking," then the facilitator will not have acted conscionably - but will have acted through drives of ego and illusions of self-importance. When such instances arise, regardless of the nature of the therapeutic mode or technique, the facilitator will have encroached upon the subject's Choice of Free Will and created adverse Karmic involvement for both subject and facilitator.

With practice and devotion, the practitioner of Loving Touch Therapy™ can gain prophetic insights into the nature and dynamics of mortal consciousness, and assist many in breaking the bonds of conditioning that inhibit Conscious Evolution. But above all else, the practitioner must always remember that it is by The Grace and Benevolence of The One Infinite Creator through which acts of "Healing" in expressions of Divine Love are realized by mortal man, and that the practitioner of Loving Touch Therapy™ is but a humble servant, a Divine Tool purged of self-involvement, in The Divine Process of Healing.

CONSECRATED AMETHYST QUARTZ
FOUNDATION LAY-OUT #2 (See Diagram 2)

Amethyst is the second primary Quartz Formation to be used in a Consecrated Foundation Lay-out of Loving Touch Therapy™. Amethyst Quartz amplifies the calming, enlightening Purple Ray of The Divine Light Spectrum that can transmit wonderfully comforting sensation throughout mortal consciousness. The procedure for Foundation Lay-out #2 is as follows:

1. After The Invocation of Divine Guidance and asking the subject's permission to begin the session of Loving Touch Therapy™, perform a series of Chakra Scans to determine the nature of the subject's Chakra Orientations. Be sure that the subject is comfortable before beginning (optimum comfort and ease of facilitation is best experienced through the use of a massage table that allows the subject to recline, but any other apparatus that would allow the subject to fully recline at about three (3) feet above the floor would be appropriate). Relax. Breathe slowly, gently inhaling through the nose and slowly exhaling from the mouth. Begin scanning the Primary Chakras. Relax and allow self to feel and/or see the nature of the subject's Chakra energies.

2. Intuitively and consciously record the impressions received from the subject. Remain silent and continue to relax with steady, gentle breathing, slowly inhaling through the nose and slowly exhaling from the mouth.

3. After scanning the Primary Chakras, step back from the table and begin to gaze upon each Primary Chakra starting at the Crown Chakra and working down to the Base Chakra. Hold your gaze upon each Primary Chakra for about ten (10) seconds. Allow self to relax. Breathe.

4. Now, beginning at the Third Eye Chakra, place an 18x13mm Consecrated Amethyst Quartz cabochon at the center of the Third Eye Chakra. Spiral Balance over the Third Eye Chakra, then Spiral Balance from the Crown Chakra to the Base Chakra. When complete, step back from the table and focus your gaze upon the Consecrated Amethyst Quartz cabochon at the Third Eye Chakra. As you gaze, continue the silent recitation of the words, "Channel The Light Of Yahweh,

DIAGRAM 2

Consecrated Amethyst Quartz - Foundation Lay-out #2

ORDER OF PLACEMENT

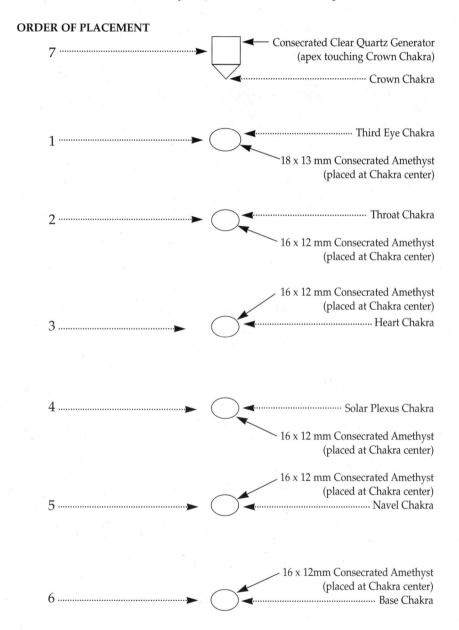

7 ....▶ ◀── Consecrated Clear Quartz Generator
(apex touching Crown Chakra)

◀.. Crown Chakra

1 ....▶ ◀.. Third Eye Chakra

18 x 13 mm Consecrated Amethyst
(placed at Chakra center)

2 ....▶ ◀.. Throat Chakra

16 x 12 mm Consecrated Amethyst
(placed at Chakra center)

16 x 12 mm Consecrated Amethyst
(placed at Chakra center)

3 ....▶ ◀.. Heart Chakra

4 ....▶ ◀.. Solar Plexus Chakra

16 x 12 mm Consecrated Amethyst
(placed at Chakra center)

16 x 12 mm Consecrated Amethyst
(placed at Chakra center)

5 ....▶ ◀.. Navel Chakra

16 x 12mm Consecrated Amethyst
(placed at Chakra center)

6 ....▶ ◀.. Base Chakra

Remove in reverse order: 7, 6, 5, 4, 3, 2, 1

179

Channel The Light Of One."

5.   After several seconds of gazing upon the 18x13mm Consecrated Amethyst cabochon at the Third Eye Chakra, return to the subject and place 16x12mm Consecrated Amethyst cabochons at each successive Chakra from the Throat Chakra to the Base Chakra. Next, place a small polished Clear Quartz Crystal Generator at the Crown Chakra with the apex pointed toward the subject.

6.   Now, perform several Spiral Balancing passes along the Chakra Cord from the Crown Chakra to the Base Chakra. Allow self to feel The Divine Light Energies passing through your hands to the subject. Allow self to feel the energies rising from the subject to meet your hands, as releases of emotional energy and memory matrices of discordance are lifted from the subject. Observe facial expressions, bodily movements and sounds and the degree to which the subject has relaxed and allowed self to fully experience the facilitation.

7.   When Spiral Balancing has been completed, stand back from the subject. Beginning at the Crown Chakra, focus your gaze upon the Clear Quartz Crystal Generator for about ten (10) to fifteen (15) seconds before slowly moving your gaze down the Chakra Cord, pausing a few seconds and focusing your gaze upon each successive Consecrated Amethyst Quartz cabochon placed upon the Chakras en route to and including the Base Chakra. Continue the silent recitation, "Channel The Light Of Yahweh, Channel The Light Of One." When the gazing has been completed (which is a process for activating each Crystal to its highest resonant potential), be seated nearby for up to five (5) minutes. Now, return to the subject and place a Consecrated Sheen Obsidian egg in each of the subject's hands.

8. Begin removing the Consecrated Crystals from the subject's body in the reverse order from which the Consecrated Crystals were placed on the subject's body: the Consecrated Clear Quartz Crystal Generator is removed first, then the Consecrated Amethyst Quartz cabochons at the Base Chakra, Navel Chakra, Solar Plexus Chakra, Heart Chakra, Throat Chakra and finally the Third Eye Chakra (Sheen Obsidian eggs are left in the subject's hands to assist in reintegration and grounding).

9. Now, while speaking in soft tones, gently encourage the subject to open his/her eyes. Gently stroke the subject's arm and shoulder to help stimulate Third Dimension recognition. Speak softly in reassuring tones to assist the subject in assimilating the experience of Loving Touch Therapy™. Remember not to rush the subject to sit up or walk, as it may take the subject a few minutes to reorient self in Third Dimension. Allow for a period of communion in which facilitator and subject discuss the shared experience of facilitation. When the subject has regained a sense of Third Dimension grounding and the discussion about the sensations, feelings, visualizations and releases experienced during facilitation has ended, assist the subject in sitting up and leaving the facilitation area.

CONSECRATED CITRINE QUARTZ
FOUNDATION LAY-OUT #3 (See Diagram 3)

Citrine is the third primary Quartz Formation to be used in sessions of Loving Touch Therapy™ as a Consecrated Foundation Lay-out. Citrine Quartz brilliantly amplifies the Golden Yellow Ray of The Spectrum of Divine Light Energy that purposefully grounds the intent and application of Divine Will into mortal consciousness. Foundation Lay-out #3 is performed as follows:

1. When The Invocation of Divine Guidance has been concluded, ask the subject for his/her permission to begin the session of Loving Touch Therapy™ (asking the subject for permission to begin the facilitation session consciously confirms the subject's willingness to actively participate in his/her own process of Soul Evolution, rules out the possibility of inadvertently compromising the subject's Choice of Free Will by performing procedures that the subject does not concur with and serves to reassure the subject that the process of Loving Touch Therapy™ is non-invasive and conducted with the utmost respect for the subject's wishes and well-being). Now, perform a series of Chakra Scans to determine the nature of the subject's Chakra Orientations. Be sure that the subject is comfortably situated before beginning. Relax. Breathe slowly, gently inhaling through the nose and slowly exhaling from the mouth. Begin Chakra Scanning. Relax and allow self to feel and/or see the nature of the subject's Chakra energies.

2. Intuitively and consciously record the impressions received from the subject. Remain silent and continue to relax with steady, gentle breathing, slowly inhaling through the nose and slowly exhaling from the mouth.

3. After scanning the Primary Chakras, step back from the table and begin to gaze upon each Primary Chakra starting at the Crown Chakra and working down the Chakra Cord to the Base Chakra. Hold your gaze at each Primary Chakra for about ten (10) seconds. Allow self to relax. Breathe.

4. Now, beginning at the Solar Plexus Chakra, place a 12x10mm Consecrated Citrine Quartz cabochon at the center of the Solar Plexus Chakra. Spiral Balance over the Solar Plexus Chakra, then Spiral Balance from the Crown Chakra to the Base

DIAGRAM 3
Consecrated Citrine Quartz - Foundation Lay-out #3

ORDER OF PLACEMENT

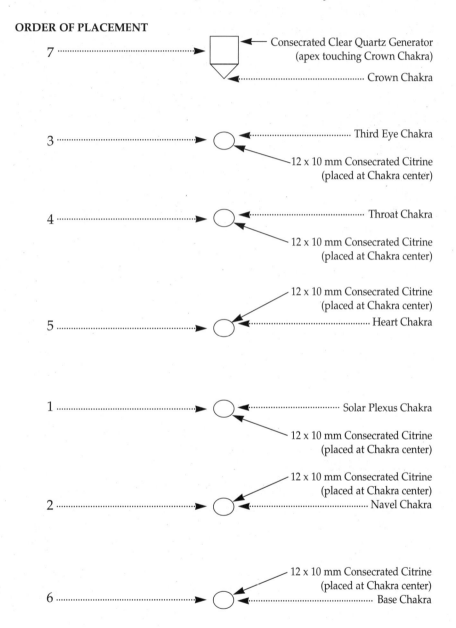

7 ···▶ ◀——— Consecrated Clear Quartz Generator
(apex touching Crown Chakra)

·· Crown Chakra

3 ···▶ ◯ ◀·· Third Eye Chakra

12 x 10 mm Consecrated Citrine
(placed at Chakra center)

4 ···▶ ◯ ◀·· Throat Chakra

12 x 10 mm Consecrated Citrine
(placed at Chakra center)

12 x 10 mm Consecrated Citrine
(placed at Chakra center)

5 ···▶ ◯ ◀·· Heart Chakra

1 ···▶ ◯ ◀·· Solar Plexus Chakra

12 x 10 mm Consecrated Citrine
(placed at Chakra center)

12 x 10 mm Consecrated Citrine
(placed at Chakra center)

2 ···▶ ◯ ◀·· Navel Chakra

12 x 10 mm Consecrated Citrine
(placed at Chakra center)

6 ···▶ ◯ ◀·· Base Chakra

Remove in reverse order: 7, 6, 5, 4, 3, 2, 1

183

Chakra. When the Spiral Balancing has been completed, step back from the table and focus your gaze upon the Consecrated Citrine Quartz cabochon at the Solar Plexus Chakra. As you gaze, continue the silent recitation of the words, "Channel The Light Of Yahweh, Channel The Light Of One."

5. After several seconds of gazing upon the 12x10mm Consecrated Citrine Quartz cabochon at the Solar Plexus Chakra, return to the subject and place a 12x10mm Consecrated Citrine Quartz cabochon at the Navel Chakra. Spiral Balance over the Naval Chakra, then Spiral Balance from Crown Chakra to the Base Chakra. When the Spiral Balance passes have been completed, step back from the facilitation table and focus your gaze upon the Consecrated Citrine Quartz cabochon at the Navel Chakra. While gazing, remember to continue silently reciting the words, "Channel The Light Of Yahweh, Channel The Light Of One."

6. After several seconds of gazing upon the Consecrated Citrine Quartz cabochon at the Navel Chakra, return to the subject and place 12x10mm Consecrated Citrine Quartz cabochons at each successive Chakra from the Third Eye Chakra to the Base Chakra (of course excluding the Solar Plexus Chakra and Navel Chakra). Next, place a small polished Clear Quartz Crystal Generator at the Crown Chakra with the apex pointed toward the subject.

7. Now, perform several Spiral Balancing passes along the Chakra Cord from the Crown Chakra to the Base Chakra. Allow self to feel The Divine Light Energies passing through your hands to the subject. Allow self to feel the energies rising from the subject to meet your hands, as releases of emotional energy and memory matrices of discordance are lifted from

the subject. Observe facial expressions, bodily movements and sounds and the degree to which the subject has relaxed and allowed self to fully experience the facilitation.

8. When the Spiral Balancing has been completed, stand back from the subject. Beginning at the Crown Chakra, focus your gaze upon the Clear Quartz Crystal Generator for about ten(10) to fifteen (15) seconds before slowly moving your gaze down the Chakra Cord, pausing a few seconds and focusing your gaze upon each successive Consecrated Citrine Quartz cabochon placed upon the Chakras en route to and including the Base Chakra. Continue the silent recitation, "Channel The Light Of Yahweh, Channel The Light Of One." When the gazing has been completed, be seated nearby for up to five (5) minutes. After the time has elapsed, return to the subject and place a Consecrated Sheen Obsidian egg in each of the subject's hands.

9. Begin removing the Consecrated Crystals from the subject's body in the reverse order from which the Consecrated Crystals were placed on the subject's body: the Consecrated Clear Quartz Crystal Generator is removed first, then the Consecrated Citrine Quartz cabochons at the Base Chakra, Heart Chakra, Throat Chakra, Third Eye Chakra, Navel Chakra and finally the Solar Plexus Chakra.

10. Now, while speaking in soft tones, gently encourage the subject to open his/her eyes. Gently stroke the subject's arm and shoulder to help stimulate Third Dimension awareness. Speak softly in reassuring tones to assist the subject in assimilating the experience of Loving Touch Therapy™. When the subject is ready, discuss the observations and experience of the Loving Touch Therapy™ session.

CONSECRATED TIGER'S EYE
FOUNDATION LAY-OUT #4 (See Diagram 4)

Tiger's Eye is the fourth member of the Quartz Family used in Consecrated Lay-outs in the practice of Loving Touch Therapy™. Amplifying the Golden Yellow Ray of The Spectrum of Divine Light Energy, Tiger's Eye also amplifies Green, Brown and Black Rays of The Divine Light Spectrum to ground the realities of Divine Will and Etheric Truth into mortal consciousness, thereby stimulating behaviors of "Godliness" and directives of Loving Kindness toward all things born of Universal Creation. Foundation Lay-out #4 is performed as follows:

1. After The Invocation of Divine Guidance has been offered and the subject has been asked for his/her permission to begin the session of Loving Touch Therapy™, perform a series of Chakra Scans to determine the nature of the subjects's Chakra Orientations. The subject should be comfortably situated before you begin Chakra Scanning. Now, relax and breathe slowly, gently inhaling through the nose and slowly exhaling from the mouth. Begin scanning the Primary Chakras. Relax. Allow self to feel and/or see the nature of the subject's Chakra energies.

2. Intuitively and consciously record the impressions received from the subject. Remain silent and continue to relax with steady, gentle breathing, slowly inhaling through the nose and slowly exhaling from the mouth.

3. After the Primary Chakras have been scanned, step back from the table and begin to gaze upon each Primary Chakra starting at the Crown Chakra and working down the Chakra Cord to the Base Chakra. Hold your gaze at each Primary Chakra for

DIAGRAM 4

Consecrated Tiger's Eye - Foundation Lay-out #4

ORDER OF PLACEMENT

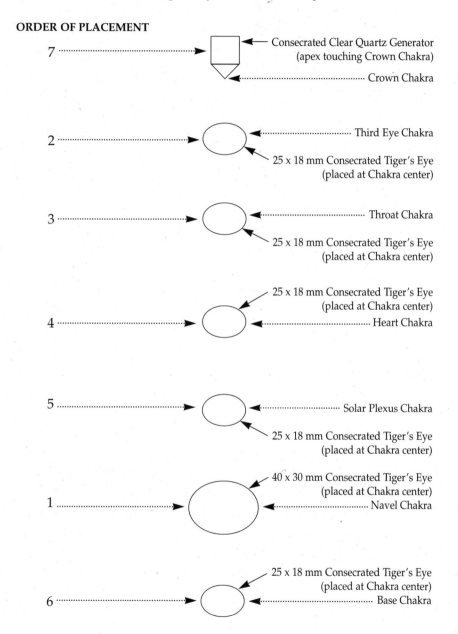

7 ....▶ Consecrated Clear Quartz Generator
(apex touching Crown Chakra)

Crown Chakra

2 ....▶ Third Eye Chakra

25 x 18 mm Consecrated Tiger's Eye
(placed at Chakra center)

3 ....▶ Throat Chakra

25 x 18 mm Consecrated Tiger's Eye
(placed at Chakra center)

25 x 18 mm Consecrated Tiger's Eye
(placed at Chakra center)

4 ....▶ Heart Chakra

5 ....▶ Solar Plexus Chakra

25 x 18 mm Consecrated Tiger's Eye
(placed at Chakra center)

40 x 30 mm Consecrated Tiger's Eye
(placed at Chakra center)

1 ....▶ Navel Chakra

25 x 18 mm Consecrated Tiger's Eye
(placed at Chakra center)

6 ....▶ Base Chakra

Remove in reverse order: 7, 6, 5, 4, 3, 2, 1

about ten (10) seconds. Allow self to relax. Breathe.

4. Now, beginning at the Navel Chakra, place a 40x30mm cabo-
    chon of Consecrated Tiger's Eye at the center of the Navel
    Chakra. Spiral Balance over the Navel Chakra, then Spiral
    Balance from the Crown Chakra to the Base Chakra. When the
    Spiral Balancing has been completed, step back from the facil-
    itation table and focus your gaze upon the Consecrated Tiger's
    Eye cabochon at the Navel Chakra. As you gaze upon the
    Consecrated Tiger's Eye cabochon, continue the silent recita-
    tion of the words, "Channel The Light Of Yahweh, Channel
    The Light Of One."

5. After gazing for several seconds, return to the subject and
    place 25x18mm Consecrated Tiger's Eye cabochons at the cen-
    ter of each successive Chakra from the Third Eye Chakra to the
    Base Chakra (excluding the Navel Chakra). Next, place a
    small polished Clear Quartz Crystal Generator, measuring
    about 1 1/2-2" in length x 1-1 1/2" in width at the base, at the
    Crown Chakra with the apex pointed toward the subject.

6. Now, perform a series of Spiral Balancing passes (no less than
    three (3) and no more than seven (7) Spiral Balancing passes
    should be performed) along the Chakra Cord from the Crown
    Chakra to the Base Chakra. Allow self to feel The Radiant
    Divine Light Energies passing through your hands, as releases
    of emotional energy and discordant memory matrices are lift-
    ed from the subject. Observe facial expressions, bodily move-
    ments and sounds made by the subject, and observe the
    degree to which the subject has relaxed and allowed self to
    fully experience the session of Loving Touch Therapy™.

7. When the Spiral Balancing has been completed, stand back

from the subject. Beginning at the Crown Chakra, focus your gaze upon the Clear Quartz Crystal Generator for about ten (10) to fifteen (15) seconds before slowly moving your gaze down the Chakra Cord, pausing a few seconds and focusing your gaze upon each successive Consecrated Tiger's Eye cabochon placed upon the Chakras en route to and including the Base Chakra. Continue the silent recitation, "Channel The Light Of Yahweh, Channel The Light Of One." When the gazing has been completed, be seated nearby for up to five (5) minutes. When the time has elapsed, return to the subject and place a Consecrated Sheen Obsidian egg in each of the subject's hands.

8. Begin to remove the Consecrated Clear Quartz Crystal Generator and Consecrated Tiger's Eye cabochons from the subject's body in the reverse order from which the Consecrated Crystal and cabochons were placed on the subject's body: first remove the Consecrated Clear Quartz Crystal Generator, then the Consecrated Tiger's Eye cabochons at the Base Chakra, Solar Plexus Chakra, Heart Chakra, Throat Chakra, Third Eye Chakra and finally the Navel Chakra.

9. Now, while speaking in soft tones, gently encourage the subject to open his/her eyes. Gently stroke the subject's arm and shoulder to help stimulate Third Dimension awareness. Speak softly in reassuring tones to assist the subject in assimilating the experience of Loving Touch Therapy™. When the subject has sufficiently reintegrated, begin a period of discussion by asking the subject how he/she is feeling, or to describe the sensations experienced during the time of facilitation, or to share any visions that might have occurred, or to speak about how past physical injuries and bodily aches and pains were affected by the session of Loving Touch Therapy™. Allow the

subject to discuss new insights that might have surfaced about emotional conflicts and the true reality of self. Allow the subject to discover his/her true conscious reality in The Light of One. And allow the experience of Loving Touch Therapy™ to follow the subject into daily life by offering the parting benediction, "God Bless, Safe Journey, Shalom."

CONSECRATED MAHOGANY OBSIDIAN
FOUNDATION LAY-OUT #5 (See Diagram 5)

The fifth Mineral used in Consecrated Lay-outs of Loving Touch Therapy™ is Mahogany Obsidian, a form of volcanic glass. Mahogany Obsidian's contribution to Conscious Evolution is found in the amplification of the Brown and Black Rays of The Divine Light Spectrum that initiate and maintain a grounded sense of cooperation in the performance of Earthly tasks. Additionally, Mahogany Obsidian transmits resonance patterns that assist mankind in releasing compulsive drives for personal survival, and integrate the Benevolence of Godliness into behaviors that address personal needs. Foundation Lay-out #5 is performed as follows:

1. Following The Invocation of Divine Guidance and asking the subject for permission to begin the session of Loving Touch Therapy™, perform a series of Chakra Scans to determine the nature of the subject's Chakra Orientations. The subject should be comfortably reclined on an appropriate facilitation table. Now, relax and breathe slowly, gently inhaling through the nose and slowly exhaling from the mouth. Relax. Allow self to feel and/or see the nature of the subject's Chakra energies.

2. Intuitively and consciously record the impressions received from the subject. Remain silent and continue to relax with steady, gentle breathing, slowly inhaling through the nose and

DIAGRAM 5

Consecrated Mahogany Obsidian - Foundation Lay-out #5

ORDER OF PLACEMENT

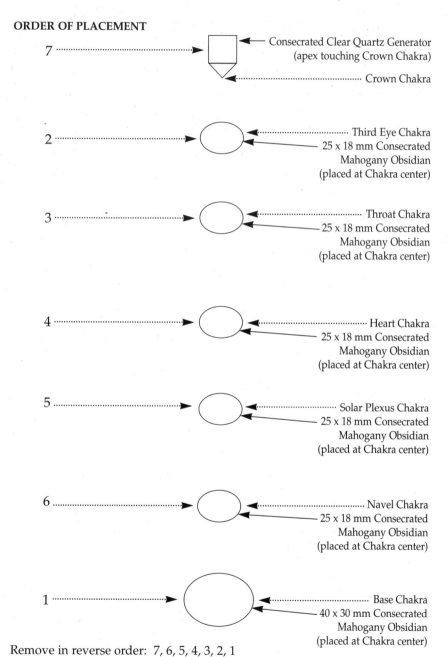

7 ....▶ Consecrated Clear Quartz Generator
(apex touching Crown Chakra)

Crown Chakra

2 ....▶ Third Eye Chakra
25 x 18 mm Consecrated
Mahogany Obsidian
(placed at Chakra center)

3 ....▶ Throat Chakra
25 x 18 mm Consecrated
Mahogany Obsidian
(placed at Chakra center)

4 ....▶ Heart Chakra
25 x 18 mm Consecrated
Mahogany Obsidian
(placed at Chakra center)

5 ....▶ Solar Plexus Chakra
25 x 18 mm Consecrated
Mahogany Obsidian
(placed at Chakra center)

6 ....▶ Navel Chakra
25 x 18 mm Consecrated
Mahogany Obsidian
(placed at Chakra center)

1 ....▶ Base Chakra
40 x 30 mm Consecrated
Mahogany Obsidian
(placed at Chakra center)

Remove in reverse order: 7, 6, 5, 4, 3, 2, 1

191

slowly exhaling from the mouth.

3. After the Primary Chakras have been scanned, step back from the table and begin to gaze upon each Primary Chakra starting at the Crown Chakra and working down the Chakra Cord to the Base Chakra. Hold your gaze at each Primary Chakra for about ten (10) seconds. Allow self to relax. Breathe.

4. Now, place a 40x30mm cabochon of Consecrated Mahogany Obsidian at the center of the Base Chakra. Spiral Balance over the Base Chakra, then Spiral Balance from the Crown Chakra to the Base Chakra. When the Spiral Balancing has been completed, step back from the table and focus your gaze upon the Consecrated Mahogany Obsidian cabochon at the Base Chakra. Continue the silent recitation, "Channel The Light Of Yahweh, Channel The Light Of One."

5. After gazing for several seconds, return to the subject and place 25x18mm cabochons of Consecrated Mahogany Obsidian at the center of each Primary Chakra from the Third Eye Chakra to the Navel Chakra. Next, place a small polished Clear Quartz Crystal Generator at the Crown Chakra with the apex pointed toward the subject.

6. Now, perform a series of Spiral Balancing passes along the Chakra Cord from the Crown Chakra to the Base Chakra. Allow self to feel The Divine Light Energies passing through your hands to the subject. Allow self to feel the energies rising from the subject to meet your hands, as releases of emotional energy and memory matrices of discordance are lifted from the subject. Pay attention to facial expressions that the subject might make, or bodily movements and sounds, and observe the degree to which the subject has relaxed and allowed self to

fully experience the session of Loving Touch Therapy™.

7. When the Spiral Balancing has been completed, stand back from the subject. Beginning at the Crown Chakra, focus your gaze upon the Clear Quartz Crystal Generator for about ten (10) to fifteen (15) seconds before slowly moving your gaze down the Chakra Cord, pausing a few seconds and focusing your gaze upon each successive Consecrated Mahogany Obsidian cabochon placed upon the Chakras en route to and including the Base Chakra. Continue the silent recitation of the phrase, "Channel The Light Of Yahweh, Channel The Light Of One." Once the gazing has been completed, be seated near the facilitation table for up to five (5) minutes. When the time has elapsed, return to the subject and place a Consecrated Sheen Obsidian egg in each of the subject's hands.

8. Begin to remove the Consecrated Generator and Consecrated Mahogany Obsidan cabochons from the subject's body in the reverse order from which the Consecrated Crystal and cabochons were placed on the subject's body: the Consecrated Polished Clear Quartz Generator is removed first, then the Consecrated Mahogany Obsidian cabochons at the Navel Chakra, Solar Plexus Chakra, Heart Chakra, Throat Chakra, Third Eye Chakra and finally the Base Chakra.

9. Now, while speaking in soft tones, gently encourage the subject to open his/her eyes. Gently stroke the subject's arm and shoulder to help stimulate Third Dimension recognition. Speak softly in reassuring tones to assist the subject in assimilating the experience of Loving Touch Therapy™. As the subject becomes more and more cognizant of Third Dimension reality, begin discussing the sensations, visualizations, insights and realizations discovered during the time of facilitation. Be

sure to allow the subject ample time to gather self before leaving the facilitation area.

CONSECRATED SNOWFLAKE OBSIDIAN
FOUNDATION LAY-OUT #6 (See Diagram 6)

Another form of volcanic glass, Snowflake Obsidian is the sixth Mineral used in Consecrated Lay-outs of Loving Touch Therapy™. The energy and appearance of Snowflake Obsidian transmits to mankind the resonant Knowingness that The Light of Truth and Love Eternal forever shine through the darkness of despair, illusion, uncertainty and the human folly of self-indulgence. Foundation Lay-out #6 is performed as follows:

1. After The Invocation of Divine Guidance has been offered and the subject has been asked for permission to begin the Loving Touch Therapy™ session, perform a series of Chakra Scans to determine the subject's Chakra Orientations. Be sure that the subject is comfortably reclined before beginning the Chakra Scans. Now, relax and breathe slowly, gently inhaling through the nose and slowly exhaling from the mouth. Begin Chakra Scanning. Relax. Allow self to feel and/or see the nature of the subject's Chakra energies.

2. Intuitively and consciously record the impressions received from the subject. Remain silent and continue to relax with steady, gentle breathing, slowly inhaling through the nose and slowly exhaling from the mouth.

3. After the Primary Chakras have been scanned, step back from the facilitation table and begin to gaze upon each Primary Chakra starting at the Crown Chakra and working down the

DIAGRAM 6

Consecrated Snowflake Obisidian - Foundation Lay-out #6

ORDER OF PLACEMENT

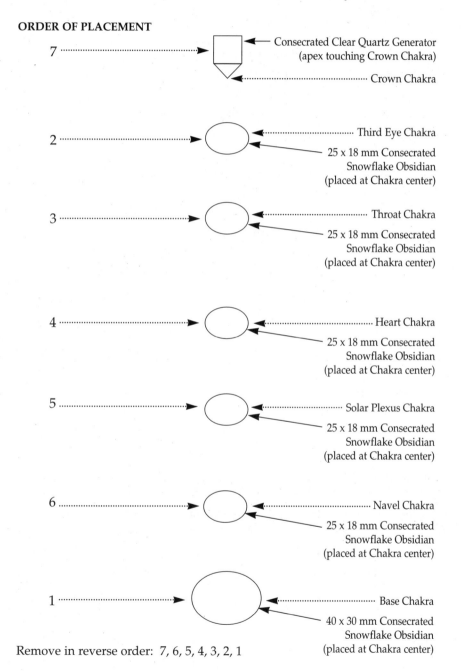

7 ··▶ Consecrated Clear Quartz Generator
(apex touching Crown Chakra)

··· Crown Chakra

2 ··▶ ··············· Third Eye Chakra
25 x 18 mm Consecrated
Snowflake Obsidian
(placed at Chakra center)

3 ··▶ ··············· Throat Chakra
25 x 18 mm Consecrated
Snowflake Obsidian
(placed at Chakra center)

4 ··▶ ··············· Heart Chakra
25 x 18 mm Consecrated
Snowflake Obsidian
(placed at Chakra center)

5 ··▶ ··············· Solar Plexus Chakra
25 x 18 mm Consecrated
Snowflake Obsidian
(placed at Chakra center)

6 ··▶ ··············· Navel Chakra
25 x 18 mm Consecrated
Snowflake Obsidian
(placed at Chakra center)

1 ··▶ ··············· Base Chakra
40 x 30 mm Consecrated
Snowflake Obsidian
Remove in reverse order: 7, 6, 5, 4, 3, 2, 1   (placed at Chakra center)

195

Chakra Cord to the Base Chakra. Hold your gaze at each Primary Chakra for about ten (10) seconds. Allow self to relax. Breathe.

4. Now, place a 40x30mm cabochon of Consecrated Snowflake Obsidian at the center of the Base Chakra. Spiral Balance over the Base Chakra, then Spiral Balance from the Crown Chakra to the Base Chakra. When the Spiral Balancing has been completed, step back from the table and fix your gaze upon the Consecrated Snowflake Obsidian cabochon at the Base Chakra. Continue the silent recitation, "Channel The Light Of Yahweh, Channel The Light Of One."

5. After gazing for several seconds to further activate The Divine Light Energies amplified through the Consecrated Snowflake Obsidian cabochon, return to the subject and place 25x18mm cabochons of Consecrated Snowflake Obsidian at the center of each Primary Chakra from the Third Eye Chakra to the Navel Chakra. Next, place a small polished Clear Quartz Crystal Generator at the Crown Chakra with the apex pointed toward the subject.

6. Now, perform a series of Spiral Balancing passes along the Chakra Cord from the Crown Chakra to the Base Chakra. Allow self to feel The Divine Light Energies passing through your hands to the subject. Allow self to feel the energies rising from the subject to meet your hands, as releases of emotional energy and discordant memory matrices are lifted from the subject. Observe the subject's facial expressions during the course of the facilitation session. Pay attention to bodily movements and sounds, and observe the degree to which the subject has relaxed and allowed self to fully experience the session of Loving Touch Therapy™.

7. When the Spiral Balancing has been completed, stand back from the subject and focus your gaze upon the Clear Quartz Crystal Generator at the Crown Chakra. Hold your gaze upon the Quartz Crystal Generator for about ten (10) to fifteen (15) seconds before slowly moving your gaze down the Chakra Cord, pausing a few seconds and refocusing your gaze upon each successive Consecrated Snowflake Obsidian cabochon placed upon the Primary Chakras en route to and including the Base Chakra. Continue the silent recitation, "Channel The Light Of Yahweh, Channel The Light Of One." When the gazing has been completed, be seated near the facilitation table for up to five (5) minutes. When the time has elapsed, return to the subject and place a Consecrated Sheen Obsidian egg in each of the subject's hands.

8. Begin to remove the Consecrated Crystal and cabochons from the subject's body in the reverse order from which the Consecrated Crystal Generator and Consecrated Snowflake Obsidian cabochons were placed on the subject's body: Consecrated polished Clear Quartz Crystal Generator is removed first, then the Consecrated Snowflake Obsidian cabochons at the Navel Chakra, Solar Plexus Chakra, Heart Chakra, Throat Chakra, Third Eye Chakra and finally the Base Chakra.

9. Now, as you speak in soft tones, gently encourage the subject to open his/her eyes. Gently stroke the subject's arm and shoulder to help stimulate the subject's awareness of Third Dimension reality. Speak softly in reassuring tones to assist the subject in assimilating the experience of Loving Touch Therapy™. As the subject becomes more and more aware of Third Dimension reality, begin discussing the facilitation experience, but remember to discuss only those areas of incarnate

experience that the subject is ready and willing to accept.

CONSECRATED LAPIS LAZULI
FOUNDATION LAY-OUT #7 (See Diagram 7)

Lapis Lazuli is the seventh Mineral used in Consecrated Lay-outs of Loving Touch Therapy™. Amplifying a Deep Blue Ray of The Spectrum of Divine Light Energy, along with intermittent Golden Rays of Divine Light Energy, Lapis Lazuli can escort mortal consciousness into the innermost sanctums of personal truth, thereby assisting mortal man in uncovering the true motivations for behaviors, while simultaneously illuminating man's discovery of true self with the evolved perception of Etheric Truth. Foundation Lay-out #7 is performed as follows:

1. Following The Invocation of Divine Guidance, ask the subject for permission to begin the Loving Touch Therapy™ session. Now, perform a series of Chakra Scans to determine the nature of the subject's Chakra Orientations. Care should be taken to be sure that the subject is comfortable before beginning the Chakra Scans. Now, relax and breathe slowly, gently inhaling through the nose and slowly exhaling from the mouth. Begin your Chakra Scans. Relax. Allow self to feel and/or see the nature of the subject's Chakra energies.

2. Intuitively and consciously record the impression received from the subject. Remain silent and continue to relax with steady, gentle breathing, slowly inhaling through the nose and slowly exhaling from the mouth.

3. After the Primary Chakras have been scanned, step back from the table and begin to gaze upon each Primary Chakra starting at the Crown Chakra and working down the Chakra Cord to

DIAGRAM 7

Consecrated Lapis Lazuli - Foundation Lay-out #7

ORDER OF PLACEMENT

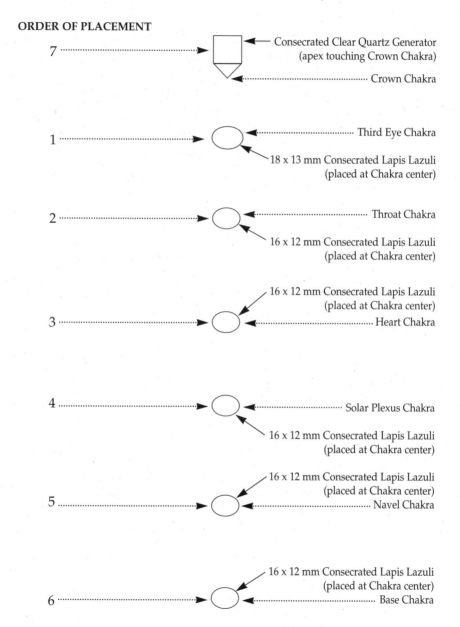

7 ....➤ ◀— Consecrated Clear Quartz Generator
(apex touching Crown Chakra)

◀.. Crown Chakra

1 ....➤ ◀.. Third Eye Chakra

18 x 13 mm Consecrated Lapis Lazuli
(placed at Chakra center)

2 ....➤ ◀.. Throat Chakra

16 x 12 mm Consecrated Lapis Lazuli
(placed at Chakra center)

16 x 12 mm Consecrated Lapis Lazuli
(placed at Chakra center)
3 ....➤ ◀.. Heart Chakra

4 ....➤ ◀.. Solar Plexus Chakra

16 x 12 mm Consecrated Lapis Lazuli
(placed at Chakra center)

16 x 12 mm Consecrated Lapis Lazuli
(placed at Chakra center)
5 ....➤ ◀.. Navel Chakra

16 x 12 mm Consecrated Lapis Lazuli
(placed at Chakra center)
6 ....➤ ◀.. Base Chakra

Remove in reverse order: 7, 6, 5, 4, 3, 2, 1

the Base Chakra. Hold your gaze at each Primary Chakra for about ten (10) seconds before moving to the next Chakra. Allow self to relax. Breathe.

4. Now, place an 18x13mm cabochon of Consecrated Lapis Lazuli at the center of the Third Eye Chakra. Spiral Balance over the Third Eye Chakra, then Spiral Balance from the Crown Chakra to the Base Chakra. When the Spiral Balancing has been completed, step back from the facilitation table and fix your gaze upon the Consecrated Lapis Lazuli cabochon at the Third Eye Chakra. Continue the silent recitation of the phrase, "Channel The Light Of Yahweh, Channel The Light Of One."

5. After gazing for several seconds, return to the subject and place a 16x12mm cabochon of Consecrated Lapis Lazuli at the center of each successive Primary Chakra from the Throat Chakra to the Base Chakra. Next, place a small polished Consecrated Clear Quartz Crystal Generator at the Crown Chakra with the apex pointed toward the subject.

6. Now, perform a series of Spiral Balancing passes along the Chakra Cord from the Crown Chakra to the Base Chakra. Allow self to feel The Divine Light Energies passing through your hands to the subject. Allow self to feel the energies rising from the subject to meet your hands, as releases of emotional energy and memory matrices of discordance are lifted from the subject. Observe the subject's facial expressions, bodily movements and the sounds made during the course of the facilitation. Observe the degree to which the subject has relaxed and allowed self to fully experience the session of Loving Touch Therapy™.

7. After completing the Spiral Balancing passes, stand back from

the subject and focus your gaze upon the Consecrated Quartz Generator at the Crown Chakra. Hold your gaze upon the Consecrated Generator for about ten (10) to fifteen (15) seconds before slowly moving your gaze down the Chakra Cord, pausing a few seconds and refocusing your gaze upon each successive Consecrated Lapis Lazuli cabochon placed upon the Chakras en route to and including the Base Chakra. Continue the silent recitation, "Channel The Light Of Yahweh, Channel The Light Of One." When the gazing has been completed, be seated near the facilitation table for up to five (5) minutes. When the time has elapsed, return to the subject and place a Consecrated Sheen Obsidian egg in each of the subject's hands.

8. Begin removing the Consecrated Quartz Generator and Consecrated Lapis Lazuli cabochons from the subject's body in the reverse order from which the Consecrated Quartz Generator and Consecrated Lapis Lazuli cabochons were placed on the subject's body: first remove the Consecrated Clear Quartz Crystal Generator, then remove the Consecrated Lapis Lazuli cabochons from the Base Chakra, Navel Chakra, Solar Plexus Chakra, Heart Chakra, Throat Chakra and finally the Third Eye Chakra.

9. Now, while speaking in soft tones, gently encourage the subject to open his/her eyes. Gently stroke the subject's arm and shoulder to help stimulate Third Dimension recognition. Speak softly in reassuring tones to assist the subject in fully assimilating and grounding the experience of Loving Touch Therapy™ into his/her conscious being. When the subject becomes sufficiently grounded in Third Dimension reality, begin discussing the facilitation experience.

CONSECRATED BLUE LACE AGATE
FOUNDATION LAY-OUT #8 (See Diagram 8)

Blue Lace Agate is the eighth Mineral from the Quartz/Mineral Kingdom used in Consecrated Lay-outs of Loving Touch Therapy™. Amplifying the soft, gentle Light Blue Ray of The Spectrum of Divine Light Energy, Blue Lace Agate transmits calming, comforting resonant energies to mortal consciousness that facilitate states of peaceful communion between elements of personal self, quieting turbulent energies of emotion and allowing gentle articulation of personal truths. The procedure for Foundation Lay-out #8 is as follows:

1. After The Invocation of Divine Guidance has been offered and the subject has been asked for permission to begin the session of Loving Touch Therapy™, perform a series of Chakra Scans to determine the nature of the subject's Chakra Orientations. After seeing that the subject is comfortable on the facilitation table, begin the procedure by allowing self to relax. Breathe slowly, gently inhaling through the nose and slowly exhaling from the mouth. Begin scanning the Primary Chakras. Relax. Allow self to feel and/or see the nature of the subject's Chakra energies.

2. Intuitively and consciously record the impressions received from the subject. Remain silent and continue to relax with steady gentle breathing, slowly inhaling through the nose and slowly exhaling from the mouth.

3. After scanning the Primary Chakras, step back from the table and begin to gaze upon each Primary Chakra starting at the Crown Chakra and working down the Chakra Cord to the Base Chakra. Hold your gaze at each Primary Chakra for

DIAGRAM 8
Consecrated Blue Lace Agate - Foundation Lay-out #8

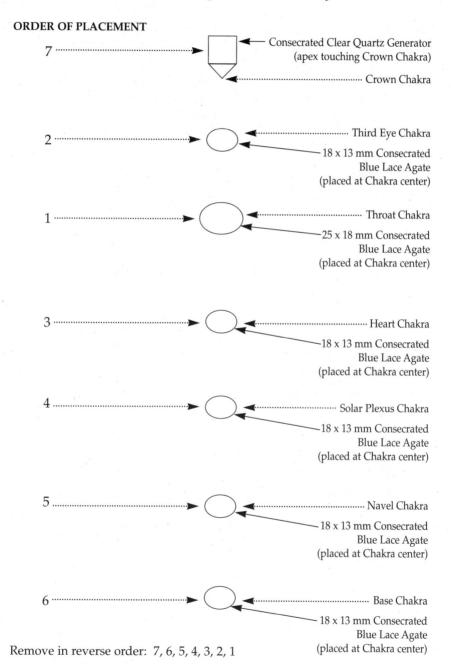

7 ··➤ Consecrated Clear Quartz Generator
(apex touching Crown Chakra)

Crown Chakra ·····································

2 ··➤ Third Eye Chakra ·····························

18 x 13 mm Consecrated
Blue Lace Agate
(placed at Chakra center)

1 ··➤ Throat Chakra ·····························

25 x 18 mm Consecrated
Blue Lace Agate
(placed at Chakra center)

3 ··➤ Heart Chakra ·····························

18 x 13 mm Consecrated
Blue Lace Agate
(placed at Chakra center)

4 ··➤ Solar Plexus Chakra ·····························

18 x 13 mm Consecrated
Blue Lace Agate
(placed at Chakra center)

5 ··➤ Navel Chakra ·····························

18 x 13 mm Consecrated
Blue Lace Agate
(placed at Chakra center)

6 ··➤ Base Chakra ·····························

18 x 13 mm Consecrated
Blue Lace Agate
(placed at Chakra center)

Remove in reverse order: 7, 6, 5, 4, 3, 2, 1

about ten (10) seconds before moving to the next Chakra. Allow self to relax. Breathe.

4. Now, place a 25x18mm cabochon of Consecrated Blue Lace Agate at the center of the Throat Chakra. Spiral Balance over the Throat Chakra, then Spiral Balance from the Crown Chakra to the Base Chakra. When the Spiral Balancing passes have been completed, step back from the table and focus your gaze upon the Consecrated Blue Lace Agate cabochon at the Throat Chakra. Continue the silent recitation, "Channel The Light Of Yahweh, Channel The Light Of One."

5. After gazing for several seconds, return to the subject and place an 18x13mm cabochon of Consecrated Blue Lace Agate at the center of each remaining Primary Chakra, (except the Crown Chakra), beginning at the Third Eye Chakra and working down to and including the Base Chakra. Next, place a small polished Clear Quartz Crystal Generator at the Crown Chakra with the apex pointed toward the subject.

6. Now, perform a series of Spiral Balancing passes along the Chakra Cord from the Crown Chakra to the Base Chakra. Allow self to feel The Divine Light Energies passing through your hands to the subject. Allow self to feel the energies rising from the subject to meet your hands, as releases of emotional energy and discordant memory matrices are lifted from the subject. Observe facial expressions, bodily movements and sounds made by the subject during the facilitation. Observe the degree to which the subject has relaxed and allowed self to fully experience the session of Loving Touch Therapy™.

7. After completing the Spiral Balancing passes, stand back from

the subject and fix your gaze upon the Consecrated Quartz Generator for about ten (10) to fifteen (15) seconds. Slowly begin moving your gaze down the Chakra Cord, pausing a few seconds and holding your gaze upon each successive Consecrated Blue Lace Agate cabochon placed upon the Chakras en route to and including the Base Chakra. Continue the silent recitation, "Channel The Light Of Yahweh, Channel The Light Of One." When the gazing has been completed, be seated near the facilitation table for up to five (5) minutes. When the sitting period has elapsed, return to the subject and place a Consecrated Sheen Obsidian egg in each of the subject's hands.

8. Begin removing the Consecrated Generator and Consecrated Blue Lace Agate cabochons from the subject's body in the reverse order from which the Consecrated Crystal and Consecrated Blue Lace Agate cabochons were placed on the subject's body: remove the Consecrated Clear Quartz Crystal Generator first, then remove the Consecrated Blue Lace Agate cabochons from the Base Chakra, Navel Chakra, Solar Plexus Chakra, Heart Chakra, Third Eye Chakra and finally the Throat Chakra.

9. Now, as you speak in soft tones, gently encourage the subject to open his/her eyes. Gently stroke the subject's arm and shoulder to help stimulate third Dimension awareness. Speak softly in reassuring tones to assist the subject in fully assimilating and grounding the experience of Loving Touch Therapy™ into his/her conscious being. When the subject has regained sufficient grounding in Third Dimension reality, begin discussing the experience of the Loving Touch Therapy™ session.

CONSECRATED UNAKITE
FOUNDATION LAY-OUT #9 (See Diagram 9)

Unakite is the ninth Mineral from the Quartz Family to be used in Consecrated Lay-outs of Loving Touch Therapy™. Amplifying the "Peachy" Pink and Lime Green Rays of The Divine Light Spectrum, Unakite gently grounds the acceptance of the "Intuitive Voice" or the Benevolent Guidance of the God-Self into mortal consciousness by facilitating the release of emotional discord and fears associated with Heart Chakra function. The energies amplified through Unakite also set the stage for cooperative functions between the evolved states of Heart Chakra and Solar Plexus Chakra operation. Foundation Lay-out #9 is performed as follows:

1. After The Invocation of Divine Guidance has been offered and the subject has been asked for permission to begin the session of Loving Touch Therapy™, perform a series of Chakra Scans to determine the subject's Chakra Orientations. Before you begin the Chakra Scans, be sure that the subject is comfortably situated on the facilitation table. Now, relax. Breathe slowly, gently inhaling through the nose and slowly exhaling from the mouth. Relax. Begin scanning the Primary Chakras. Allow self to feel and/or see the nature of the subject's Chakra energies.

2. Intuitively and consciously record the impressions you receive from the subject. Remain silent and continue to relax with steady, gentle breathing, slowly inhaling through the nose and slowly exhaling from the mouth.

3. After the Primary Chakras have been scanned, step back from the table and begin to gaze upon each Primary Chakra starting at the Crown Chakra and working down the Chakra Cord to

DIAGRAM 9

Consecrated Unakite - Foundation Lay-out #9

ORDER OF PLACEMENT

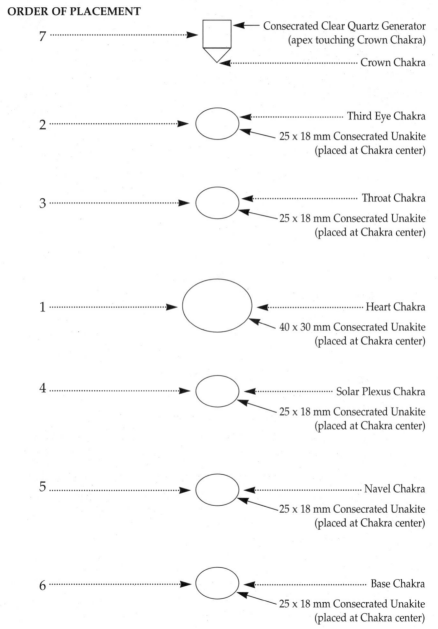

7 ··▶ — Consecrated Clear Quartz Generator
(apex touching Crown Chakra)

·· Crown Chakra

2 ··▶ ·· Third Eye Chakra

— 25 x 18 mm Consecrated Unakite
(placed at Chakra center)

3 ··▶ ·· Throat Chakra

— 25 x 18 mm Consecrated Unakite
(placed at Chakra center)

1 ··▶ ·· Heart Chakra

— 40 x 30 mm Consecrated Unakite
(placed at Chakra center)

4 ··▶ ·· Solar Plexus Chakra

— 25 x 18 mm Consecrated Unakite
(placed at Chakra center)

5 ··▶ ·· Navel Chakra

— 25 x 18 mm Consecrated Unakite
(placed at Chakra center)

6 ··▶ ·· Base Chakra

— 25 x 18 mm Consecrated Unakite
(placed at Chakra center)

Remove in reverse order: 7, 6, 5, 4, 3, 2, 1

207

the Base Chakra. Relax. Breathe.

4. Now, beginning at the Heart Chakra, place a 40x30mm cabo-
    chon of Consecrated Unakite at the center of the Heart Chakra.
    Spiral Balance over the Heart Chakra, then Spiral Balance from
    the Crown Chakra to the Base Chakra (remember to continue
    the silent recitation, "Channel The Light Of Yahweh, Channel
    The Light Of One," whenever Spiral Balancing is performed).
    When the Spiral Balancing passes have been completed, move
    away from the facilitation table, and focus your gaze upon the
    Consecrated Unakite cabochon at the center of the Heart
    Chakra. As you gaze upon the Unakite cabochon, continue the
    silent recitation.

5. After gazing for ten (10) to fifteen (15) seconds, return to the
    subject and place 25x18mm cabochons of Consecrated Unakite
    at the center of each Primary Chakra (except the Heart
    Chakra) from the Third Eye Chakra to the Base Chakra. Next,
    place a small polished Clear Quartz Crystal Generator at the
    Crown Chakra with the apex pointed toward the subject.

6. Now, perform Spiral Balancing passes along the Chakra Cord
    from the Crown Chakra to the Base Chakra. Allow self to feel
    The Divine Light Energies passing through your hands to the
    subject. Allow self to feel the energies rising from the subject
    to meet your hands, as releases of emotional energy and dis-
    cordant memory matrices are lifted from the subject. Observe
    the facial expressions, bodily movements and sounds made by
    the subject during the facilitation session. Pay attention to the
    degree to which the subject has relaxed and allowed self to
    experience the facilitation.

7. When the Spiral Balancing passes have been completed, stand

back from the subject. Beginning at the Crown Chakra, focus your gaze upon the Clear Quartz Generator for about ten (10) to fifteen (15) seconds before slowly moving your gaze down the Chakra Cord, pausing a few seconds and focusing your gaze upon each successive Consecrated Unakite cabochon placed upon the Primary Chakras en route to and including the Base Chakra. Continue the silent recitation. When the gazing has been completed, be seated nearby for up to five (5) minutes. When the time has elapsed, return to the subject and place a Consecrated Sheen Obsidian egg in each of the subject's hands.

8. Begin removing the Consecrated Crystal and cabochons from the subject's body in the reverse order from which the Consecrated Crystal Generator and Consecrated Unakite cabochons were placed on the subject's body: the Consecrated Quartz Crystal Generator is removed first, followed by the Consecrated Unakite cabochons at the Base Chakra, Navel Chakra, Solar Plexus Chakra, Throat Chakra, Third Eye Chakra and finally the Heart Chakra.

9. Now, while speaking in soft tones, gently encourage the subject to open his/her eyes. Gently stroke the subject's arm and shoulder to help stimulate Third Dimension recognition. Speak softly in reassuring tones to assist the subject in assimilating the experience of Loving Touch Therapy™. When the subject is sufficiently grounded in the reality of Third Dimension, begin discussing the feelings, sensations and impressions experienced during the facilitation session.

CONSECRATED RHODONITE
FOUNDATION LAY-OUT #10 (See Diagram 10)

Rhodonite is the tenth member of the Quartz/Mineral Family used in Consecrated Lay-outs of Loving Touch Therapy™. The black dendritic inclusions of Rhodonite along with The Divine Light Energy of the Pink Ray facilitate the release of emotional trauma associated with issues of self-worth, while elevating the resonance of lower energy states to accept and implement the reality of Evolved Self. Foundation Lay-out #10 is performed as follows:

1. Offer The Invocation of Divine Guidance and ask the subject for permission to begin the Loving Touch Therapy™ session. Be sure that the subject is comfortably reclined on the facilitation table before proceeding. Now, relax and breathe slowly, gently inhaling through the nose and slowly exhaling from the mouth. Relax. Begin scanning the Primary Chakras from the Crown Chakra to the Base Chakra. Allow self to feel and/or see the nature of the subject's Chakra energies.

2. Intuitively and consciously record the impressions you receive from the subject. Remain silent and continue to relax with steady, gentle breathing, slowly inhaling through the nose and slowly exhaling from the mouth.

3. After scanning the Primary Chakras, step back from the table and begin gazing upon each Primary Chakra, starting at the Crown Chakra and working down the Chakra Cord to the Base Chakra. Relax. Breathe.

4. Now, beginning at the Heart Chakra, place a 40x30mm cabochon of Consecrated Rhodonite at the center of the Heart Chakra. Spiral Balance over the Heart Chakra, then Spiral

DIAGRAM 10
Consecrated Rhodonite - Foundation Lay-out #10

ORDER OF PLACEMENT

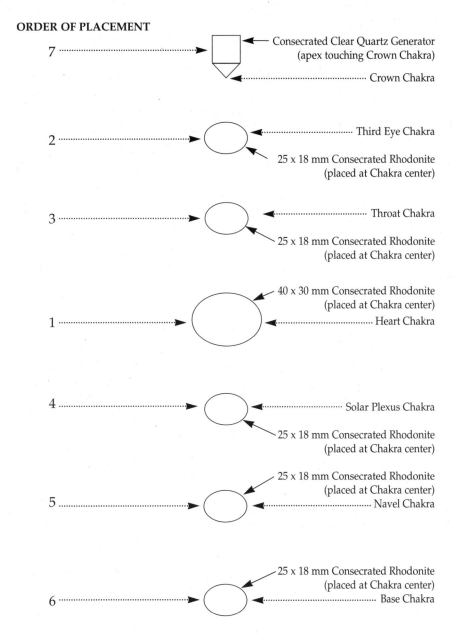

7 ···▶ ◀── Consecrated Clear Quartz Generator
(apex touching Crown Chakra)

◀··· Crown Chakra

2 ···▶ ◀··· Third Eye Chakra

25 x 18 mm Consecrated Rhodonite
(placed at Chakra center)

3 ···▶ ◀··· Throat Chakra

25 x 18 mm Consecrated Rhodonite
(placed at Chakra center)

40 x 30 mm Consecrated Rhodonite
(placed at Chakra center)

1 ···▶ ◀··· Heart Chakra

4 ···▶ ◀··· Solar Plexus Chakra

25 x 18 mm Consecrated Rhodonite
(placed at Chakra center)

25 x 18 mm Consecrated Rhodonite
(placed at Chakra center)

5 ···▶ ◀··· Navel Chakra

25 x 18 mm Consecrated Rhodonite
(placed at Chakra center)

6 ···▶ ◀··· Base Chakra

Remove in reverse order: 7, 6, 5, 4, 3, 2, 1

Balance from the Crown Chakra to the Base Chakra. When the Spiral Balancing passes have been completed, move away from the table and focus your gaze upon the Consecrated Rhodonite cabochon at the center of the Heart Chakra. While gazing upon the Consecrated Rhodonite cabochon, continue the silent recitation, "Channel The Light Of Yahweh, Channel The Light Of One."

5. After gazing for about ten (10) to fifteen (15) seconds, return to the subject and place 25x18mm cabochons of Consecrated Rhodonite at the center of each Primary Chakra (except the Heart Chakra) from the Third Eye Chakra to the Base Chakra. Next, place a small polished Clear Quartz Crystal Generator at the Crown Chakra with the apex pointed toward the subject.

6. Now, perform Spiral Balancing passes along the Chakra Cord from the Crown Chakra to the Base Chakra. Allow self to feel The Radiant, Divine Light Energies passing through your hands to the subject. Allow self to feel the energies rising from the subject to meet your hands, as releases of emotional energy and memory matrices of discordance are lifted from the subject's consciousness. Carefully observe the facial expressions, bodily movements and sounds made by the subject during the facilitation session. Observe the degree to which the subject has relaxed and allowed self to experience the energies of Transformation transmitted through Loving Touch Therapy™.

7. When the Spiral Balancing passes have been completed, stand away from the facilitation table. Beginning at the Crown Chakra, fix your gaze upon the Consecrated Clear Quartz Crystal Generator for about ten (10) to fifteen (15) seconds before slowly moving your gaze down the Chakra Cord, pausing a few seconds and focusing your gaze upon each succes-

sive Consecrated Rhodonite cabochon placed upon the Primary Chakras en route to and including the Base Chakra. Continue the silent recitation. When the gazing has been completed, be seated near the facilitation table for up to five (5) minutes. When the time has elapsed, return to the subject and place a Consecrated Sheen Obsidian egg in each of the subject's hands.

8. Begin to remove the Consecrated Generator and cabochons from the subject's body in the reverse order from which the Consecrated Crystal Generator and Consecrated Rhodonite cabochons were place on the subject's body: first remove the Consecrated Quartz Generator at the Crown Chakra, followed by the Consecrated Rhodonite cabochons at the Base Chakra, Navel Chakra, Solar Plexus Chakra, Throat Chakra, Third Eye Chakra and finally the Heart Chakra.

9. Now, as you speak in a soft voice, gently encourage the subject to open his/her eyes. Gently stroke the subject's arm and shoulder to help stimulate recognition of Third Dimension reality. Speak softly in reassuring tones to assist the subject in assimilating the experience of Loving Touch Therapy™. When the subject is sufficiently grounded in the reality of Third Dimension, begin discussing the experience of the facilitation session.

CONSECRATED ROSE QUARTZ W/MALACHITE
FOUNDATION LAY-OUT #11 (See Diagram 11)

Foundation Lay-out #11 utilizes the energies of the Pink and Green Rays of The Divine Light Spectrum as amplified by Rose Quartz and Malachite. The comforting, compassionate energy transmitted by Rose Quartz serves to soften, cleanse and transmute the energies of emotional trauma lifted to the surface by the energies transmitted through Malachite. The procedure for performing Foundation Lay-out #11 is as follows:

1. After offering The Invocation of Divine Guidance and asking the subject for permission to begin the session of Loving Touch Therapy™, perform a series of Chakra Scans to determine the nature of the subject's Chakra Orientations. After being sure that the subject is comfortably situated on the facilitation table, begin the procedure by allowing self to relax. Breathe slowly, gently inhaling through the nose and slowly exhaling from the mouth. Begin scanning the Primary Chakras. Relax. Allow self to feel and/or see the nature of the subject's Chakra energies.

2. Intuitively and consciously record the impressions received from the subject. Remain in silence and continue to relax with steady, gentle breathing, slowly inhaling through the nose and slowly exhaling from the mouth.

3. After scanning the Primary Chakras, step back from the table and begin to gaze upon each Primary Chakra starting at the Crown Chakra and working down the Chakra Cord to the Base Chakra. Hold your gaze at each Primary Chakra for about ten (10) seconds before moving to the next Chakra. Allow self to relax. Breathe.

4. Now, beginning at the Heart Chakra, place a 40x30mm Consecrated Rose Quartz cabochon at the center of the Heart Chakra. Spiral Balance over the Heart Chakra, then Spiral Balance from the Crown Chakra to the Base Chakra. When the Spiral Balancing passes have been completed, step back from the facilitation table and focus your gaze upon the Consecrated Rose Quartz cabochon at the Heart Chakra. While gazing

DIAGRAM 11

Consecrated Rose Quartz w/Malachite - Foundation Lay-out #11

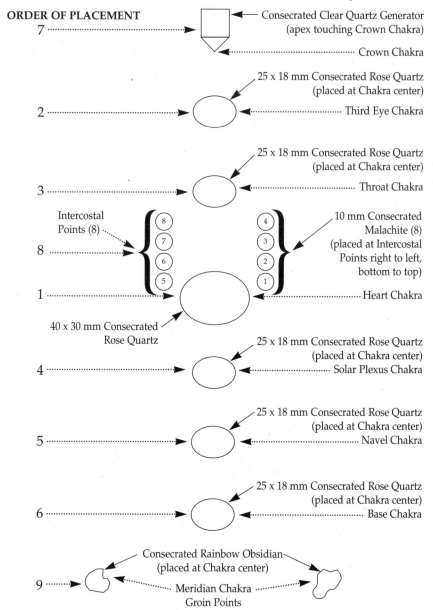

ORDER OF PLACEMENT

7 ·········· → ◄— Consecrated Clear Quartz Generator
(apex touching Crown Chakra)

········· Crown Chakra

25 x 18 mm Consecrated Rose Quartz
(placed at Chakra center)

2 ·········· → ◄········· Third Eye Chakra

25 x 18 mm Consecrated Rose Quartz
(placed at Chakra center)

3 ·········· → ◄········· Throat Chakra

Intercostal Points (8) ········· { 8 7 6 5 }   { 4 3 2 1 }   10 mm Consecrated Malachite (8)
(placed at Intercostal Points right to left, bottom to top)

8 ·········· →

1 ·········· → ◄········· Heart Chakra

40 x 30 mm Consecrated Rose Quartz

25 x 18 mm Consecrated Rose Quartz
(placed at Chakra center)

4 ·········· → ◄········· Solar Plexus Chakra

25 x 18 mm Consecrated Rose Quartz
(placed at Chakra center)

5 ·········· → ◄········· Navel Chakra

25 x 18 mm Consecrated Rose Quartz
(placed at Chakra center)

6 ·········· → ◄········· Base Chakra

Consecrated Rainbow Obsidian
(placed at Chakra center)

9 ·········· → ◄········· Meridian Chakra ·········· →
Groin Points

Remove in reverse order: 8, 7, 6, 5, 4, 3, 2, 1, 9

upon the Consecrated Rose Quartz cabochon at the Heart Chakra, continue the silent recitation, "Channel The Light Of Yahweh, Channel The Light Of One."

5. After several seconds of gazing, return to the subject and place 25x18mm Consecrated Rose Quartz cabochons at the center of each successive Primary Chakra from the Third Eye Chakra to the Base Chakra (excluding the Heart Chakra). Next, place a small polished Clear Quartz Crystal Generator at the Crown Chakra with the apex pointed toward the subject.

6. Now, perform several Spiral Balancing passes (3-5) along the Chakra Cord from the Crown Chakra to the Base Chakra. When the Spiral Balancing has been completed, step back from the table and focus your gaze upon the Consecrated Quartz Generator at the Crown Chakra. Hold your gaze upon the Consecrated Generator for about ten (10) to fifteen (15) seconds before slowly moving your gaze down the Chakra Cord, pausing a few seconds and focusing your gaze upon each successive Consecrated Rose Quartz cabochon placed upon the Chakras en route to and including the Base Chakra. Continue the silent recitation, "Channel The Light Of Yahweh, Channel The Light Of One."

7. When the Spiral Balancing passes have been completed, return to the subject and begin placing eight (8) 10mm round Consecrated Malachite cabochons at the intercostal points above the Heart Chakra (See Illustration 17), then place a polished, free-form Consecrated Rainbow Obsidian at each Meridian Chakra Groin Point (free-form Rainbow Obsidian should be of equal weight, ranging between 20mgs to 75mgs each).

Illustration 17: Location of Intercostal Points

FRONTAL VIEW

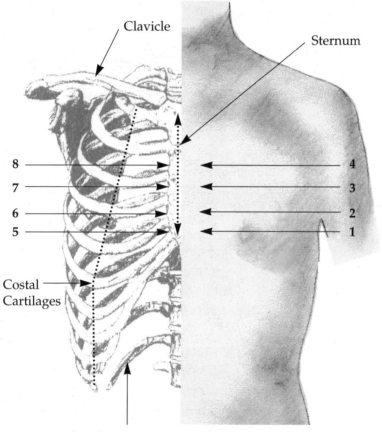

Intercostal Points are located at the juncture
between the Costal Cartilages and the Sternum.

8. Now, Spiral Balance over the Heart Chakra and the Consecrated Malachite at the intercostal points. When complete, stand back from the facilitation table and focus your gaze upon the Consecrated Rose Quartz and Consecrated Malachite cabochons in the Heart Chakra area.

9. Return to the subject and Spiral Balance along the Chakra Cord from the Crown Chakra to the Base Chakra. Allow self to feel The Divine Light Energies passing through your hands to the subject. Allow self to feel the energies rising from the subject to meet your hands, as releases of emotional energy and discordant energy matrices are lifted from the subject's consciousness. Observe facial expressions, bodily movements and sounds made by the subject during the session. And observe the degree to which the subject has relaxed and allowed self to experience the Loving Touch Therapy™ facilitation.

10. When the Spiral Balancing has been completed, stand back from the subject. Beginning at the Crown Chakra, fix your gaze upon the Consecrated Quartz Generator for about ten (10) to fifteen (15) seconds before slowly moving your gaze down the Chakra Cord, pausing a few seconds and refocusing your gaze upon each successive Consecrated cabochon and free-form shape placed upon the Chakras en route to and including the Meridian Chakra Groin Points and Base Chakra. Continue the silent recitation, "Channel The Light Of Yahweh, Channel The Light Of One." When the gazing has been completed, be seated near the facilitation table for up to five (5) minutes. After the time has elapsed, return to the subject and place a Consecrated Sheen Obsidian egg in each of the subject's hands.

11. With the exception of the free-form Consecrated Rainbow Obsidian, begin removing the Consecrated Generator and Consecrated Rose Quartz and Malachite cabochons from the subject's body in the reverse order from which the Consecrated Generator and cabochons were placed on the subject's body: remove the Consecrated Malachite cabochons first from bottom to top, then remove the Consecrated Clear Quartz Generator, followed by the Consecrated Rose Quartz cabochons from the Base Chakra, Navel Chakra, Solar Plexus Chakra, Throat Chakra, Third Eye Chakra and Heart Chakra, and finally, remove the free-form Consecrated Rainbow Obsidian from the Meridian Chakra Groin Points.

12. Now, while speaking in soft, comforting tones, gently encourage the subject to open his/her eyes. Gently stroke the subject's arm and shoulder to help stimulate awareness of Third Dimension reality. Speak softly in reassuring tones to assist the subject in assimilating the experience of Loving Touch Therapy™. When the subject demonstrates a grounded sense of Third Dimension recognition, discuss the events and experience of the facilitation.

CONSECRATED
ROSE QUARTZ, MALACHITE, EMERALD & RUBY
FOUNDATION LAY-OUT #12 (See Diagram 12)

The addition of Consecrated Emerald & Ruby cabochons to Foundation Lay-out #11 provides Foundation Lay-out #12 with a heightened resonance pitch that facilitates conscious well-being through evolved Heart Chakra states, while simultaneously stimulating and grounding a sense of Faith and Devotion to Evolved Spiritual Truth in mortal consciousness. To perform Foundation Lay-out #12, begin by following steps 1-8 of Foundation Lay-out

#11. Now, continue with the following steps:

9. Return to the subject and Spiral Balance along the Chakra Cord from the Crown Chakra to the Base Chakra. When the Spiral Balancing passes have been completed, stand back from the subject and beginning at the Crown Chakra, focus your gaze upon the Consecrated Quartz Generator for about ten (10) to fifteen (15) seconds before slowly moving your gaze down the Chakra Cord, pausing a few seconds and refocusing your gaze upon each successive Consecrated cabochon and free-form shape placed upon the Chakras en route to and including the Meridian Chakra Groin Points and the Base Chakra.

10. When the gazing has been completed, return to the subject and place a 7x5mm cabochon of Consecrated Emerald on top of the 40x30mm Consecrated Rose Quartz cabochon at the center of the Heart Chakra. Next, place a 6x4mm cabochon of Consecrated Ruby on top of the 25x18mm Consecrated Rose Quartz cabochon at the center of the Base Chakra.

11. Now, Spiral Balance for twenty (20) to thirty (30) seconds over the Heart Chakra area, then immediately Spiral Balance for twenty (20) to thirty (30) seconds over the Base Chakra. When Spiral Balancing has been completed, stand back from the table and fix your gaze squarely upon the Consecrated Emerald at the center of the Heart Chakra. After about fifteen (15) seconds, slowly move down the Chakra Cord and refocus your gaze squarely upon the Consecrated Ruby at the center of the Base Chakra for about fifteen (15) seconds.

12. When gazing has been completed, return to the subject and Spiral Balance along the Chakra Cord from the Crown Chakra to the Base Chakra. Continue the silent recitation, "Channel

DIAGRAM 12

Consecrated Rose Quartz w/Malachite, Emerald & Ruby - Foundation Lay-out #12

ORDER OF PLACEMENT

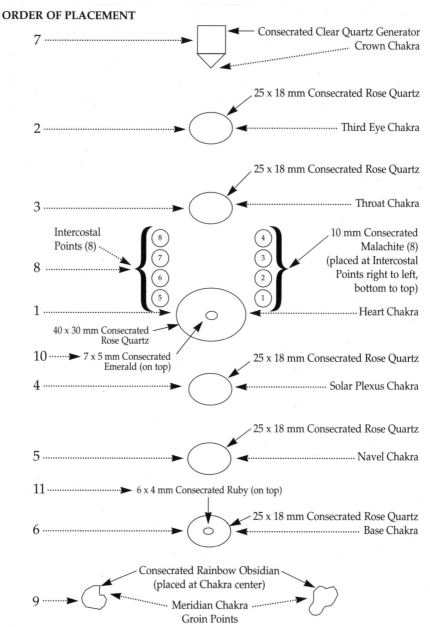

7 ··▶ ◀── Consecrated Clear Quartz Generator
··········· Crown Chakra

2 ··▶ 25 x 18 mm Consecrated Rose Quartz
◀···································· Third Eye Chakra

3 ··▶ 25 x 18 mm Consecrated Rose Quartz
◀····································· Throat Chakra

Intercostal Points (8)
8 ··▶
8 7 6 5 | 4 3 2 1
10 mm Consecrated Malachite (8) (placed at Intercostal Points right to left, bottom to top)

1 ··▶ ◀·································· Heart Chakra

40 x 30 mm Consecrated Rose Quartz

10 ·······▶ 7 x 5 mm Consecrated Emerald (on top)

4 ··▶ 25 x 18 mm Consecrated Rose Quartz
◀··································· Solar Plexus Chakra

5 ··▶ 25 x 18 mm Consecrated Rose Quartz
◀··································· Navel Chakra

11 ··▶ 6 x 4 mm Consecrated Ruby (on top)

6 ··▶ 25 x 18 mm Consecrated Rose Quartz
◀··································· Base Chakra

Consecrated Rainbow Obsidian (placed at Chakra center)

9 ·······▶ ◀········· Meridian Chakra ·········▶
Groin Points

Remove in reverse order: 11, 10, 8, 7, 6, 5, 4, 3, 2, 1, 9

221

The Light Of Yahweh, Channel The Light Of One." Allow self to feel The Radiant Divine Light Energies passing through your hands to the subject. Allow self to feel the energies rising from the subject to meet your hands, as releases of discordant energy matrices and emotional energy systems are lifted from the subject's consciousness. Observe the facial expression, bodily movements and sounds made by the subject during the facilitation session. Observe the degree to which the subject has relaxed and allowed self to experience the Loving Touch Therapy™ facilitation.

13. When the Spiral Balancing passes have been completed, stand back from the subject. Beginning at the Crown Chakra, fix your gaze upon the Consecrated Quartz Generator for about ten (10) to fifteen (15) seconds before slowly moving your gaze down the Chakra Cord, pausing a few seconds and refocusing your gaze upon each successive Consecrated cabochon and free-form shape placed upon the Chakras en route to and including the Meridian Chakra Groin Points and the Base Chakra. Continue the silent recitation. When the gazing has been completed, be seated near the table for up to five (5) minutes. After the time has elapsed, return to the subject and place a Consecrated Sheen Obsidian egg in each of the subject's hands.

14. With the exception of the free-form Consecrated Rainbow Obsidian, begin removing the Consecrated Generator and other Consecrated cabochons from the subject's body in the reverse order from which the Consecrated Crystal and cabochons were placed on the subject's body: first remove the Consecrated Ruby from the Base Chakra and the Consecrated Emerald from the Heart Chakra, then remove the Consecrated Malachite from the Heart Chakra area from bottom to top, fol-

lowed by the Consecrated Quartz Generator and the Consecrated Rose Quartz cabochons at the Base Chakra, Navel Chakra, Solar Plexus Chakra, Throat Chakra, Third Eye Chakra and Heart Chakra and remove the free-form Consecrated Rainbow Obsidian from the Meridian Chakra Groin Points last.

15. Now, while speaking in a soft voice, gently encourage the subject to open his/her eyes. Gently stroke the subject's arm and shoulder to help stimulate awareness of Third Dimension reality. Speak softly in reassuring tones to assist the subject in assimilating the experience of Loving Touch Therapy™. When the subject has regained a grounded sense of Third Dimension awareness, begin discussing the experience of Loving Touch Therapy™ facilitation.

As was discussed earlier in this chapter, strict attention must be paid to following the precise Crystal/Mineral placements and Lay-out orders given. To facilitate the most evolved states of conscious well-being, the practitioner of Loving Touch Therapy™ must be committed to following the steps of each Foundation Lay-out sequence without deviation, for to change the order of Crystal/Mineral placement, or to ignore The Invocation of Divine Guidance or the silent recitation, or to perform Foundation Lay-outs out of sequence will adversely impact upon the subject, diminishing the overall transformative properties of Loving Touch Therapy™. Without exception, those soul incarnates who participate in sessions of Loving Touch Therapy™ as dutiful servants to the needs of Creation will do so with open Heart Chakras and become the facilitators for the children of God yet to be born.

After receiving each of the twelve (12) Foundation Lay-outs, Foundation Lay-outs #11 and #12 may be performed several times on the same subject, or depending upon the subject's individual need, previous Foundation Lay-outs (Lay-outs 1-10) may now be used to effect changes in areas of consciousness requiring specific attention. Study the properties of the Crystals and Minerals in the Foundation Lay-outs to best determine how to most effectively assist the subject in his/her journey toward The Realization of Self.

APPLIED LOVING TOUCH THERAPY™

CHAPTER 10

The Consecrated Foundation Lay-outs of Loving Touch Therapy™ presented in Chapter 9 were developed to stimulate states of Conscious Evolution through the release and Transformation of dysfunctional energy systems within mortal consciousness. Care is advised in the use and application of Crystals and Minerals in practices of Healing Facilitation, as imperceptible damage to the auric and electrical systems of mortal being can result from indiscriminate use of Crystals and Minerals. The damage sustained from the improper or indiscriminate use of Crystals and Minerals may seemingly go unnoticed, but will inevitably have adverse effects upon the process of Conscious Evolution. Additionally, the use of Crystals and Minerals in Loving Touch Therapy™ and other practices of Healing Facilitation that have not been specifically and properly prepared as facilitation tools will diminish the integrity of the practice of Healing Facilitation and in fact may contribute to serious physical, mental, emotional and spiritual dysfunctions.

APPLIED LOVING TOUCH THERAPY™

The Consecrated Crystal/Mineral Lay-outs that follow were developed to refine and heighten states of Conscious Evolution by escorting mortal consciousness through the dark corridors of personal dysfunctions to The Radiant Realization of God-Conscious

Being. Using specialized Crystals and Minerals to facilitate states of Liberation from the illusions of personal self, the Consecrated Lay-outs that follow can assist mortal consciousness in identifying and transforming core motivations for dysfunctional thought and behavior patterns, thereby freeing self to experience The Transcendental Wonder of Evolved Self.

Under no circumstances are the Consecrated Lay-outs that follow to be used on ANY SUBJECT, regardless of how "advanced or knowledgeable" the subject might think self to be, before first completing the twelve (12) week, twelve (12) Consecrated Foundation Lay-out sequence. There can be no exceptions to this basic premise, as without the proper preparation derived from the Consecrated Foundation Lay-outs, the subject will be unable to fully assimilate The Evolved Consciousness States facilitated by the Applied Consecrated Lay-outs. Even subjects who have worked with Crystals and Minerals for ten (10), twenty (20) or thirty (30) years or more must begin at Consecrated Foundation Lay-out #1 to fully appreciate the process of Loving Touch Therapy™.

Of equal importance is the fact that the practitioner of Loving Touch Therapy™ must be fully competent in reading Chakra Orientations, performing Spiral Balancing and knowing the Crystal/Mineral patterns and placements within each Lay-out sequence. The best advise here is to memorize necessary information and practice the techniques as often as possible to gain needed confidence and proficiency. It is also important that the facilitator of Loving Touch Therapy™ fully understand the properties of the Crystals and Minerals used in the Consecrated Foundation Lay-outs before using the Consecrated Lay-outs outlined in this chapter.

PHASE I:
Applied Consecrated Lay-out #1
(See Diagram 13)

The six (6) Applied Consecrated Lay-outs that follow are progressions built upon Consecrated Foundation Lay-out #12. To perform Applied Consecrated Lay-out #1, begin by following steps 1-12 for Consecrated Foundation Lay-out #12.

13. When the Spiral Balancing passes have been completed, stand back from the table, and beginning at the Crown Chakra, focus your gaze upon the Consecrated Quartz Crystal Generator for about ten (10) to fifteen (15) seconds before slowly moving your gaze down the Chakra Cord, pausing a few seconds and refocusing upon each successive Consecrated cabochon and free-form shape placed upon the Primary Chakras en route to and including the Meridian Chakra Groin Points and the Base Chakra.

14. Now, return to the subject. With 10mm round cabochons of Consecrated Malachite held between the index fingers and thumbs, place the Consecrated cabochons of Malachite behind both ears of the subject at the juncture of the upper jaw, neck and skull (Consecrated Malachite should be held with the flat side of the cabochon against the thumb or index finger and the convex side of the cabochon against the subject's skin). Hold the Consecrated Malachite in place for twenty (20) to thirty (30) seconds. Remember to continue the silent recitation, "Channel The Light Of Yahweh, Channel The Light Of One."

15. Remove the Consecrated Malachite from behind the subject's ears and place the Consecrated Malachite on either side (but not touching) the Consecrated Rose Quartz cabochon at the

DIAGRAM 13

Applied Consecrated Lay-out #1

ORDER OF PLACEMENT

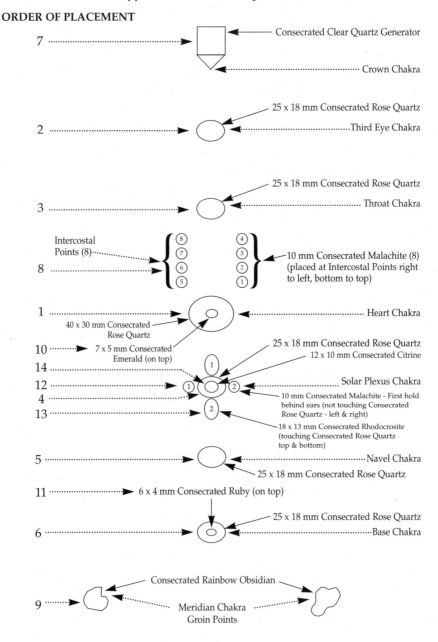

Remove in reverse order: 14-10, 8-1, 9

Solar Plexus Chakra. Next, place one (1) 18x13mm cabochon of Rhodocrosite above and touching the Consecrated Rose Quartz cabochon at the Solar Plexus Chakra and one (1) 18x13mm Consecrated Rhodocrosite cabochon below and touching the Consecrated Rose Quartz cabochon at the Solar Plexus Chakra. And place one (1) 12x10mm Consecrated Citrine cabochon on top and in the center of the Consecrated Rose Quartz at the Solar Plexus Chakra.

16. Spiral Balance over the Solar Plexus Chakra, then Spiral Balance from the Crown Chakra to the Base Chakra. When the Spiral Balancing passes have been completed, stand back from the subject and focus your gaze upon the Consecrated cabochons at the Solar Plexus Chakra. After fifteen (15) to twenty (20) seconds, begin at the Crown Chakra and focus your gaze upon the Consecrated Quartz Generator for between ten (10) and fifteen (15) seconds before slowly moving your gaze down the Chakra Cord, pausing a few seconds and fixing your gaze upon the Consecrated cabochons placed upon each Chakra en route to and including the Meridian Chakra Groin Points and the Base Chakra. Continue the silent recitation. When the gazing has been completed, be seated near the facilitation table for up to five (5) minutes. When the time has elapsed, return to the subject and place a Consecrated Sheen Obsidian egg in each of the subject's hands.

17. With the exception of the free-form Consecrated Rainbow Obsidian at the Meridian Chakra Groin Points, begin removing the Consecrated Generator and Consecrated cabochons from the subject's body in the reverse order from which the Consecrated Generator and cabochons were placed on the subject's body: first remove the Consecrated Citrine, Rhodocrosite and Malachite cabochons from the Solar Plexus Chakra,

followed by the Consecrated Ruby at the Base Chakra, Consecrated Emerald and Consecrated Malachite at the Heart Chakra area (remove Malachite from bottom to top), followed by the Consecrated Generator at the Crown Chakra and the Consecrated Rose Quartz cabochons at the Base Chakra, Navel Chakra, Solar Plexus Chakra, Throat Chakra, Third Eye Chakra and Heart Chakra, and remove the free-form Consecrated Rainbow Obsidian from the Meridian Chakra Groin Points last.

18. Now, while speaking in a soft voice, gently encourage the subject to open his/her eyes. Gently stroke the subject's arm and shoulder to help stimulate awareness of Third Dimension reality. Speak softly in reassuring tones to assist the subject in assimilating the experience of Loving Touch Therapy™. When the subject has regained a sense of Third Dimension reality, begin discussing the experience of the Loving Touch Therapy™ facilitation.

APPLIED CONSECRATED LAY-OUT #2
(See Diagram 14)

To perform Applied Consecrated Lay-out #2, follow steps 1-12 for Consecrated Foundation Lay-out #12, then steps 13, 14 and 15 for Applied Consecrated Lay-out #1.

16. Now, Spiral Balance over the Solar Plexus Chakra, then Spiral Balance from the Crown Chakra to the Base Chakra. After completing the Spiral Balancing passes, stand back from the facilitation table and begin focusing your gaze upon the Consecrated cabochons at the Solar Plexus Chakra for fifteen (15) to twenty (20) seconds. When the time has elapsed, beginning at the Crown Chakra, focus your gaze upon the Conse-

DIAGRAM 14

Applied Consecrated Lay-out #2

ORDER OF PLACEMENT

7 ....► Consecrated Clear Quartz Generator

Crown Chakra

2 ....► 25 x 18 mm Consecrated Rose Quartz

Third Eye Chakra

3 ....► 25 x 18 mm Consecrated Rose Quartz

Throat Chakra

Intercostal Points (8) ....► ⑧ ⑦ ⑥ ⑤   ④ ③ ② ①   10 mm Consecrated Malachite (8) (placed at Intercostal Points right to left, bottom to top)

8 ....►

1 ....► Heart Chakra

40 x 30 mm Consecrated Rose Quartz

10 ....► 7 x 5 mm Consecrated Emerald (on top)   18 x 13 mm Consecrated Rhodocrosite (top & bottom)

14 ....   25 x 18 mm Consecrated Rose Quartz

12 ....► ① ① ②   Solar Plexus Chakra

4 ....   10 mm Consecrated Malachite (left & right - not touching)

13 ....► ②

5 ....   12 x 10 mm Consecrated Citrine (on top)

① 18 x 13 mm Consecrated Tiger's Eye (4)

16 ....► ③ ④   Navel Chakra

15 ....► 12 x 10 mm Consecrated Citrine (on top)   ②   25 x 18 mm Consecrated Rose Quartz

6 ....► 25 x 18 mm Consecrated Rose Quartz

Base Chakra

11 ....► 6 x 4 mm Consecrated Ruby (on top)

Consecrated Rainbow Obsidian

9 ....►

Meridian Chakra Groin Points

Remove in reverse order: 16-10, 8-1, 9

233

crated Quartz Generator for about fifteen (15) seconds before slowly moving your gaze down the Chakra Cord, pausing a few seconds and focusing your gaze upon the Consecrated cabochons placed upon each successive Chakra en route to and including the Meridian Chakra Groin Points and the Base Chakra.

17. When the gazing has been completed, return to the subject and place one (1) 12x10mm Consecrated cabochon on top and in the center of the Consecrated Rose Quartz cabochon at the Navel Chakra, followed by the placement of four (4) 18x13mm cabochons of Consecrated Tiger's Eye at the four (4) compass points around and touching the Consecrated Rose Quartz at the Navel Chakra (top, bottom, left, right). Spiral Balance over the Navel Chakra, then Spiral Balance from the Crown Chakra to the Base Chakra.

18. When the Spiral Balancing passes have been completed, stand back from the subject and focus your gaze upon the Consecrated cabochons at the Navel Chakra for twenty (20) seconds. When the time has elapsed, beginning at the Crown Chakra, focus your gaze upon the Consecrated Quartz Generator for about fifteen (15) seconds before slowly moving your gaze down the Chakra Cord, pausing a few seconds and fixing your gaze upon the Consecrated cabochons placed upon each successive Chakra en route to and including the Meridian Chakra Groin Points and the Base Chakra. When the gazing has been completed, be seated near the facilitation table for up to five (5) minutes. After the time has elapsed, return to the subject and place a Consecrated Sheen Obsidian egg in each of the subject's hands.

19. With the exception of the free-form Consecrated Rainbow

Obsidian at the Meridian Chakra Groin Points, begin to remove the Consecrated Generator and Consecrated cabochons from the subject's body in the reverse order from which the Consecrated Generator and cabochons were placed on the subject's body: remove the Consecrated cabochons of Tiger's Eye and Citrine at the Navel Chakra first, then remove the Consecrated Citrine, Rhodocrosite and Malachite at the Solar Plexus Chakra, followed by the Consecrated Ruby at the Base Chakra, Consecrated Emerald and Malachite at the Heart Chakra area, the Consecrated Quartz Generator at the Crown Chakra, the Consecrated Rose Quartz cabochons at the Base Chakra, Navel Chakra, Solar Plexus Chakra, Throat Chakra, Third Eye Chakra and Heart Chakra, and remove the free-form Rainbow Obsidian last.

20. Now, speak in a soft voice and gently encourage the subject to open his/her eyes. Gently stroke the subject's arm and shoulder to help stimulate the subject's awareness of Third Dimension reality. Speak softly in reassuring tones to assist the subject in assimilating the experience of Loving Touch Therapy™. When the subject has regained a grounded sense of Third Dimension reality, begin discussing the experience of the Loving Touch Therapy™ session.

APPLIED CONSECRATED LAY-OUT #3
(See Diagram 15)

To perform Applied Consecrated Lay-out #3, follow steps 1-17 for Applied Consecrated Lay-out #2.

18. When the Spiral Balancing passes have been completed, stand back from the table and focus your gaze upon the Consecrated cabochons at the Navel Chakra for twenty (20) seconds. At the

DIAGRAM 15

Applied Consecrated Lay-out #3

ORDER OF PLACEMENT

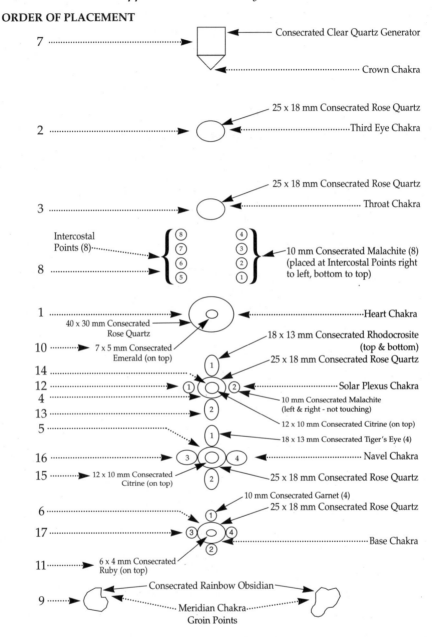

7 .... ▶ Consecrated Clear Quartz Generator

Crown Chakra

25 x 18 mm Consecrated Rose Quartz

2 .... ▶ Third Eye Chakra

25 x 18 mm Consecrated Rose Quartz

3 .... ▶ Throat Chakra

Intercostal Points (8) ....

8 .... ▶

10 mm Consecrated Malachite (8) (placed at Intercostal Points right to left, bottom to top)

1 .... ▶ Heart Chakra

40 x 30 mm Consecrated Rose Quartz

18 x 13 mm Consecrated Rhodocrosite (top & bottom)

10 ········· ▶ 7 x 5 mm Consecrated Emerald (on top)

25 x 18 mm Consecrated Rose Quartz

14 ....

12 .... ▶ Solar Plexus Chakra

4 ....

10 mm Consecrated Malachite (left & right - not touching)

13 .... ▶

12 x 10 mm Consecrated Citrine (on top)

5 ....

18 x 13 mm Consecrated Tiger's Eye (4)

16 ········· ▶ Navel Chakra

15 ········· ▶ 12 x 10 mm Consecrated Citrine (on top)

25 x 18 mm Consecrated Rose Quartz

10 mm Consecrated Garnet (4)

25 x 18 mm Consecrated Rose Quartz

6 ....

17 .... ▶ Base Chakra

11 ········· ▶ 6 x 4 mm Consecrated Ruby (on top)

Consecrated Rainbow Obsidian

9 ········· ▶ Meridian Chakra Groin Points

Remove in reverse order: 17-10, 8-1, 9

236

end of the twenty (20) seconds, focus your gaze upon the Consecrated Quartz Generator at the Crown Chakra for about fifteen (15) seconds. Now, slowly move your gaze down the Chakra Cord, pausing a few seconds and fixing your gaze upon the Consecrated cabochons placed upon each Chakra en route to and including the Meridian Chakra Groin Points and the Base Chakra.

19. When the gazing has been completed, return to the subject and place four (4) 10mm round cabochons of Consecrated Garnet at the four (4) compass points around and touching (top, bottom, left, right) the Consecrated Rose Quartz cabochon at the Base Chakra. Spiral Balance over the Base Chakra, then Spiral Balance from the Crown Chakra to the Base Chakra. When the Spiral Balancing passes have been completed, step back from the facilitation table and focus your gaze upon the Consecrated cabochons at the Base Chakra for twenty (20) seconds. When the time has elapsed, refocus your gaze upon the Consecrated Quartz Generator at the Crown Chakra. Hold your gaze for about fifteen (15) seconds before slowly moving your gaze down the Chakra Cord, pausing a few seconds and fixing your gaze upon the Consecrated cabochons placed upon each Chakra en route to and including the Meridian Chakra Groin Points and the Base Chakra. When the gazing has been completed, be seated nearby for up to five (5) minutes. At the end of five (5) minutes, return to the subject and place a Consecrated Sheen Obsidian egg in each of the subject's hands.

20. Remembering to leave the free-form Consecrated Rainbow Obsidian at the Meridian Chakra Groin Points until last, begin removing the Consecrated Generator and Consecrated cabochons from the subject's body in the reverse order from which the Consecrated Generator and cabochons were placed on the

subject's body: remove the Consecrated Garnet at the Base Chakra first, then remove the Consecrated Citrine and Tiger's Eye at the Navel Chakra, followed by the Consecrated Citrine, Rhodocrosite and Malachite at the Solar Plexus Chakra, then the Consecrated Ruby at the Base Chakra, the Consecrated Emerald and Malachite at the Heart Chakra, the Consecrated Generator at the Crown Chakra, the Consecrated Rose Quartz cabochons at the Base Chakra, Navel Chakra, Solar Plexus Chakra, Throat Chakra, Third Eye Chakra and the Heart Chakra, and finally remove the free-form Consecrated Rainbow Obsidian at the Meridian Chakra Groin Points last.

21. Now, as you speak in a soft voice, gently encourage the subject to open his/her eyes. Gently stroke the subject's arm and shoulder to help stimulate the subject's sense of Third Dimensional reality. Speak softly in reassuring tones to assist the subject in assimilating the experience of Loving Touch Therapy™. When the subject has regained a grounded sense of Third Dimension reality, begin discussing the experience of the Loving Touch Therapy™ session.

APPLIED CONSECRATED LAY-OUT #4

(See Diagram 16)

To perform Applied Consecrated Lay-out #4, follow steps 1-18 for Applied Consecrated Lay-out #3.

19. When the gazing has been completed, return to the subject and place four (4) 10mm round cabochons of Consecrated Garnet at the four (4) compass points around and touching (top, bottom, left, right) the Consecrated Rose Quartz cabochon at the Base Chakra. Spiral Balance over the Base Chakra, then Spiral Balance from the Crown Chakra to the Base Chakra. When the

DIAGRAM 16

Applied Consecrated Lay-out #4

ORDER OF PLACEMENT

7 ....► Consecrated Clear Quartz Generator

◄.. Crown Chakra

19 ·············► 12 x 10 mm Consecrated Peach Moonstone

25 x 18 mm Consecrated Rose Quartz

2 ....► ◄..Third Eye Chakra

18 ·············► 18 x 13 mm Consecrated Lapis Lazuli (on top)

25 x 18 mm Consecrated Rose Quartz

3 ....► ◄.. Throat Chakra

Intercostal Points (8)···········
8 ....►

⑧ ④
⑦ ③
⑥ ②
⑤ ①

◄ 10 mm Consecrated Malachite (8) (placed at Intercostal Points right to left, bottom to top)

1 ....► ◄..Heart Chakra

40 x 30 mm Consecrated Rose Quartz

18 x 13 mm Consecrated Rhodocrosite (top & bottom)

10 ·········► 7 x 5 mm Consecrated Emerald (on top)

25 x 18 mm Consecrated Rose Quartz

14 ....
12 ....► ① ② ◄.................................Solar Plexus Chakra
4 ....►
13 ....► ②

10 mm Consecrated Malachite (left & right - not touching)

12 x 10 mm Consecrated Citrine (on top)

5 ....► ①

18 x 13 mm Consecrated Tiger's Eye (4)

16 ....► ③ ④ ◄.................................. Navel Chakra

15 ·········► 12 x 10 mm Consecrated Citrine (on top)

②

25 x 18 mm Consecrated Rose Quartz

10 mm Consecrated Garnet (4)

25 x 18 mm Consecrated Rose Quartz

6 ....► ①

17 ....► ③ ④ ◄.................................. Base Chakra

②

11 ·········► 6 x 4 mm Consecrated Ruby (on top)

Consecrated Rainbow Obsidian

9 ·········► ◄.................... Meridian Chakra ············►
Groin Points

Remove in reverse order: 19-10, 8-1, 9

239

Spiral Balancing passes have been completed, step back from the subject and focus your gaze upon the Consecrated cabochons at the Base Chakra for twenty (20) seconds. At the end of twenty (20) seconds, refocus your gaze upon the Consecrated Quartz Crystal Generator at the Crown Chakra. Hold your gaze for about fifteen (15) seconds before slowly moving your gaze down the Chakra Cord, pausing a few seconds and focusing your gaze upon the Consecrated cabochons placed upon each successive Primary Chakra en route to and including the Meridian Chakra Groin Points and the Base Chakra.

20. When the gazing has been completed, return to the subject and place an 18x13mm cabochon of Consecrated Lapis Lazuli on top and in the center of the Consecrated Rose Quartz cabochon at the Third Eye Chakra and a 12x10mm cabochon of Consecrated Peach Moonstone above and touching the Consecrated Rose Quartz at the Third Eye Chakra. Spiral Balance over the Third Eye Chakra, then Spiral Balance from the Crown Chakra to the Base Chakra. When the Spiral Balancing has been completed, step back from the subject and focus your gaze upon the Consecrated cabochons at the Third Eye Chakra. Hold your gaze for twenty (20) seconds, then refocus your gaze upon the Consecrated Generator at the Crown Chakra for fifteen (15) seconds. Slowly begin moving your gaze down the Chakra Cord, pausing a few seconds to focus your gaze upon the Consecrated cabochons placed on each successive Primary Chakra en route to and including the Meridian Chakra Groin Points and the Base Chakra. When the gazing has been completed, be seated near the facilitation table for up to five (5) minutes. When the time has elapsed, return to the subject and place a Consecrated Sheen Obsidian egg in each of the subject's hands.

21. Leave the Consecrated Rainbow Obsidian in place and begin to remove the other Consecrated Crystals and Minerals from the subject's body in the reverse order from which the Consecrated Crystal and Mineral cabochons were placed on the subject's body: remove the Consecrated Peach Moonstone and Lapis Lazuli cabochons at the Third Eye Chakra first, then remove the Consecrated Garnets at the Base Chakra, the Consecrated Citrine and Tiger's Eye at the Navel Chakra, the Consecrated Citrine, Rhodocrosite and Malachite at the Solar Plexus Chakra, the Consecrated Ruby at the Base Chakra, the Consecrated Emerald at the Heart Chakra, the Consecrated Quartz Generator at the Crown Chakra, the Consecrated Rose Quartz cabochons at the Base Chakra, Navel Chakra, Solar Plexus Chakra, Throat Chakra, Third Eye Chakra and the Heart Chakra and finally remove the free-form Consecrated Rainbow Obsidian at the Meridian Chakra Groin Points.

22. Now, in a soft voice, gently encourage the subject to open his/her eyes. Gently stroke the subject's arm and shoulder to help stimulate the subject's sense of Third Dimension reality. Speak softly in reassuring tones to assist the subject in assimilating the experience of Loving Touch Therapy™. When the subject has sufficiently regained a grounded sense of Third Dimension reality, begin discussing the experience of the Loving Touch Therapy™ facilitation.

APPLIED CONSECRATED LAY-OUT #5
(See Diagram 17)

To perform Applied Consecrated Lay-out #5, follow steps 1-19 for Applied Consecrated Lay-out #4.

20. When the gazing has been completed, return to the subject and

DIAGRAM 17

Applied Consecrated Lay-out #5

ORDER OF PLACEMENT

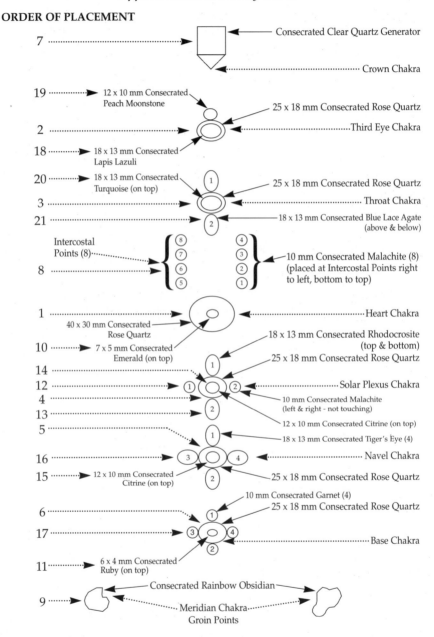

Remove in reverse order: 21-10, 8-1, 9

place an 18x13mm cabochon of Consecrated Lapis Lazuli on top and in the center of the Consecrated Rose Quartz cabochon at the Third Eye Chakra and a 12x10mm cabochon of Consecrated Peach Moonstone above and touching the Consecrated Rose Quartz at the Third Eye Chakra. Spiral Balance over the Third Eye Chakra, then Spiral Balance from the Crown Chakra to the Base Chakra. When the Spiral Balancing passes have been completed, step back from the subject and focus your gaze upon the Consecrated cabochons at the third Eye Chakra. Hold your gaze for twenty (20) seconds, then refocus your gaze upon the Consecrated Quartz Generator at the Crown Chakra for fifteen (15) seconds. After fifteen (15) seconds, slowly begin moving your gaze down the Chakra Cord, pausing a few seconds to focus your gaze upon the Consecrated cabochons placed on each successive Primary Chakra en route to and including the Meridian Chakra Groin Points and the Base Chakra. Continue the silent recitation.

21. When the gazing has been completed, return to the subject and place an 18x13mm cabochon of Consecrated Turquoise on top and in the center of the Consecrated Rose Quartz cabochon at the Throat Chakra, one (1) 18x13mm Consecrated Blue Lace Agate cabochon above and touching the Consecrated Rose Quartz at the Throat Chakra and one (1) 18x13mm Consecrated Blue Lace Agate cabochon below and touching the Consecrated Rose Quartz cabochon at the Throat Chakra. Spiral Balance over the Throat Chakra, then Spiral Balance from the Crown Chakra to the Base Chakra. When the Spiral Balancing passes have been completed, step back from the subject and fix your gaze upon the Consecrated cabochons at the Throat Chakra for twenty (20) seconds. After twenty (20) seconds, refocus your gaze upon the Consecrated Quartz Crystal Generator at the Crown Chakra for fifteen (15) seconds before slowly moving

your gaze down the Chakra Cord, pausing a few seconds to focus your gaze upon the Consecrated cabochons placed on each successive Primary Chakra en route to and including the Meridian Chakra Groin Points and the Base Chakra. When the gazing has been completed, be seated nearby for up to five (5) minutes. When the time has elapsed, return to the subject and place a Consecrated Sheen Obsidian egg in each of the subject's hands.

22. Leave the Consecrated Rainbow Obsidian in place and begin to remove the other Consecrated Crystals and cabochons from the subject's body in the reverse order from which the Consecrated Crystals and cabochons were placed on the subject's body: remove the Consecrated Blue Lace Agate and Turquoise at the Throat Chakra first, then remove the Consecrated Peach Moonstone and Lapis Lazuli cabochons at the Third Eye Chakra next, followed by the Consecrated Garnets at the Base Chakra, the Consecrated Citrine and Tiger's Eye cabochons at the Navel Chakra, the Consecrated Citrine, Rhodocrosite and Malachite at the Solar Plexus Chakra, the Consecrated Ruby cabochon at the Base Chakra, the Consecrated Emerald and Malachite cabochons at the Heart Chakra, the Consecrated Quartz Crystal Generator at the Crown Chakra, the Consecrated Rose Quartz cabochons at the Base Chakra, Navel Chakra, Solar Plexus Chakra, Throat Chakra, Third Eye Chakra and the Heart Chakra and remove the free-form Consecrated Rainbow Obsidian at the Meridian Chakra Groin Points last.

23. Now, speaking in a soft voice, encourage the subject to open his/her eyes. Gently stroke the subject's arm and shoulder to help stimulate the subject's sense of Third Dimension reality. Speak softly in reassuring tones to assist the subject in assimi-

lating the experience of Loving Touch Therapy™. When the subject has regained a grounded sense of Third Dimension reality, begin discussing the experience of the Loving Touch Therapy™ session.

APPLIED CONSECRATED LAY-OUT #6
(See Diagram 18)

Applied Consecrated Lay-out #6 is performed by first following steps 1-20 for Applied Consecrated Lay-out #5.

21. When the gazing has been completed, return to the subject and place an 18x13mm cabochon of Consecrated Turquoise on top and in the center of the Consecrated Rose Quartz cabochon at the Throat Chakra, one (1) 18x13mm Consecrated Blue Lace Agate cabochon above and touching the Consecrated Rose Quartz at the Throat Chakra and one (1) 18x13mm cabochon of Consecrated Blue Lace Agate below and touching the Consecrated Rose Quartz at the Throat Chakra. Spiral Balance over the Throat Chakra, then Spiral Balance from the Crown Chakra to the Base Chakra. When the Spiral Balancing passes have been completed, stand back from the subject and focus your gaze upon the Consecrated cabochons at the Throat Chakra for twenty (20) seconds. When the time has elapsed, refocus your gaze upon the Consecrated Quartz Generator at the Crown Chakra for fifteen (15) seconds before slowly moving your gaze down the Chakra Cord, pausing a few seconds to fix your gaze upon the Consecrated cabochons placed on each Chakra en route to and including the Meridian Chakra Groin Points and the Base Chakra.

22. When the gazing has been completed, return to the subject and place four (4) 18x13mm cabochons of Consecrated Aventurine

DIAGRAM 18

Applied Consecrated Lay-out #6

ORDER OF PLACEMENT

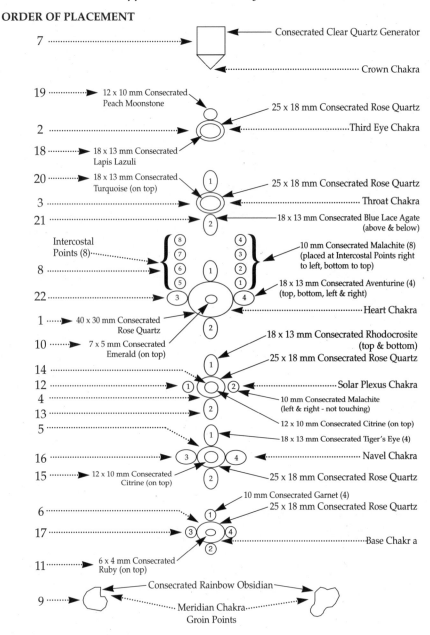

7 ···▶ ◀————— Consecrated Clear Quartz Generator

·· Crown Chakra

19 ··········▶ 12 x 10 mm Consecrated Peach Moonstone

25 x 18 mm Consecrated Rose Quartz

2 ···▶ ◀···Third Eye Chakra

18 ··········▶ 18 x 13 mm Consecrated Lapis Lazuli

20 ··········▶ 18 x 13 mm Consecrated Turquoise (on top)

25 x 18 mm Consecrated Rose Quartz

3 ···▶ ◀··· Throat Chakra

21 ···▶ ————— 18 x 13 mm Consecrated Blue Lace Agate (above & below)

Intercostal Points (8)·········

8 ···▶ 10 mm Consecrated Malachite (8) (placed at Intercostal Points right to left, bottom to top)

22 ···▶ 18 x 13 mm Consecrated Aventurine (4) (top, bottom, left & right)

·· Heart Chakra

1 ·····▶ 40 x 30 mm Consecrated Rose Quartz

10 ·······▶ 7 x 5 mm Consecrated Emerald (on top)

18 x 13 mm Consecrated Rhodocrosite (top & bottom)

25 x 18 mm Consecrated Rose Quartz

14 ···

12 ···▶ ◀···Solar Plexus Chakra

4 ··· 10 mm Consecrated Malachite (left & right - not touching)

13 ···▶

5 ··· 12 x 10 mm Consecrated Citrine (on top)

18 x 13 mm Consecrated Tiger's Eye (4)

16 ···▶ ◀···Navel Chakra

15 ··········▶ 12 x 10 mm Consecrated Citrine (on top)

25 x 18 mm Consecrated Rose Quartz

10 mm Consecrated Garnet (4)

25 x 18 mm Consecrated Rose Quartz

6 ···

17 ···▶ ···Base Chakr a

11 ··········▶ 6 x 4 mm Consecrated Ruby (on top)

————— Consecrated Rainbow Obsidian —————

9 ·······▶ ·········· Meridian Chakra·········· Groin Points

Remove in reverse order: 22-10, 8-1, 9

246

at the four (4) compass points around and touching the Consecrated Rose Quartz at the Heart Chakra. Spiral Balance over the Heart Chakra, then Spiral Balance from the Crown Chakra to the Base Chakra. When the Spiral Balancing passes have been completed, step back from the subject and fix your gaze upon the Consecrated cabochons at and around the Heart Chakra area for twenty (20) seconds. After the time has elapsed, refocus your gaze upon the Consecrated Quartz Crystal Generator at the Crown Chakra for fifteen (15) seconds before slowly moving your gaze down the Chakra Cord, pausing a few seconds to focus your gaze upon the Consecrated cabochons placed on each Chakra en route to and including the Meridian Chakra Groin Points and the Base Chakra. When the gazing has been completed, be seated near the facilitation table for up to five (5) minutes. At the end of five (5) minutes, return to the subject and place a Consecrated Sheen Obsidian egg in each of the subject's hands.

23. Leave the Consecrated Rainbow Obsidian in place and begin to remove the other Consecrated Crystals and cabochons in the reverse order from which the Consecrated Crystals and cabochons were placed on the subject's body: remove the Consecrated Aventurine at the Heart Chakra first, then remove the Consecrated Blue Lace Agate and Turquoise at the Throat Chakra, followed by the Consecrated Peach Moonstone and Lapis Lazuli cabochons at the Third Eye Chakra, the Consecrated Garnets at the Base Chakra, the Consecrated Citrine and Tiger's Eye cabochons at the Navel Chakra, the Consecrated Citrine, Rhodocrosite and Malachite at the Solar Plexus Chakra, the Consecrated Ruby cabochon at the Base Chakra, the Consecrated Emerald and Malachite cabochons at the Heart Chakra, the Consecrated Clear Quartz Crystal Generator at the Crown Chakra, the Consecrated Rose Quartz

cabochons at the Base Chakra, the Navel Chakra, the Solar Plexus Chakra, the Throat Chakra, the Third Eye Chakra and the Heart Chakra and remove the free-form Rainbow Obsidian at the Meridian Chakra Groin Points last.

4.   Now, speaking in a soft voice, encourage the subject to open his/her eyes. Gently stroke the subject's arm and shoulder to help stimulate the subject's sense of Third Dimension reality. Speak softly in reassuring tones to assist the subject in assimilating the experience of Loving Touch Therapy™. When the subject demonstrates a grounded sense of Third Dimension reality, begin discussing the experience of the Loving Touch Therapy™ session.

PHASE II:
APPLIED CONSECRATED LAY-OUT #7
(See Diagram 19)

The eight (8) Applied Consecrated Lay-outs that follow are each developed from Consecrated Foundation Lay-out #12. To perform Applied Consecrated Lay-out #7, begin by following steps 1-12 for Consecrated Foundation Lay-out #12.

13.   When the Spiral Balancing passes have been completed, stand back from the subject, and beginning at the Crown Chakra, focus your gaze upon the Consecrated Quartz Generator for ten (10) to fifteen (15) seconds before slowly moving your gaze down the Chakra Cord, pausing a few seconds and refocusing your gaze upon the Consecrated cabochons and free-form shapes placed upon each successive Primary Chakra en route to and including the Meridian Chakra Groin Points and the Base Chakra.

DIAGRAM 19

Applied Consecrated Lay-out #7

ORDER OF PLACEMENT

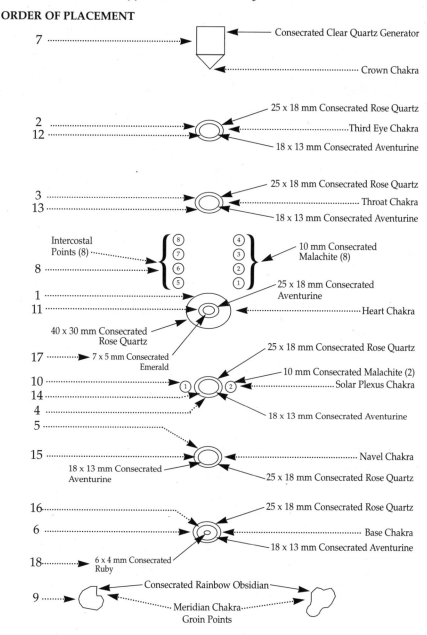

7 ···▶ ◀── Consecrated Clear Quartz Generator

··· Crown Chakra

25 x 18 mm Consecrated Rose Quartz

2 ···▶ ◀··Third Eye Chakra
12 ··▶ ◀──

── 18 x 13 mm Consecrated Aventurine

25 x 18 mm Consecrated Rose Quartz

3 ···▶ ◀·· Throat Chakra
13 ··▶ ◀──

── 18 x 13 mm Consecrated Aventurine

Intercostal Points (8) ·········· ⑧ ④ ── 10 mm Consecrated
                                  ⑦ ③   Malachite (8)
8 ···▶ ⑥ ②
                                  ⑤ ①
                                        25 x 18 mm Consecrated
1 ···▶   Aventurine
11 ··▶ ◀·· Heart Chakra

40 x 30 mm Consecrated
Rose Quartz

17 ·············▶ 7 x 5 mm Consecrated
                    Emerald   25 x 18 mm Consecrated Rose Quartz

10 ·· ① ② ── 10 mm Consecrated Malachite (2)
14 ··   ◀··Solar Plexus Chakra
4 ···
5 ··· ── 18 x 13 mm Consecrated Aventurine

15 ···▶ ◀·· Navel Chakra
18 x 13 mm Consecrated ──
Aventurine   25 x 18 mm Consecrated Rose Quartz

16···   25 x 18 mm Consecrated Rose Quartz

6 ···▶ ◀·· Base Chakra
                                        ── 18 x 13 mm Consecrated Aventurine

18·············▶ 6 x 4 mm Consecrated
                    Ruby

── Consecrated Rainbow Obsidian ──
9 ········▶
·········· Meridian Chakra··········
Groin Points

Remove in reverse order: 18-10, 8-1, 9

249

14. When the gazing has been completed, return to the subject and place 10mm round cabochons of Consecrated Malachite behind both ears of the subject at the juncture of the upper jaw, neck and skull. Hold the Consecrated Malachite in place for twenty (20) to thirty (30) seconds before removing the Consecrated Malachite cabochons and placing the cabochons to the left and right but not touching the Consecrated Rose Quartz cabochon at the Solar Plexus Chakra.

15. Next, remove the Consecrated Ruby cabochon at the Base Chakra along with the Consecrated Emerald at the Heart Chakra and set aside.

16. Now, place a 25x18mm cabochon of Consecrated Aventurine on top and in the center of the Consecrated Rose Quartz at the Heart Chakra. Spiral Balance over the Heart Chakra, then Spiral Balance from the Crown Chakra to the Base Chakra. When the Spiral Balancing has been completed, stand back from the subject and focus your gaze upon the Consecrated Aventurine and the Consecrated Rose Quartz cabochons at the Heart Chakra for fifteen (15) to twenty (20) seconds before refocusing your gaze upon the Consecrated Quartz Generator at the Crown Chakra. Hold your gaze for fifteen (15) seconds before slowly moving your gaze down the Chakra Cord, pausing a few seconds and focusing your gaze upon the Consecrated cabochons at each successive Primary Chakra en route to and including the Meridian Chakra Groin Points and the Base Chakra.

17. When the gazing has been completed, return to the subject and place 18x13mm cabochons of Consecrated Aventurine on top and in the center of each 25x18mm cabochon of Rose Quartz from the Third Eye Chakra to the Base Chakra. Next, place the

7x5mm cabochon of Consecrated Emerald on top and in the center of the 25x18mm cabochon of Consecrated Aventurine at the Heart Chakra and place the 6x4mm cabochon of Consecrated Ruby on top and in the center of the 18x13mm cabochon of Consecrated Aventurine at the Base Chakra. Now, Spiral Balance from the Crown Chakra to the Base Chakra. When the Spiral Balancing passes have been completed, stand back from the subject and beginning at the Crown Chakra, focus your gaze upon the Consecrated Quartz Crystal Generator for fifteen (15) seconds before slowly moving your gaze down the Chakra Cord, pausing a few seconds and refocusing your gaze upon the Consecrated cabochons and freeform shapes at each successive Primary Chakra en route to and including the Meridian Chakra Groin Points and the Base Chakra. When the gazing has been completed, be seated near the facilitation table for up to five (5) minutes. When the time has elapsed, return to the subject and place a Consecrated Sheen Obsidian egg in each of the subject's hands.

18. Leave the free-form Consecrated Rainbow Obsidian shapes in place and begin to remove the Consecrated Crystals and cabochons in the reverse order from which the Consecrated Crystals and cabochons were placed on the subject's body: first remove the Consecrated Ruby at the Base Chakra and the Consecrated Emerald at the Heart Chakra, then remove the Consecrated Aventurine cabochons at the Base Chakra, Navel Chakra, Solar Plexus Chakra, Throat Chakra, Third Eye Chakra and the Heart Chakra, followed by the Consecrated Malachite at the Solar Plexus Chakra, the Consecrated Malachite at the Heart Chakra, the Consecrated Quartz Crystal Generator at the Crown Chakra, the Consecrated Rose Quartz cabochons at the Base Chakra, Navel Chakra, Solar Plexus Chakra, Throat Chakra, Third Eye Chakra and the

Heart Chakra and the Consecrated Rainbow Obsidian free-form shapes are removed last.

19. Now, while speaking in a soft voice, gently encourage the subject to open his/her eyes. Gently stroke the subject's arm and shoulder to help hasten an awareness of Third Dimension reality. Speak softly in reassuring tones to assist the subject in fully assimilating the experience of Loving Touch Therapy™. When the subject has regained a grounded sense of Third Dimension reality, begin discussing the experience of the Loving Touch Therapy™ session.

APPLIED CONSECRATED LAY-OUT #8
(See Diagram 20)

To perform Applied Consecrated Lay-out #8, begin by following steps 1-15 for Applied Consecrated Lay-out #7.

16. Now, place an 18x13mm cabochon of Consecrated Amethyst on top and in the center of the Consecrated Rose Quartz cabochon at the Third Eye Chakra. Spiral Balance over the Third Eye Chakra, then Spiral Balance from the Crown Chakra to the Base Chakra. When the Spiral Balancing passes have been completed, stand back from the subject and fix your gaze upon the Consecrated Amethyst and Rose Quartz cabochons at the Third Eye Chakra for fifteen (15) to twenty (20) seconds. After the time has elapsed, refocus your gaze upon the Consecrated Quartz Generator at the Crown Chakra. Hold your gaze for fifteen seconds before slowly moving your gaze down the Chakra Cord, pausing a few seconds and focusing your gaze upon the Consecrated cabochons placed at each successive Primary Chakra en route to and including the Meridian Chakra Groin Points and the Base Chakra.

DIAGRAM 20

Applied Consecrated Lay-out #8

ORDER OF PLACEMENT

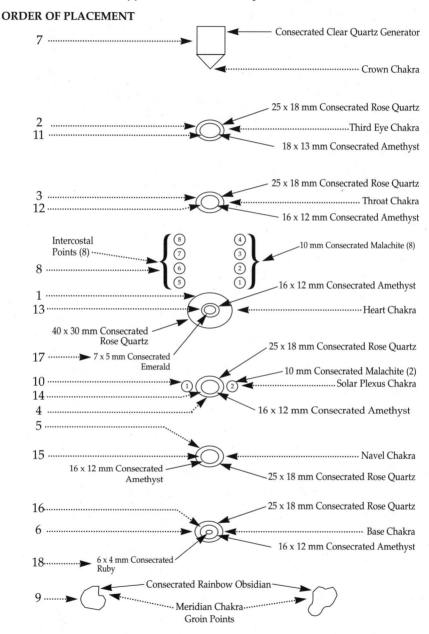

7 ....▶ Consecrated Clear Quartz Generator

Crown Chakra ....◀

25 x 18 mm Consecrated Rose Quartz

2 ....▶
11 ....▶ Third Eye Chakra ◀............................

18 x 13 mm Consecrated Amethyst

25 x 18 mm Consecrated Rose Quartz

3 ....▶
12 ....▶ Throat Chakra ◀............................

16 x 12 mm Consecrated Amethyst

Intercostal Points (8) ....▶

⑧ ④
⑦ ③
⑥ ②
⑤ ①

10 mm Consecrated Malachite (8)

8 ....▶

16 x 12 mm Consecrated Amethyst

1 ....▶
13 .... Heart Chakra ◀............................

40 x 30 mm Consecrated Rose Quartz

17 ....▶ 7 x 5 mm Consecrated Emerald

25 x 18 mm Consecrated Rose Quartz

10 mm Consecrated Malachite (2)

10 ....▶
14 ....
4 .... ① ② Solar Plexus Chakra ◀............................

16 x 12 mm Consecrated Amethyst

5 ....

15 ....▶ Navel Chakra ◀............................

16 x 12 mm Consecrated Amethyst

25 x 18 mm Consecrated Rose Quartz

16 ....▶ 25 x 18 mm Consecrated Rose Quartz

6 ....▶ Base Chakra ◀............................

16 x 12 mm Consecrated Amethyst

18 ....▶ 6 x 4 mm Consecrated Ruby

Consecrated Rainbow Obsidian

9 ....▶ Meridian Chakra ....▶
Groin Points

Remove in reverse order: 18-10, 8-1, 9

253

When the gazing has been completed, return to the subject and place 16x12mm cabochons of Consecrated Amethyst on top and in the center of each 25x18mm cabochon of Consecrated Rose Quartz at each Primary Chakra from the Throat Chakra to the Base Chakra. Next, place the 7x5mm cabochon of Consecrated Emerald on top and in the center of the 16x12mm cabochon of Consecrated Amethyst at the Heart Chakra and place the 6x4mm cabochon of Consecrated Ruby on top and in the center of the 16x12mm cabochon of Consecrated Amethyst at the Base Chakra. Now, Spiral Balance from the Crown Chakra to the Base Chakra. When the Spiral Balancing passes have been completed, stand back from the subject and beginning at the Crown Chakra, focus your gaze upon the Consecrated Quartz Crystal Generator for fifteen (15) seconds before slowly moving your gaze down the Chakra Cord, pausing a few seconds and refocusing your gaze upon the Consecrated cabochons and free-form shapes placed at each Chakra en route to and including the Meridian Chakra Groin Points and the Base Chakra. When the gazing has been completed, be seated nearby for up to five (5) minutes. When the time has elapsed, return to the subject and place Consecrated Sheen Obsidian eggs in each of the subject's hands.

18. Leaving the free-form Consecrated Rainbow Obsidian shapes in place, begin to remove the Consecrated Crystal Generator and Consecrated cabochons in the reverse order from which the Consecrated Crystals and cabochons were placed on the subject's body: first remove the Consecrated Ruby at the Base Chakra and the Consecrated Emerald at the Heart Chakra, then remove the Consecrated Amethyst cabochons at the Base Chakra, Navel Chakra, Solar Plexus Chakra, Heart Chakra, Throat Chakra and the Third Eye Chakra, followed by the Consecrated Malachite at the Solar Plexus Chakra, the

Consecrated Malachite at the Heart Chakra, the Consecrated Quartz Crystal Generator at the Crown Chakra, the Consecrated Rose Quartz cabochons at the Base Chakra, Navel Chakra, Solar Plexus Chakra, Throat Chakra, Third Eye Chakra and the Heart Chakra and the Consecrated Rainbow Obsidian free-form shapes are removed from the Meridian Chakra Groin Points last.

19. Now, in a soft voice, gently encourage the subject to open his/her eyes. Gently stroke the subject's arm and shoulder to help stimulate recognition of Third Dimension reality. Speak softly in reassuring tones to assist the subject in assimilating the experience of Loving Touch Therapy™. When the subject demonstrates a grounded sense of Third Dimension reality, begin discussing the experience of the Loving Touch Therapy™ session.

APPLIED CONSECRATED LAY-OUT #9
(See Diagram 21)

Applied Consecrated Lay-out #9 is performed by first following steps 1-15 for Applied Consecrated Lay-out #7.

16. Now, place a 12x10mm cabochon of Consecrated Citrine on top and in the center of the Consecrated Rose Quartz cabochon at the Solar Plexus Chakra. Spiral Balance over the Solar Plexus Chakra, then Spiral Balance from the Crown Chakra to the Base Chakra. Next, place a 12x10mm cabochon of Consecrated Citrine on top and in the center of the Consecrated Rose Quartz at the Navel Chakra. Spiral Balance over the Navel Chakra, then Spiral Balance from the Crown Chakra to the Base Chakra. When Spiral Balancing passes have been completed, stand back from the facilitation table and focus

DIAGRAM 21

Applied Consecrated Lay-out #9

ORDER OF PLACEMENT

7 .... Consecrated Clear Quartz Generator

Crown Chakra

25 x 18 mm Consecrated Rose Quartz

2
13 .... Third Eye Chakra

12 x 10 mm Consecrated Citrine

25 x 18 mm Consecrated Rose Quartz

3
14 .... Throat Chakra

12 x 10 mm Consecrated Citrine

Intercostal Points (8) .... { ⑧ ⑦ ⑥ ⑤   ④ ③ ② ① } 10 mm Consecrated Malachite (8)

8 ....

12 x 10 mm Consecrated Citrine

1
15 .... Heart Chakra

40 x 30 mm Consecrated Rose Quartz

17 .... 7 x 5 mm Consecrated Emerald

25 x 18 mm Consecrated Rose Quartz

10 mm Consecrated Malachite (2)

10 ....① ② Solar Plexus Chakra
11

4 .... 12 x 10 mm Consecrated Citrine
5

12 .... Navel Chakra

12 x 10 mm Consecrated Citrine

25 x 18 mm Consecrated Rose Quartz

16 .... 25 x 18 mm Consecrated Rose Quartz

6 .... Base Chakra

18 .... 6 x 4 mm Consecrated Ruby

12 x 10 mm Consecrated Citrine

Consecrated Rainbow Obsidian

9 .... Meridian Chakra
Groin Points

Remove in reverse order: 18-10, 8-1, 9

your gaze upon the Consecrated Citrine and Rose Quartz cabochons at the Solar Plexus Chakra for fifteen (15) to twenty (20) seconds. After the time has elapsed, refocus your gaze and concentrate upon the Consecrated Quartz Generator at the Crown Chakra. Hold your gaze for fifteen (15) seconds before slowly moving your gaze down the Chakra Cord, pausing a few seconds and focusing your gaze upon the Consecrated cabochons placed at each successive Primary Chakra en route to and including the Meridian Chakra Groin Points and the Base Chakra.

17. When the gazing has been completed, return to the subject and place 12x10mm cabochons of Consecrated Citrine on top and in the center of each cabochon of Consecrated Rose Quartz at each Primary Chakra from the Third Eye Chakra to the Base Chakra (of course excluding the Solar Plexus Chakra and the Navel Chakra). Next, place the 7x5mm cabochon of Consecrated Emerald on top and in the center of the Consecrated Rose Quartz cabochon at the Heart Chakra and place the 6x4mm cabochon of Consecrated Ruby on top and in the center of the Consecrated Rose Quartz cabochon at the Base Chakra. Now, Spiral Balance from the Crown Chakra to the Base Chakra. When the Spiral Balancing passes have been completed, stand back from the subject and beginning at the Crown Chakra, focus your gaze upon the Consecrated Quartz Crystal Generator for fifteen (15) seconds before slowly moving your gaze down the Chakra Cord, pausing a few seconds and refocusing your gaze upon the Consecrated cabochons and free-form shapes placed at each successive Primary Chakra en route to and including the Meridian Chakra Groin Points and the Base Chakra. When the gazing has been completed, be seated near the facilitation table for up to five (5) minutes. When the time has elapsed, return to the subject and place a Consecrated

Sheen Obsidian egg in each of the subject's hands.

18. Leaving the free-form Consecrated Rainbow Obsidian shapes in place, begin to remove the Consecrated Quartz Crystal Generator and Consecrated cabochons in the reverse order from which the Consecrated Generator and cabochons were placed on the subject's body: first remove the Consecrated Ruby at the Base Chakra and the Consecrated Emerald at the Heart Chakra, then remove the Consecrated Citrine cabochons at the Base Chakra, Heart Chakra, Throat Chakra, Third Eye Chakra, Navel Chakra and Solar Plexus Chakra, followed by the Consecrated Malachite at the Solar Plexus Chakra, the Consecrated Malachite at the Heart Chakra, the Consecrated Quartz Generator at the Crown Chakra, the Consecrated Rose Quartz cabochons at the Base Chakra, Navel Chakra, Solar Plexus Chakra, Throat Chakra, Third Eye Chakra and the Heart Chakra and the Consecrated Rainbow Obsidian free-form shapes are removed from the Meridian Chakra Groin Points last.

19. Now, speaking in a soft voice, gently encourage the subject to open his/her eyes. Gently stroke the subject's arm and shoulder to help stimulate the subject's awareness of Third Dimension reality. Speak softly in reassuring tones to assist the subject in assimilating the experience of Loving Touch Therapy™. When the subject is sufficiently grounded in the reality of Third Dimension, begin discussing the experience of the Loving Touch Therapy™ session.

APPLIED CONSECRATED LAY-OUT #10
(See Diagram 22)

To perform Applied Consecrated Lay-out #10, begin by following steps 1-15 for Applied Consecrated Lay-out #7.

16. Now, place a 25x18mm cabochon of Consecrated Tiger's Eye on top and in the center of the 25x18mm cabochon of Consecrated Rose Quartz at the Navel Chakra. Spiral Balance over the Navel Chakra, then Spiral Balance from the Crown Chakra to the Base Chakra. When the Spiral Balancing passes have been completed, stand back from the facilitation table and focus your gaze upon the Consecrated cabochons of Tiger's Eye and Rose Quartz at the Navel Chakra for fifteen (15) to twenty (20) seconds before refocusing your gaze upon the Consecrated Quartz Generator at the Crown Chakra. Hold your gaze for about fifteen (15) seconds before slowly moving your gaze down the Chakra Cord, pausing a few seconds and fixing your gaze upon the Consecrated cabochons and free-form shapes placed at each successive Primary Chakra en route to and including the Meridian Chakra Groin Points and the Base Chakra.

17. When the gazing has been completed, return to the subject and place 18x13mm cabochons of Consecrated Tiger's Eye on top and in the center of each remaining Consecrated Rose Quartz cabochon from the Third Eye Chakra to the Base Chakra. Next, place a 7x5mm cabochon of Consecrated Emerald on top and in the center of the 18x13mm cabochon of Consecrated Tiger's Eye at the Heart Chakra and place the 6x4mm cabochon of Consecrated Ruby on top and in the center of the 18x13mm cabochon of Consecrated Tiger's Eye at the Base Chakra. Now, Spiral Balance from the Crown Chakra to the

DIAGRAM 22

Applied Consecrated Lay-out #10

ORDER OF PLACEMENT

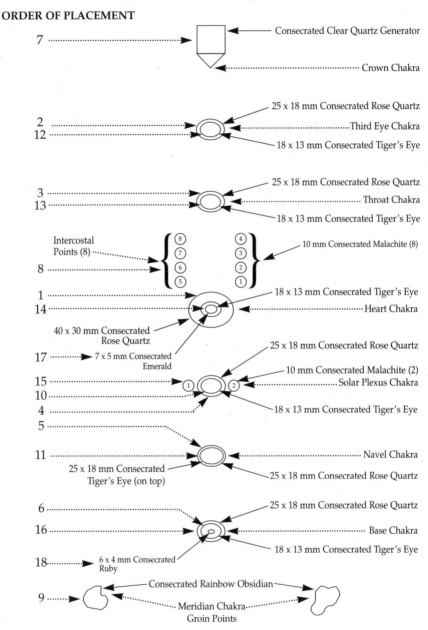

7 .... Consecrated Clear Quartz Generator

.... Crown Chakra

2 ....
12 .... 25 x 18 mm Consecrated Rose Quartz
....Third Eye Chakra
.... 18 x 13 mm Consecrated Tiger's Eye

3 ....
13 .... 25 x 18 mm Consecrated Rose Quartz
.... Throat Chakra
.... 18 x 13 mm Consecrated Tiger's Eye

Intercostal Points (8) ·············
8 .... 10 mm Consecrated Malachite (8)

1 .... 18 x 13 mm Consecrated Tiger's Eye
14 .... Heart Chakra

40 x 30 mm Consecrated Rose Quartz
17 ············▶ 7 x 5 mm Consecrated Emerald
25 x 18 mm Consecrated Rose Quartz
15 .... 10 mm Consecrated Malachite (2)
10 .... Solar Plexus Chakra
4 ....
5 .... 18 x 13 mm Consecrated Tiger's Eye

11 .... Navel Chakra
25 x 18 mm Consecrated Tiger's Eye (on top)
25 x 18 mm Consecrated Rose Quartz

6 .... 25 x 18 mm Consecrated Rose Quartz
16 .... Base Chakra
.... 18 x 13 mm Consecrated Tiger's Eye
18············▶ 6 x 4 mm Consecrated Ruby

9 ·······▶ Consecrated Rainbow Obsidian
·············· Meridian Chakra··············
Groin Points

Remove in reverse order: 18-10, 8-1, 9

260

Base Chakra. When the Spiral Balancing passes have been completed, stand back from the subject and beginning at the Crown Chakra, focus your gaze upon the Consecrated Clear Quartz Generator for fifteen (15) seconds before slowly moving your gaze down the Chakra Cord, pausing a few seconds and refocusing your gaze upon the Consecrated cabochons and free-form shapes placed at each successive Primary Chakra en route to and including the Meridian Chakra Groin Points and the Base Chakra. When the gazing has been completed, be seated nearby for up to five (5) minutes. When the time has elapsed, return to the subject and place a Consecrated Sheen Obsidian egg in each of the subject's hands.

18. Leave the free-form Consecrated Rainbow Obsidian shapes in place and begin to remove the Consecrated cabochons from the subject's body in the reverse order from which the Consecrated cabochons were placed on the subject's body: first, remove the Consecrated Ruby at the Base Chakra and the Consecrated Emerald at the Heart Chakra, then remove the Consecrated Tiger's Eye cabochons at the Base Chakra, Solar Plexus Chakra, Heart Chakra, Throat Chakra, Third Eye Chakra and Navel Chakra, followed by the Consecrated Malachite at the Solar Plexus Chakra, the Consecrated Malachite at the Heart Chakra, the Consecrated Clear Quartz Generator at the Crown Chakra, the Consecrated Rose Quartz cabochons at the Base Chakra, Navel Chakra, Solar Plexus Chakra, Throat Chakra, Third Eye Chakra and the Heart Chakra, and the Consecrated Rainbow Obsidian free-form shapes at the Meridian Chakra Groin Points last.

19. Now, while speaking in a soft voice, gently encourage the subject to open his/her eyes. Gently stroke the subject's arm and shoulder to help stimulate the subject's awareness of Third

Dimension reality. Speak softly in reassuring tones to assist the subject in assimilating the experience of Loving Touch Therapy™. When the subject is sufficiently surrounded in the reality of Third Dimension, begin discussing the experience of the Loving Touch Therapy™ session.

APPLIED CONSECRATED LAY-OUT #11
(See Diagram 23)

Applied Consecrated Lay-out #11 is performed by first following steps 1-15 for applied Consecrated Lay-out #7.

16. Now, place a 25x18mm cabochon of Consecrated Mahogany Obsidian on top and in the center of the 25x18mm cabochon of Consecrated Rose Quartz at the Base Chakra. Spiral Balance over the Base Chakra, then Spiral Balance from the Crown Chakra to the Base Chakra. When the Spiral Balancing passes have been completed, stand back from the subject and focus your gaze upon the Consecrated cabochons of Mahogany Obsidian and Rose Quartz at the Base Chakra for fifteen (15) to twenty (20) seconds before refocusing your gaze upon the Consecrated Quartz Generator at the Crown Chakra. Hold your gaze for about fifteen (15) seconds before slowly moving your gaze down the Chakra Cord, pausing a few seconds and fixing your gaze upon the Consecrated cabochons and free-form shapes placed at each successive Chakra en route to and including the Meridian Chakra Groin Points and the Base Chakra.

17. When the gazing has been completed, return to the subject and place 18x13mm cabochons of Consecrated Mahogany Obsidian on top and in the center of each remaining 25x18mm and 40x30mm cabochon of Consecrated Rose Quartz from the Third Eye Chakra to the Navel Chakra. Next, place the

DIAGRAM 23

Applied Consecrated Lay-out #11

ORDER OF PLACEMENT

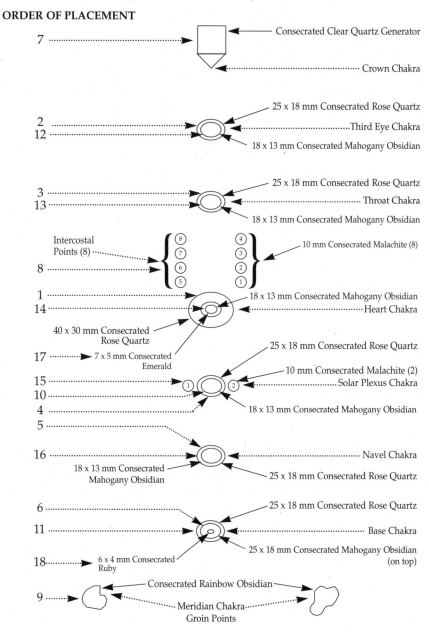

Remove in reverse order: 18-10, 8-1, 9

7x5mm cabochon of Consecrated Emerald on top and in the center of the 18x13mm cabochon of Consecrated Mahogany Obsidian at the Heart Chakra and place the 6x4mm cabochon of Consecrated Ruby on top and in the center of the 18x13mm cabochon of Consecrated Mahogany Obsidian at the Base Chakra. Now, Spiral Balance from the Crown Chakra to the Base Chakra. When the Spiral Balancing passes have been completed, stand back from the facilitation table. Beginning at the Crown Chakra, focus your gaze upon the Consecrated Clear Quartz Crystal Generator for fifteen (15) seconds before slowly moving your gaze down the Chakra Cord, pausing a few seconds and refocusing your gaze upon the Consecrated cabochons and free-form shapes placed at each successive Chakra en route to and including the Meridian Chakra Groin Points and the Base Chakra. When the gazing has been completed, be seated near the facilitation table for up to five (5) minutes. When the time has elapsed, return to the subject and place a Consecrated Sheen Obsidian egg in each of the subject's hands.

18. Leave the free-form Consecrated Rainbow Obsidian shapes in place and begin to remove the Consecrated Generator and cabochons in the reverse order from which the Consecrated Generator and cabochons were placed on the subject's body: first remove the Consecrated Ruby at the Base Chakra and the Consecrated Emerald at the Heart Chakra, then remove the Consecrated Mahogany Obsidian cabochons at the Navel Chakra, Solar Plexus Chakra, Heart Chakra, Throat Chakra, Third Eye Chakra and Base Chakra, followed by the Consecrated Malachite at the Solar Plexus Chakra, the Consecrated Malachite at the Heart Chakra, the Consecrated Quartz Crystal Generator at the Crown Chakra, the Consecrated Rose Quartz cabochons at the Base Chakra, Navel Chakra, Solar

Plexus Chakra, Throat Chakra, Third Eye Chakra and Heart Chakra, and the Consecrated Rainbow Obsidian free-form shapes at the Meridian Chakra Groin Points last.

19. Now, as you speak in a soft voice, gently encourage the subject to open his/her eyes. Gently stroke the subject's arm and shoulder to help stimulate the subject's awareness of Third Dimension reality. Speak softly in reassuring tones to assist the subject in assimilating the experience of Loving Touch Therapy™. When the subject has regained grounded perceptions of Third Dimension reality, begin discussing the experiences of the Loving Touch Therapy™ session.

APPLIED CONSECRATED LAY-OUT #12
(See Diagram 24)

Applied Consecrated Lay-out #12 is performed in the same manner as Applied Consecrated Lay-out #11, but substituting the same size cabochons of Consecrated Snowflake Obsidian for the Consecrated Mahogany Obsidian cabochons.

APPLIED CONSECRATED LAY-OUT #13
(See Diagram 25)

To perform Applied Consecrated Lay-out #13, begin by following steps 1-15 for Applied Consecrated Lay-out #7.

16. Now, place an 18x13mm cabochon of Consecrated Lapis Lazuli on top and in the center of the 25x18mm cabochon of Consecrated Rose Quartz at the Third Eye Chakra. Spiral Balance over the Third Eye Chakra, then Spiral Balance from the Crown Chakra to the Base Chakra. When the Spiral

DIAGRAM 24

Applied Consecrated Lay-out #12

ORDER OF PLACEMENT

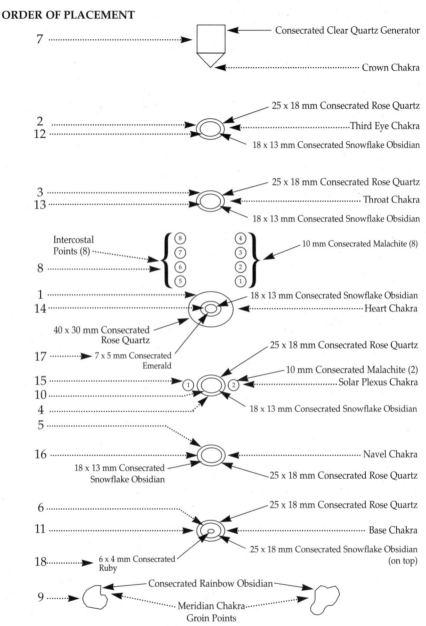

7 ···▶ Consecrated Clear Quartz Generator

Crown Chakra

25 x 18 mm Consecrated Rose Quartz

2 ···▶ Third Eye Chakra
12 ···▶

18 x 13 mm Consecrated Snowflake Obsidian

25 x 18 mm Consecrated Rose Quartz

3 ···
13 ···

Throat Chakra

18 x 13 mm Consecrated Snowflake Obsidian

Intercostal
Points (8) ·········· 8 4 10 mm Consecrated Malachite (8)
7 3
8 ····························· 6 2
5 1

1 ···▶ 18 x 13 mm Consecrated Snowflake Obsidian
14 ··· Heart Chakra

40 x 30 mm Consecrated
Rose Quartz
25 x 18 mm Consecrated Rose Quartz

17 ········▶ 7 x 5 mm Consecrated
Emerald 10 mm Consecrated Malachite (2)

15 ··· 1 2 Solar Plexus Chakra
10 ···

4 ··· 18 x 13 mm Consecrated Snowflake Obsidian
5 ···

16 ··· Navel Chakra

18 x 13 mm Consecrated
Snowflake Obsidian 25 x 18 mm Consecrated Rose Quartz

25 x 18 mm Consecrated Rose Quartz

6 ···
11 ··· Base Chakra

25 x 18 mm Consecrated Snowflake Obsidian
(on top)

18············▶ 6 x 4 mm Consecrated
Ruby

Consecrated Rainbow Obsidian
9 ·······▶

Meridian Chakra
Groin Points

Remove in reverse order: 18-10, 8-1, 9

266

DIAGRAM 25

Applied Consecrated Lay-out #13

ORDER OF PLACEMENT

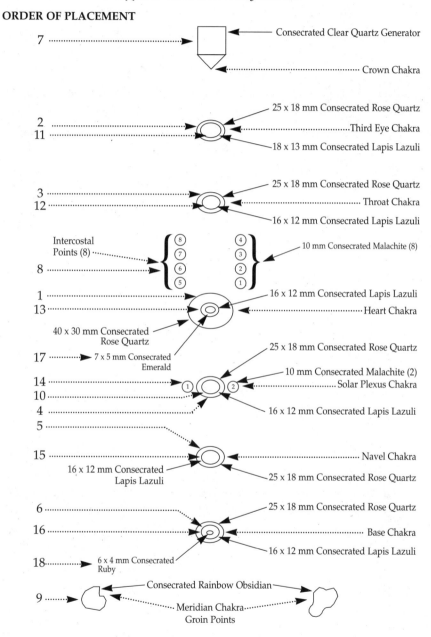

7 ··▶ ◀——— Consecrated Clear Quartz Generator

◀·· Crown Chakra

25 x 18 mm Consecrated Rose Quartz

2 ··▶
11 ·· ◀·· Third Eye Chakra

18 x 13 mm Consecrated Lapis Lazuli

25 x 18 mm Consecrated Rose Quartz

3 ··▶
12 ·· ◀·· Throat Chakra

16 x 12 mm Consecrated Lapis Lazuli

Intercostal Points (8) ··········· ⑧ ④ ——— 10 mm Consecrated Malachite (8)
⑦ ③
8 ··▶ ⑥ ②
⑤ ①

1 ··▶ ——— 16 x 12 mm Consecrated Lapis Lazuli
13 ·· ◀·· Heart Chakra

40 x 30 mm Consecrated Rose Quartz

17 ·········▶ 7 x 5 mm Consecrated Emerald

25 x 18 mm Consecrated Rose Quartz

14 ··▶ ① ② ——— 10 mm Consecrated Malachite (2)
10 ·· ◀·· Solar Plexus Chakra
4 ···

5 ··· 16 x 12 mm Consecrated Lapis Lazuli

15 ··· ◀·· Navel Chakra

16 x 12 mm Consecrated Lapis Lazuli

25 x 18 mm Consecrated Rose Quartz

25 x 18 mm Consecrated Rose Quartz

6 ···
16 ·· ◀·· Base Chakra

16 x 12 mm Consecrated Lapis Lazuli

18 ···········▶ 6 x 4 mm Consecrated Ruby

◀——— Consecrated Rainbow Obsidian ———▶
9 ········▶ ◀·············· Meridian Chakra ·············▶
Groin Points

Remove in reverse order: 18-10, 8-1, 9

267

Balancing passes have been completed, stand back from the subject and focus your gaze upon the cabochons of Consecrated Lapis Lazuli and Rose Quartz at the Third Eye Chakra for fifteen (15) to twenty (20) seconds before refocusing your gaze upon the Consecrated Quartz Generator at the Crown Chakra. Hold your gaze upon the Consecrated Generator for about fifteen (15) seconds before slowly moving your gaze down the Chakra Cord, pausing a few seconds and fixing your gaze upon the Consecrated cabochons and free-form shapes placed at each successive Chakra en route to and including the Meridian Chakra Groin Points and Base Chakra.

17. When the gazing has been completed, return to the subject and place 16x12mm cabochons of Consecrated Lapis Lazuli on top and in the center of each remaining cabochon of Consecrated Rose Quartz from the Throat Chakra to the Base Chakra. Next, place the 7x5mm cabochon of Consecrated Emerald on top and in the center of the 16x12mm cabochon of Lapis Lazuli at the Heart Chakra and place the 6x4mm cabochon of Consecrated Ruby on top and in the center of the 16x12mm cabochon of Consecrated Lapis Lazuli at the Base Chakra. Now, Spiral Balance from the Crown Chakra to the Base Chakra. When the Spiral Balancing passes have been completed, stand back from the subject and beginning at the Crown Chakra, focus your gaze upon the Consecrated Clear Quartz Crystal Generator for fifteen (15) seconds before slowly moving your gaze down the Chakra Cord, pausing a few seconds and refocusing your gaze upon the Consecrated cabochons and free-form shapes placed at each successive Chakra en route to and including the Meridian Chakra Groin Points and the Base Chakra. When the gazing has been completed, be seated near-by for up to five (5) minutes. When the time has elapsed, return to the subject and place a Consecrated Sheen Obsidian

egg in each of the subject's hands.

18. Leaving the free-form Consecrated Rainbow Obsidian shapes in place, begin to remove the Consecrated Crystals and cabochons in the reverse order from which the Consecrated Crystals and cabochons were placed on the subject's body: first remove the Consecrated Ruby at the Base Chakra and the Consecrated Emerald at the Heart Chakra, then remove the Consecrated Lapis Lazuli cabochons at the Base Chakra, Navel Chakra, Solar Plexus Chakra, Heart Chakra, Throat Chakra and Third Eye Chakra, followed by the Consecrated Malachite at the Solar Plexus Chakra, the Consecrated Malachite at the Heart Chakra, the Consecrated Clear Quartz Crystal Generator at the Crown Chakra, the Consecrated Rose Quartz cabochons at the Base Chakra, Navel Chakra, Solar Plexus Chakra, Throat Chakra, Third Eye Chakra and Heart Chakra, and the Consecrated Rainbow Obsidian free-form pieces at the Meridian Chakra Groin Points last.

19. Now, as you speak in a soft voice, gently encourage the subject to open his/her eyes. Gently stroke the subject's arm and shoulder to help stimulate the subject's awareness of Third Dimension reality. Speak softly in reassuring tones to assist the subject in assimilating the experience of Loving Touch Therapy™. When the subject has regained a grounded perception of Third Dimension reality, begin discussing the details and sensations experienced during the session of Loving Touch Therapy™.

APPLIED CONSECRATED LAY-OUT #14
(See Diagram 26)

Applied Consecrated Lay-out #14 is performed by first following steps 1-15 for Applied Consecrated Lay-out #7.

16. Now, place a 25x18mm cabochon of Consecrated Blue Lace Agate on top and in the center of the 25x18mm cabochon of Consecrated Rose Quartz at the Throat Chakra. Spiral Balance over the Throat Chakra, then Spiral Balance from the Crown Chakra to the Base Chakra. When the spiral Balancing passes have been completed, stand back from the facilitation table and focus your gaze upon the Consecrated cabochons of Blue Lace Agate and Rose Quartz for fifteen (15) to twenty (20) seconds before refocusing your gaze and fixing it upon the Consecrated Quartz Generator at the Crown Chakra. Hold your gaze upon the Consecrated Quartz Generator for about fifteen (15) seconds before slowly moving your gaze down the Chakra Cord, pausing a few seconds and focusing your gaze upon the Consecrated cabochons and free-form shapes placed at each successive Chakra en route to and including the Meridian Chakra Groin Points and Base Chakra.

17. When the gazing has been completed, return to the subject and place 18x13mm cabochons of Consecrated Blue Lace Agate on top and in the center of each remaining cabochon of Consecrated Rose Quartz from the Third Eye Chakra to the Base Chakra. Next, place the 7x5mm cabochon of Consecrated Emerald on top and in the center of the 18x13mm cabochon of Consecrated Blue Lace Agate at the Heart Chakra and place the 6x4mm cabochon of Consecrated Ruby on top and in the center of the 18x13mm cabochon of Consecrated Blue Lace Agate at the Base Chakra. Now, Spiral Balance from the Crown

DIAGRAM 26

Applied Consecrated Lay-out #14

ORDER OF PLACEMENT

7 ....► ◄———— Consecrated Clear Quartz Generator

.... Crown Chakra

25 x 18 mm Consecrated Rose Quartz

2 ....►⬭◄.. Third Eye Chakra
12 ....

18 x 13 mm Consecrated Blue Lace Agate

25 x 18 mm Consecrated Rose Quartz

3 ....►⬭◄.. Throat Chakra
11 ....

25 x 18 mm Consecrated Blue Lace Agate
(on top)

Intercostal Points (8) ....► ⑧ ④
⑦ ③   10 mm Consecrated Malachite (8)
8 ....► ⑥ ②
⑤ ①

1 ....► ⬬ ◄ 18 x 13 mm Consecrated Blue Lace Agate
13 .... Heart Chakra

40 x 30 mm Consecrated Rose Quartz

17 ....► 7 x 5 mm Consecrated Emerald

25 x 18 mm Consecrated Rose Quartz

14 ....►① ⬭ ②◄ 10 mm Consecrated Malachite (2)
10 .... Solar Plexus Chakra
4 ....

18 x 13 mm Consecrated Blue Lace Agate

5 ....

15 ....►⬭◄.. Navel Chakra
18 x 13 mm Consecrated Blue Lace Agate
25 x 18 mm Consecrated Rose Quartz

6 .... 25 x 18 mm Consecrated Rose Quartz

16 ....►⬬◄.. Base Chakra

18 x 13 mm Consecrated Blue Lace Agate

18 ....► 6 x 4 mm Consecrated Ruby

Consecrated Rainbow Obsidian
9 ....► ◄
.......................Meridian Chakra........................►
Groin Points

Remove in reverse order: 18-10, 8-1, 9

271

Chakra to the Base Chakra. When the Spiral Balancing passes have been completed, stand back from the subject. Beginning at the Crown Chakra, focus your gaze upon the Consecrated Clear Quartz Generator for fifteen (15) seconds before slowly moving your gaze down the Chakra Cord, pausing a few seconds and refocusing your gaze upon the Consecrated cabochons and free-form shapes placed at each successive Chakra en route to and including the Meridian Chakra Groin Points and the Base Chakra. When the gazing has been completed, be seated nearby for up to five (5) minutes. When the time has elapsed, return to the subject and place a Consecrated Sheen Obsidian egg in each of the subject's hands.

18. Leaving the free-form shapes of Consecrated Rainbow Obsidian in place, begin to remove the Consecrated cabochons in the reverse order from which the Consecrated cabochons were placed on the subject's body: first, remove the Consecrated Ruby at the Base Chakra and the Consecrated Emerald at the Heart Chakra, then remove the Consecrated Blue Lace Agate cabochons at the Base Chakra, Navel Chakra, Solar Plexus Chakra, Heart Chakra, Third Eye Chakra and Throat Chakra, followed by the Consecrated Malachite at the Solar Plexus Chakra and the Consecrated Malachite at the Heart Chakra, the Consecrated Clear Quartz Crystal Generator at the Crown Chakra, the Consecrated Rose Quartz cabochons at the Base Chakra, Navel Chakra, Solar Plexus Chakra, Throat Chakra, Third Eye Chakra and Heart Chakra, and the Consecrated Rainbow Obsidian free-form shapes at the Meridian Chakra Groin Points are removed last.

19. Now, while speaking in a soft voice, gently encourage the subject to open his/her eyes. Gently stroke the subject's arm and shoulder to help stimulate the subject's awareness of Third

Dimension reality. Speak softly in reassuring tones to assist the subject in assimilating the experience of Loving Touch Therapy™. When the subject has regained a grounded sense of Third Dimension reality, begin discussing the details and sensations experienced during the session of Loving Touch Therapy™.

PHASE III :
APPLIED CONSECRATED LAY-OUT #15
(See Diagram 27)

Each of the four Applied Consecrated Lay-outs that follow are developed from the first fifteen (15) steps for Applied Consecrated Lay-out #7. To perform Applied Consecrated Lay-out #15, first complete steps 1-15 for Applied Consecrated Lay-out #7.

16. Now, place a 25x18mm cabochon of Consecrated Unakite on top and in the center of the 40x30mm cabochon of Consecrated Rose Quartz at the Heart Chakra. Spiral Balance over the Heart Chakra, then Spiral Balance from the Crown Chakra to the Base Chakra. When the Spiral Balancing passes have been completed, stand back from the facilitation table and focus your gaze upon the Consecrated cabochons of Unakite and Rose Quartz at the Heart Chakra for fifteen (15) to twenty (20) seconds before refocusing your gaze and fixing it upon the Consecrated Quartz Generator at the Crown Chakra. Hold your gaze upon the Consecrated Quartz Generator for about fifteen (15) seconds before slowly moving your gaze down the Chakra Cord, pausing a few seconds and focusing your gaze upon the Consecrated cabochons and free-form shapes placed at each successive Chakra en route to and including the Meridian Chakra Groin Points and the Base Chakra.

DIAGRAM 27

Applied Consecrated Lay-out #15

ORDER OF PLACEMENT

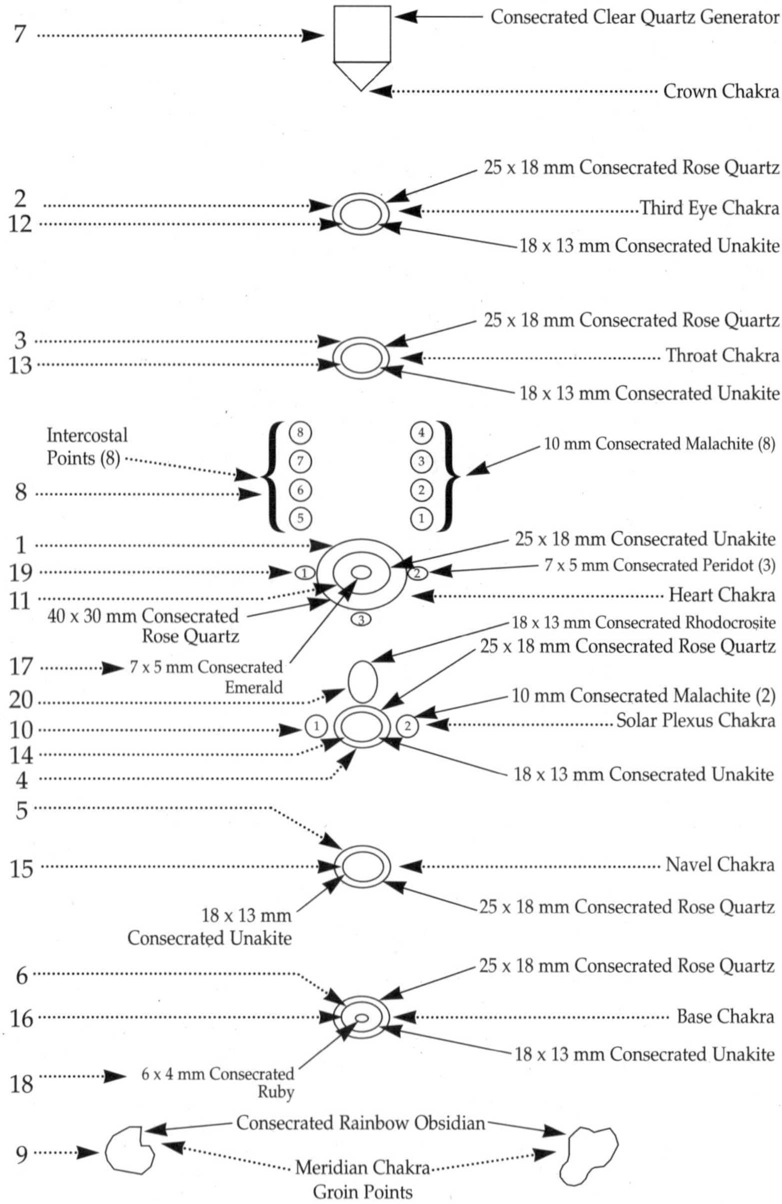

7 ⋯⋯⋯⋯⋯⋯⋯⋯⋯⋯⋯⋯⋯⋯⋯⋯► Consecrated Clear Quartz Generator

Crown Chakra

25 x 18 mm Consecrated Rose Quartz

2 ⋯⋯⋯⋯⋯⋯⋯⋯⋯⋯⋯► Third Eye Chakra
12 ⋯⋯⋯⋯⋯⋯⋯⋯⋯⋯►

18 x 13 mm Consecrated Unakite

25 x 18 mm Consecrated Rose Quartz

3 ⋯⋯⋯⋯⋯⋯⋯⋯⋯⋯⋯► Throat Chakra
13 ⋯⋯⋯⋯⋯⋯⋯⋯⋯⋯►

18 x 13 mm Consecrated Unakite

Intercostal Points (8) ⋯⋯⋯ ⑧ ④ 10 mm Consecrated Malachite (8)
⑦ ③
8 ⋯⋯⋯⋯⋯⋯⋯⋯⋯⋯► ⑥ ②
⑤ ①

1 ⋯⋯⋯⋯⋯⋯⋯⋯⋯⋯► 25 x 18 mm Consecrated Unakite
19 ⋯⋯⋯⋯⋯⋯⋯⋯⋯► ① ② 7 x 5 mm Consecrated Peridot (3)
11 ⋯⋯⋯⋯⋯⋯⋯⋯⋯► Heart Chakra
40 x 30 mm Consecrated ③
Rose Quartz 18 x 13 mm Consecrated Rhodocrosite
25 x 18 mm Consecrated Rose Quartz
17 ⋯⋯⋯► 7 x 5 mm Consecrated
Emerald 10 mm Consecrated Malachite (2)
20 ⋯⋯⋯⋯⋯⋯⋯⋯⋯⋯ Solar Plexus Chakra
10 ⋯⋯⋯⋯⋯⋯⋯⋯⋯► ① ②
14 ⋯⋯⋯⋯⋯⋯⋯⋯⋯⋯
4 ⋯⋯⋯⋯⋯⋯⋯⋯⋯⋯ 18 x 13 mm Consecrated Unakite
5 ⋯⋯⋯⋯⋯⋯⋯⋯⋯⋯

15 ⋯⋯⋯⋯⋯⋯⋯⋯⋯⋯ Navel Chakra
18 x 13 mm 25 x 18 mm Consecrated Rose Quartz
Consecrated Unakite

25 x 18 mm Consecrated Rose Quartz

6 ⋯⋯⋯⋯⋯⋯⋯⋯⋯⋯
16 ⋯⋯⋯⋯⋯⋯⋯⋯⋯⋯ Base Chakra

18 x 13 mm Consecrated Unakite

18 ⋯⋯⋯► 6 x 4 mm Consecrated
Ruby

Consecrated Rainbow Obsidian
9 ⋯⋯⋯►
Meridian Chakra
Groin Points

Remove in reverse order: 20-10, 8-1, 9

17. When the gazing has been completed, return to the subject and place 18x13mm cabochons of Consecrated Unakite on top and in the center of each Consecrated Rose Quartz cabochon from the Third Eye Chakra to the Base Chakra (excluding the Heart Chakra). Next, place the 7x5mm cabochon of Consecrated Emerald on top and in the center of the 18x13mm cabochon of Consecrated Unakite at the Heart Chakra, and place the 6x4mm cabochon of Consecrated Ruby on top and in the center of the 18x13mm cabochon of Consecrated Unakite at the Base Chakra. Now, Spiral Balance from the Crown Chakra to the Base Chakra. When the Spiral Balancing has been completed, stand back from the subject. Beginning at the Crown Chakra, focus your gaze upon the Consecrated Clear Quartz Generator for fifteen (15) seconds before slowly moving your gaze down the Chakra Cord, pausing a few seconds and refocusing your gaze upon the Consecrated cabochons and freeform shapes placed at each successive Chakra en route to and including the Meridian Chakra Groin Points and the Base Chakra.

18. When the gazing has been completed, return to the subject and place three (3) 7x5mm cabochons of Consecrated Peridot around and touching the 40x30mm cabochon of Consecrated Rose Quartz at the Heart Chakra in the following order and position: 1st cabochon placed on the left (facilitator's left) side of the 40x30mm cabochon of Consecrated Rose Quartz; 2nd cabochon placed on the right (facilitator's right) side of the 40x30mm cabochon of Consecrated Rose Quartz; 3rd cabochon placed below the 40x30mm cabochon of Consecrated Rose Quartz. Next, place an 18x13mm cabochon of Consecrated Rhodocrosite above and touching the 25x18mm cabochon of Consecrated Rose Quartz at the Solar Plexus Chakra. Now, Spiral Balance from the Crown Chakra to the Base Chakra.

When the Spiral Balancing has been completed, stand back from the subject and focus your gaze upon the Clear Quartz Generator for about fifteen (15) seconds before slowly moving your gaze down the Chakra Cord, pausing a few seconds and refocusing your gaze upon the Consecrated cabochons and free-form shapes at each Chakra en route to and including the Meridian Chakra Groin Points and the Base Chakra. When the gazing has been completed, be seated near the facilitation table for up to five (5) minutes before returning to the subject and placing Consecrated Sheen Obsidian eggs in each of the subject's hands.

19. Leaving the free-form shapes of Consecrated Rainbow Obsidian in place, begin removing the Consecrated Crystals and cabochons in the reverse order from which the Consecrated Crystals and cabochons were placed on the subject's body: first, remove the Consecrated Rhodocrosite at the Solar Plexus Chakra and the Consecrated Peridot at the Heart Chakra, then remove the Consecrated Ruby at the Base Chakra and the Consecrated Emerald at the Heart Chakra, followed by the Consecrated Unakite cabochons at the Base Chakra, Navel Chakra, Solar Plexus Chakra, Throat Chakra, Third Eye Chakra, and Heart Chakra, the Consecrated Malachite at the Solar Plexus Chakra and the Consecrated Malachite at the Heart Chakra, the Consecrated Quartz Crystal Generator at the Crown Chakra, the Consecrated Rose Quartz cabochons at the Base Chakra, Navel Chakra, Solar Plexus Chakra, Throat Chakra, Third Eye Chakra and Heart Chakra, and the Consecrated Rainbow Obsidian free-form shapes at the Meridian Chakra Groin Points are removed last.

20. Now, while speaking in a soft voice, gently encourage the subject to open his/her eyes. Gently stroke the subject's arm and

shoulder to help stimulate the subject's awareness of Third Dimension reality. Speak softly in reassuring tones to assist the subject in assimilating the experience of Loving Touch Therapy™. When the subject has regained a grounded sense of Third Dimension reality, begin discussing the details and sensations experienced during the session of Loving Touch Therapy™. Be sure that the subject is well grounded before allowing the subject to leave the facilitation area.

APPLIED CONSECRATED LAY-OUT #16
(See Diagram 28)

To perform Applied Consecrated Lay-out #16, first complete steps 1-15 for Applied Consecrated Lay-out #7.

16. Now, place a 25x18mm cabochon of Consecrated Rhodonite on top and in the center of the 40x30mm cabochon of Consecrated Rose Quartz at the Heart Chakra. Spiral Balance over the Heart Chakra, then Spiral Balance from the Crown Chakra to the Base Chakra. When the Spiral Balancing passes have been completed, stand back from the subject and focus your gaze upon the cabochons of Consecrated Rhodonite and Rose Quartz at the Heart Chakra for fifteen (15) to twenty (20) seconds before refocusing and fixing your gaze upon the Consecrated Quartz Generator at the Crown Chakra. Hold your gaze upon the Consecrated Quartz Generator for about fifteen (15) seconds before slowly moving your gaze down the Chakra Cord, pausing a few seconds and focusing your gaze upon the Consecrated cabochons and free-form shapes placed at each successive Chakra en route to and including the Meridian Chakra Groin Points and the Base Chakra.

17. When the gazing has been completed, return to the subject and

place 18x13mm cabochons of Consecrated Rhodonite on top and in the center of each 25x18mm cabochon of Consecrated Rose Quartz from the Third Eye Chakra to the Base Chakra. Next, place the 7x5mm cabochon of Consecrated Emerald on top and in the center of the 18x13mm cabochon of Consecrated Rhodonite at the Heart Chakra, and place the 6x4mm cabochon of Consecrated Ruby on top and in the center of the 18x13mm cabochon of Consecrated Rhodonite at the Base Chakra. Now, Spiral Balance from the Crown Chakra to the Base Chakra. When the Spiral Balancing passes have been completed, move away from the subject and focus your gaze upon the Consecrated Quartz Generator at the Crown Chakra. Hold your gaze upon the Consecrated Quartz Generator for about fifteen (15) seconds before slowly moving your gaze down the Chakra Cord, pausing a few seconds and focusing your gaze upon the Consecrated cabochons and free-form shapes placed at each successive Chakra en route to and including the Meridian Chakra Groin Points and the Base Chakra.

18. When the gazing has been completed, return to the subject and place three (3) 7x5mm cabochons of Consecrated Peridot around and touching the 40x30mm cabochon of Consecrated Rose Quartz at the Heart Chakra in the following order and position: 1st cabochon of Consecrated Peridot is placed on the left (facilitator's left) side of the Consecrated Rose Quartz; 2nd cabochon of Consecrated Peridot is placed on the right (facilitator's right) side of the Consecrated Rose Quartz; 3rd cabochon of Consecrated Peridot is placed below the Consecrated Rose Quartz cabochon. Next, place an 18x13mm cabochon of Consecrated Rhodocrosite above and touching the 25x18mm cabochon of Consecrated Rose Quartz at the Solar Plexus Chakra. Now, Spiral Balance from the Crown Chakra to the

DIAGRAM 28

Applied Consecrated Lay-out #16

ORDER OF PLACEMENT

7 ···► — Consecrated Clear Quartz Generator

··· Crown Chakra

2 ·······································► — 25 x 18 mm Consecrated Rose Quartz
12 ······································► ·······························Third Eye Chakra
— 18 x 13 mm Consecrated Rhodonite

3 ·····································► — 25 x 18 mm Consecrated Rose Quartz
13 ···································► ······························· Throat Chakra
— 18 x 13 mm Consecrated Rhodonite

Intercostal Points (8) ·········► { ⑧ ⑦ ⑥ ⑤   ④ ③ ② ① } ◄— 10 mm Consecrated Malachite (8)

8 ·······························►

1 ·································► — 25 x 18 mm Consecrated Rhodonite
19 ·······························► ① ② ◄— 7 x 5 mm Consecrated Peridot (3)
11 ························· ③ ·························· Heart Chakra
40 x 30 mm Consecrated Rose Quartz

— 18 x 13 mm Consecrated Rhodocrosite
— 25 x 18 mm Consecrated Rose Quartz
17 ·········► 7 x 5 mm Consecrated Emerald
20 ································► — 10 mm Consecrated Malachite (2)
10 ·····························► ① ② ◄·················· Solar Plexus Chakra
14 ······························
4 ·······························► — 18 x 13 mm Consecrated Rhodonite
5 ·······························

15 ·····························► ◄·················· Navel Chakra
18 x 13 mm Consecrated Rhodonite
— 25 x 18 mm Consecrated Rose Quartz

6 ·····························► — 25 x 18 mm Consecrated Rose Quartz
16 ···························► ◄·················· Base Chakra
— 18 x 13 mm Consecrated Rhodonite
18 ·········► 6 x 4 mm Consecrated Ruby

— Consecrated Rainbow Obsidian —
9 ·····► ◄·········· Meridian Chakra ·········►
Groin Points

Remove in reverse order: 20-10, 8-1, 9

279

Base Chakra. When the Spiral Balancing has been completed, stand back from the subject and focus your gaze upon the Consecrated Quartz Generator at the Crown Chakra. Hold your gaze for about fifteen (15) seconds before slowly moving your gaze down the Chakra Cord, pausing a few seconds and focusing your gaze upon the Consecrated cabochons and free-form shapes at each Chakra en route to and including the Meridian Chakra Groin Points and the Base Chakra. When the gazing has been completed, be seated for up to five (5) minutes before returning to the subject and placing Consecrated Sheen Obsidian eggs in each of the subject's hands.

19. Leaving the free-form shapes of Consecrated Rainbow Obsidian in place, begin removing the Consecrated Crystals and cabochons in the reverse order from which the Consecrated Crystals and cabochons were placed on the subject's body: first, remove the Consecrated Rhodocrosite at the Solar Plexus Chakra and the Consecrated Peridot at the Heart Chakra, then remove the Consecrated Ruby at the Base Chakra and the Consecrated Emerald at the Heart Chakra, followed by the Consecrated Rhodonite cabochons at the Base Chakra, Navel Chakra, Solar Plexus Chakra, Throat Chakra, Third Eye Chakra and Heart Chakra, the Consecrated Malachite at the Solar Plexus Chakra and the Consecrated Malachite at the Heart Chakra, the Consecrated Quartz Crystal Generator at the Crown Chakra, the Consecrated Rose Quartz cabochons at the Base Chakra, Navel Chakra, Solar Plexus Chakra, Throat Chakra, Third Eye Chakra and the Heart Chakra, and the Consecrated Rainbow Obsidian free-form shapes at the Meridian Chakra Groin Points are removed last.

20. Now, speak in a soft voice and encourage the subject to open his/her eyes. Gently stroke the subject's arm and shoulder to

help stimulate awareness of physical reality. Speak softly in reassuring tones to assist the subject in assimilating the experience of Loving Touch Therapy™. When the subject has regained a grounded sense of Third Dimension reality, begin discussing your observations, details and the sensations experienced during the session of Loving Touch Therapy™. Remember to be sure that the subject is well grounded before allowing the subject to leave the facilitation area.

APPLIED CONSECRATED LAY-OUT #17
(See Diagram 29)

To perform Applied Consecrated Lay-out #17, begin by completing steps 1-15 for Applied Consecrated Lay-out #7.

16. Now, place a 25x18mm cabochon of Consecrated Red Jasper on top and in the center of the 40x30mm cabochon of Consecrated Rose Quartz at the Heart Chakra. Spiral Balance over the Heart Chakra, then Spiral Balance from the Crown Chakra to the Base Chakra. When the Spiral Balancing passes have been completed, stand back from the subject and focus your gaze upon the cabochons of Consecrated Red Jasper and Rose Quartz at the Heart Chakra for fifteen (15) seconds before refocusing and fixing your gaze upon the Consecrated Generator at the Crown Chakra. Hold your gaze for about fifteen (15) seconds before slowly moving your gaze down the Chakra Cord, pausing a few seconds and focusing your gaze upon the Consecrated cabochons and free-form shapes placed at each successive Chakra en route to and including the Meridian Chakra Groin Points and the Base Chakra.

17. When the gazing has been completed, return to the subject and place 18x13mm cabochons of Consecrated Red Jasper on top

DIAGRAM 29
Applied Consecrated Lay-out #17

ORDER OF PLACEMENT

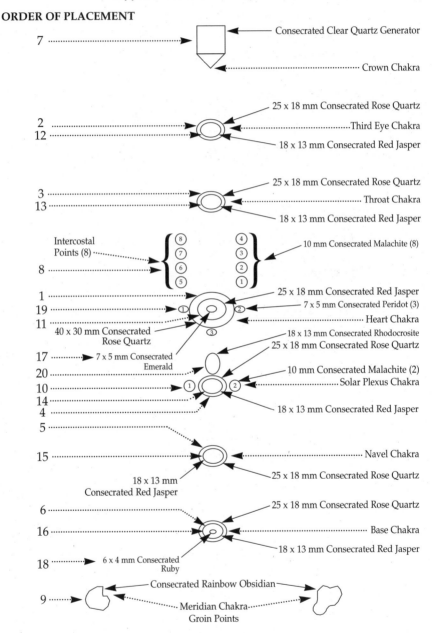

7 ....➤ Consecrated Clear Quartz Generator

.... Crown Chakra

25 x 18 mm Consecrated Rose Quartz

2 ....➤ Third Eye Chakra
12 ....➤

18 x 13 mm Consecrated Red Jasper

25 x 18 mm Consecrated Rose Quartz

3 ....➤ Throat Chakra
13 ....➤

18 x 13 mm Consecrated Red Jasper

Intercostal Points (8) .... ⑧ ④ 10 mm Consecrated Malachite (8)
⑦ ③
8 ....➤ ⑥ ②
⑤ ①

1 ....➤ 25 x 18 mm Consecrated Red Jasper
19 ....➤ ① ② 7 x 5 mm Consecrated Peridot (3)
11 .... Heart Chakra
40 x 30 mm Consecrated ③ 18 x 13 mm Consecrated Rhodocrosite
Rose Quartz 25 x 18 mm Consecrated Rose Quartz

17 ....➤ 7 x 5 mm Consecrated
Emerald 10 mm Consecrated Malachite (2)
20 .... ① ② Solar Plexus Chakra
10 ....➤
14 ....
4 .... 18 x 13 mm Consecrated Red Jasper
5 ....

15 .... Navel Chakra

18 x 13 mm 25 x 18 mm Consecrated Rose Quartz
Consecrated Red Jasper

6 .... 25 x 18 mm Consecrated Rose Quartz

16 .... Base Chakra

18 x 13 mm Consecrated Red Jasper

18 ....➤ 6 x 4 mm Consecrated
Ruby

Consecrated Rainbow Obsidian
9 ....➤
Meridian Chakra
Groin Points

Remove in reverse order: 20-10, 8-1, 9

282

and in the center of each 25x18mm cabochon of Consecrated Rose Quartz from the Third Eye Chakra to the Base Chakra. Next, place the 7x5mm cabochon of Consecrated Emerald on top and in the center of the 18x13mm cabochon of Consecrated Red Jasper at the Heart Chakra, and place the 6x4mm cabochon of Consecrated Ruby on top and in the center of the 18x13mm cabochon of Consecrated Red Jasper at the Base Chakra. Now, Spiral Balance from the Crown Chakra to the Base Chakra. When the Spiral Balancing passes have been completed, move away from the subject and focus your gaze upon the Consecrated Quartz Crystal Generator at the Crown Chakra. Hold your gaze upon the Consecrated Generator for about fifteen (15) seconds before slowly moving your gaze down the Chakra Cord, pausing a few seconds and focusing your gaze upon the Consecrated cabochons and free-form shapes placed at each successive Chakra en route to and including the Meridian Chakra Groin Points and the Base Chakra.

18. When the gazing has been completed, return to the subject and place three (3) 7x5mm cabochons of Consecrated Peridot around and touching the 40x30mm cabochon of Consecrated Rose Quartz at the Heart Chakra in the following order and position: 1st cabochon of Consecrated Peridot is place on the left (facilitator's left) side of the Consecrated Rose Quartz; 2nd cabochon of Consecrated Peridot is place on the right (facilitator's right) side of the Consecrated Rose Quartz; 3rd cabochon of Consecrated Peridot is placed below the Consecrated Rose Quartz cabochon. Next, place an 18x13mm cabochon of Consecrated Rhodocrosite above and touching the 25x18mm cabochon of Consecrated Rose Quartz at the Solar Plexus Chakra. Now, Spiral Balance from the Crown Chakra to the Base Chakra. When the Spiral Balancing passes have been

completed, stand back from the subject and focus your gaze upon the Consecrated Quartz Generator at the Crown Chakra. Hold your gaze for about fifteen (15) seconds before slowly moving your gaze down the Chakra Cord, pausing a few seconds and focusing your gaze upon the Consecrated cabochons and free-form shapes placed at each successive Chakra en route to and including the Meridian Chakra Groin Points and the Base Chakra. When the gazing has been completed, be seated for up to five (5) minutes before returning to the subject and placing Consecrated Sheen Obsidian eggs in each of the subject's hands.

19. Leaving the free-form shapes of Consecrated Rainbow Obsidian in place, begin removing the Consecrated Crystals and cabochons in the reverse order from which the Consecrated Crystals and cabochons were placed on the subject's body: first, remove the Consecrated Rhodocrosite at the Solar Plexus Chakra and the Consecrated Peridot at the Heart Chakra, then remove the Consecrated Ruby at the Base Chakra and the Consecrated Emerald at the Heart Chakra, followed by the Consecrated Red Jasper cabochons at the Base Chakra, Navel Chakra, Solar Plexus Chakra, Throat Chakra, Third Eye Chakra and the Heart Chakra, the Consecrated Malachite at the Solar Plexus Chakra and the Consecrated Malachite at the Heart Chakra, the Consecrated Quartz Crystal Generator at the Crown Chakra, the Consecrated Rose Quartz cabochons at the Base Chakra, Navel Chakra, Solar Plexus Chakra, Throat Chakra, Third Eye Chakra and Heart Chakra, and the Consecrated Rainbow Obsidian free-form shapes at the Meridian Chakra Groin Points are removed last.

20. Now, speak in a soft voice and encourage the subject to open his/her eyes. Gently stroke the subject's arm and shoulder to

help stimulate awareness of physical reality. Speak softly in reassuring tones to assist the subject in assimilating the experience of Loving Touch Therapy™. When the subject has regained a grounded sense of Third Dimension reality, begin discussing the feelings and sensations experienced during the session of Loving Touch Therapy™.

APPLIED CONSECRATED LAY-OUT #18
(See Diagram 30)

To perform Applied Consecrated Lay-out #18, begin by first completing steps 1-15 for Applied Consecrated Lay-out #7.

16. Now, place an 18x13mm cabochon of Consecrated Green Jade on top and in the center of the 40x30mm cabochon of Consecrated Rose Quartz at the Heart Chakra. Spiral Balance over the Heart Chakra, then Spiral Balance from the Crown Chakra to the Base Chakra. When the Spiral Balancing passes have been completed, stand back from the subject and focus your gaze upon the cabochons of Consecrated Green Jade and Rose Quartz at the Heart Chakra for fifteen (15) to twenty (20) seconds before refocusing and fixing your gaze upon the Consecrated Quartz Crystal Generator at the Crown Chakra. Hold your gaze upon the Consecrated Generator for about fifteen (15) seconds before slowly moving your gaze down the Chakra Cord, pausing a few seconds and focusing your gaze upon the Consecrated cabochons and free-form shapes placed at each successive Chakra en route to and including the Meridian Chakra Groin Points and the Base Chakra.

17. When the gazing has been completed, return to the subject and place 16x12mm cabochons of Consecrated Green Jade on top and in the center of each 25x18mm cabochon of Consecrated

DIAGRAM 30
Applied Consecrated Lay-out #18

ORDER OF PLACEMENT

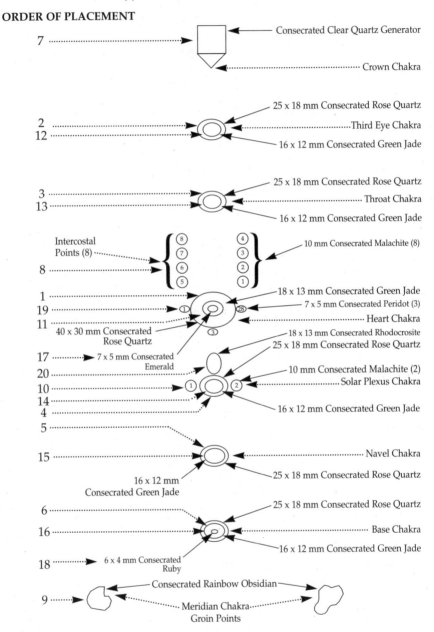

7 ....► Consecrated Clear Quartz Generator

Crown Chakra

25 x 18 mm Consecrated Rose Quartz

2 ....► Third Eye Chakra
12 ....► 16 x 12 mm Consecrated Green Jade

25 x 18 mm Consecrated Rose Quartz

3 ....► Throat Chakra
13 ....► 16 x 12 mm Consecrated Green Jade

Intercostal Points (8) .... 10 mm Consecrated Malachite (8)

8 ....►

1 ....► 18 x 13 mm Consecrated Green Jade
19 ....► 7 x 5 mm Consecrated Peridot (3)
11 ....► Heart Chakra
40 x 30 mm Consecrated Rose Quartz

17 ....► 18 x 13 mm Consecrated Rhodocrosite
7 x 5 mm Consecrated Emerald
25 x 18 mm Consecrated Rose Quartz

20 ....► 10 mm Consecrated Malachite (2)
10 ....► Solar Plexus Chakra
14 ....►
4 ....► 16 x 12 mm Consecrated Green Jade

5 ....►

15 ....► Navel Chakra

16 x 12 mm Consecrated Green Jade

25 x 18 mm Consecrated Rose Quartz

25 x 18 mm Consecrated Rose Quartz

6 ....►
16 ....► Base Chakra

16 x 12 mm Consecrated Green Jade

18 ....► 6 x 4 mm Consecrated Ruby

Consecrated Rainbow Obsidian

9 ....► Meridian Chakra
Groin Points

Remove in reverse order: 20-10, 8-1, 9

Rose Quartz from the Third Eye Chakra to the Base Chakra. Next, place the 7x5mm cabochon of Consecrated Emerald on top and in the center of the 18x13mm cabochon of Consecrated Green Jade at the Heart Chakra, then place the 6x4mm cabochon of Consecrated Ruby on top and in the center of the 16x12mm cabochon of Consecrated Green Jade at the Base Chakra. Now, Spiral Balance from the Crown Chakra to the Base Chakra. When the Spiral Balancing passes have been completed, move away from the subject and focus your gaze upon the Consecrated Clear Quartz Crystal Generator at the Crown Chakra. Hold your gaze for about fifteen (15) seconds before slowly moving your gaze down the Chakra Cord, pausing a few seconds and focusing your gaze upon the Consecrated cabochons and free-form shapes placed at each successive Chakra en route to and including the Meridian Chakra Groin Points and the Base Chakra.

18. When the gazing has been completed, return to the subject and place three (3) 7x5mm cabochons of Consecrated Peridot around and touching the 40x30mm cabochon of Consecrated Rose Quartz at the Heart Chakra in the following order and position: 1st cabochon of Consecrated Peridot is placed on the left (facilitator's left) side of the Consecrated Rose Quartz; 2nd cabochon of Consecrated Peridot is placed on the right (facilitator's right) side of the Consecrated Rose Quartz; 3rd cabochon of Consecrated Peridot is placed below the Consecrated Rose Quartz cabochon. Next, place an 18x13mm cabochon of Consecrated Rhodocrosite above and touching the 25x18mm cabochon of Consecrated Rose Quartz at the Solar Plexus Chakra. Now, Spiral Balance from the Crown Chakra to the Base Chakra. When the Spiral Balancing passes have been completed, step back from the subject and focus your gaze upon the Consecrated Quartz Crystal Generator at the Crown

Chakra. Hold your gaze for about fifteen (15) seconds before slowly moving your gaze down the Chakra Cord, pausing a few seconds and focusing your gaze upon the Consecrated cabochons and free-form shapes placed at each successive Chakra en route to and including the Meridian Chakra Groin Points and the Base Chakra. When the gazing has been completed, be seated nearby for up to five (5) minutes before returning to the subject and placing Consecrated Sheen Obsidian eggs in each of the subject's hands.

19. Leave the free-form Consecrated Rainbow Obsidian shapes in place and begin to remove the Consecrated Crystals and cabochons in the reverse order from which the Consecrated Crystals and cabochons were placed on the subject's body: first, remove the Consecrated Rhodocrosite at the Solar Plexus Chakra and the Consecrated Peridot at the Heart Chakra, then remove the Consecrated Ruby at the Base Chakra and the Consecrated Emerald at the Heart Chakra, followed by the Consecrated Green Jade cabochons at the Base Chakra, Navel Chakra, Solar Plexus Chakra, Throat Chakra, Third Eye Chakra and Heart Chakra, the Consecrated Malachite at the Solar Plexus Chakra and the Consecrated Malachite at the Heart Chakra, the Consecrated Quartz Generator at the Crown Chakra, the Consecrated Rose Quartz cabochons at the Base Chakra, Navel Chakra, Solar Plexus Chakra, Throat Chakra, Third Eye Chakra and Heart Chakra, and the Consecrated Rainbow Obsidian free-form shapes at the Meridian Chakra Groin Points are removed last.

20. Now, when the final Consecrated Crystals and cabochons have been removed from the subject's body, speak in a soft voice and encourage the subject to open his/her eyes. Gently stroke the subject's arm and shoulder to help stimulate aware-

ness of physical reality. Speak softly in reassuring tones to assist the subject in assimilating the experience of Loving Touch Therapy™. When the subject has regained a grounded sense of Third Dimension reality, begin discussing the feelings and sensations experienced during the session of Loving Touch Therapy™. Be sure that the subject is well grounded before allowing the subject to leave the facilitation area.

TRANS-CULTURAL SPIRITUALITY:
The Practice Of Divine Being

CHAPTER 11

Through Loving Touch Therapy™, avenues of Conscious Existence can be accessed that facilitate states of evolved, intuitive consciousness, but the applications of evolved states of Understanding can at times seem unclear. In life's unending circumstances of change, emotional factors frequently obscure choices and hamper one's ability to consistently engage conscionable behaviors that impact upon The Greater Good of All Creation. But in man's journey through the darkness and confusion of egocentric pursuit into The Transcendent Grace of The Light of Divine Being, the avenue by which man learns to apply The Teachings of Benevolence and Grace can be found in the principles of Trans-Cultural Spirituality.

As a synergetic system of evolved concepts common to all Spiritual and Religious Traditions, the principles of Trans-Cultural Spirituality embody the essence of Divine Conscience, the application of which affords mortal man The Blessing of Divine Being. Though linear thought patterns and societal conditioning pose formidable obstacles to the conscious expression of Divine Being, each child of God will in time evolve to acknowledge The Path of Truth that leads to The House of God, and in so doing resolve Karmic Debt and transform the experience of incarnate life from a day-to-day struggle to maintain the illusions of personal self into a glorious sustained moment of communion with The Infinite Body of God.

It is the responsibility of every child of God to embrace each day of incarnate existence one day, one step at a time, and allow self to experience the entire spectrum of feelings available in the world of man. But in the experience of life, the ultimate predestined choice of each incarnate soul is to learn how to feel the realities of incarnate existence without being consumed by emotion, the illusions of personal importance or need. The lesson each child of God will ultimately learn is how to live in man's world as an awakened child of God, not allowing self to become a product of man's world or simply an illusion of that which self might have been expected to be. When each child of God actively takes responsibility for all aspects of self, then it shall be that the once formidable obstacles posed by societal conditioning and linear thought patterns will prove to be wonderful opportunities to demonstrate The Blessings of Divine Being.

PRACTICAL TRANS-CULTURAL SPIRITUALITY

The successful application of Trans-Cultural Spirituality rests solely upon the unwavering, unilateral acceptance and comprehension of The Divine Precepts upon which it is based. Taken in its simplest form, Trans-Cultural Spirituality is the application of The Wisdom of One expressed through twelve (12) Divine Precepts: Patience, Compassion, Wisdom, Mercy, Serenity, Love, Faith, Perseverance, Courage, Conviction, Transcendence and Liberation.

THE WISDOM OF ONE

The Wisdom of One prescribes the treatment of all things born of Universal Creation with Loving Kindness, respect and the conscious acknowledgment that all things born of Universal Creation contain the same Light/Life resonant energy of The One Infinite Creator. In short, all within Universal Creation is related - we are all related, we are all one - or "Namaste," as spoken by Hindus, or "Mitake Oyasin," as spoken by the people of the Lakota Nation of North America.

When modern man employs The Wisdom of One, man's footsteps become gentle upon the bosom of The Earth Mother. When modern man embraces The Wisdom of One, hunting for sport will become a distant memory of a dark past. When all children of God learn to accept one another as true brethren, the need for standing armies, territorial boundaries and assumptions of cultural superiority will vanish like echoes upon the breath of the wind, never again to be heard.

The Wisdom of One holds that all God's children are equal, without restriction, qualification or exception. As noble as the attempt was meant to be, the founding fathers of the United States fell far short in word and deed in the proclamation that "We hold these truths to be self-evident that all men are created equal." Indeed the spirit of these words has never been realized, even in a country that was founded upon the notion of freedom and equality. After all, when the constitution was drafted, human bondage and servitude were an acceptable practice as the economic institution of slavery, even for many who drafted and signed the most profound document known to government that outlines and guarantees personal freedoms. And therein lies the inherent difference between the laws of man and The Laws of God.

Man would attempt to issue laws to control and regulate that which God has created and allowed to simply be. In effect, man would attempt to govern or otherwise direct the unfoldment of incarnate existence, while simultaneously maintaining selective, pre-emptive rights and proclaiming the course that reality must follow. In contrast, That which is God is The Conscious Essence of Creation in Harmony with the natural order of existence, as That which is God simply is.

The Wisdom of One is The Law of God as offered by The Council of Twelve. As The Law of God, The Wisdom of One is neither enforced by codes of punishment, nor does it differentiate between species, classes or by earning potential. The Wisdom of One states simply that all God's children in every dimension of existence, be it an ant, an owl, a redwood, a fish, primate or crystalline form, is worthy of The Blessings of Love. All things born of Universal Creation exist as One in The Heart of God, and warrant the same nature of Loving Kindness as mortal man would claim for personal self. As the time of readiness to embrace evolved concepts approaches, each child of God will begin to grasp the concept that all life, all Conscious States of Existence are inter-related and inter-dependent upon one another. The concept of Oneness will emerge as a viable principle necessary to sustain incarnate existence, and mortal man will come to realize that The Wisdom of One has always been a part of man's Divine Heritage, waiting for the moment to actively live again.

PATIENCE

The foundation for all states of Evolved Consciousness is the Divine Precept, Patience. As defined through The Teachings of Absolute Truth, Patience is the allowance for all things to find the appropriate moment of conscionable resolution. Stated otherwise,

Patience is the acceptance of life-conditions as being necessary to reveal The Lessons of Existence, and allowing self to embrace the experiences of life without anticipation, expectation and anxiety compelling egocentric, reactionary behaviors in response to that which is experienced. Additionally, by accepting the life-experience presented, one allows self to participate actively and conscionable in the time-table of resolution. What this means is that without attempting to impose personal will upon life-experiences, one can allow self to learn of incarnate life without struggling against it. One can learn the Transcendent reality of incarnate existence by allowing self to flow with the current of life, instead of defiantly or unwittingly swimming against it. One can learn to free self from illusions of self-importance by simply allowing self to be - ergo, by the implementation of Patience.

Now, it is not being suggested that Patience implies either a lack of commitment to resolving troubling life-conditions, or merely not involving self in the pain and suffering so rampant in man's world. Most definitely not. The Divine Precept of Patience guides man through the temporal realities of discontent, suffering and the preoccupation with personal self by offering man intuitive insights into the very process of Liberation. In other words, by implementing Divine Patience, man allows self to access states of sheer "Knowingness" and comes to realize that regardless of the nature of the life-conditions that beset one the necessary resolution will be the result of engaging behaviors that offer a positive, benevolent impact upon The Greater Good of Creation. Man learns that By The Grace of God, Patience is the beacon of Truth shining through the night of uncertainty.

At first glance, many children of God who have studied different Esoteric or Spiritual Traditions, may feel that the implementation of Divine Patience has already been a part of daily practice for some time. But upon closer inspection, it is revealed that something else instead of Divine Patience had been implemented. In fact, it is most probable that tolerance is the behavior engaged instead of the true behavior of Patience, as defined in The Teachings of Absolute Truth. You see, whenever the emotion of expectation or thoughts or behaviors of reaction are felt or enacted, tolerance for unpleasant circumstances is the resultant behavior. Though it might appear as if one has "accepted" circumstances as found, in fact one is merely waiting for the situation to change, or hoping someone will effect resolution, or praying for strength to withstand the experience one wishes would disappear. In any case, The Divine Precept of Patience will not have been implemented.

As human beings, mortal man will repeatedly confuse tolerance with Divine Patience, especially if one deems self to be "evolved." But this is not reason for disappointment or concern, as the time for each child of God to comprehend the true nature of self comes when and only when one is ready to receive it. To be sure, one will not find self immersed in life-situations that illustrate evolved concepts unless and until one is ready from the standpoint of Spiritual Evolution to receive The Teachings therein. Further, it is a natural part of Conscious Evolution "to think" self to be advanced following the study of course material that addresses issues of Spirituality. Yet until one "Knows," through the warmth of Heart-centered Truth, the question of Divine Patience or tolerance need never be asked, as if there is need to ask, then it is most likely that tolerance has been the behavior engaged. And should it be discovered that indeed one has consistently engaged in behaviors of tolerance instead of Divine Patience, simply forgive self for human frailty and acknowledge that The Path of Enlightenment traverses the world of illusion created by man, but nonetheless remains forever the road to The Temple of Liberation.

COMPASSION

The Teachings of Absolute Truth define the Evolved, Divine Precept of Compassion as the Selfless engagement of Universal Creation, giving freely of self to any and all in need. Through the application of Divine Compassion, man willingly accepts the reality of problematic life-situations and commits self to nurturing the birth of conscionable resolution, without judgment, qualification or restriction. In the presence of Compassion, man gives of self without expectation or concern for personal well-being or designs for manipulating specific outcomes in the resolution of conflict or problematic life-experiences. It is by the hand of Compassion that man learns the true meaning of giving to another, as in the experience of Compassion man learns that the gift of giving is itself A Blessing of Love.

But once again, many incarnate souls actively pursuing The Path of Enlightenment will most likely think self to have implemented acts of Divine Compassion as a matter of course. Yet under closer examination, that which was thought to be Divine Compassion was in fact expressions of concern. When man expresses concern, man imposes limits to the degree of involvement that will be allowed. Man places restrictions and passes judgments in an attempt to protect personal self from possible perceived damage or danger, while attempting to assist another in need. In effect, man will have chosen not to allow the misfortunes of others to tarnish feelings of personal self-worth, but will have made a "controlled effort" to assist another child of God in need.

Such behavior is most often the result of complex ego-schemes or defense mechanisms designed to maintain positive feelings about self through elaborate illusions of personal identity. By means of social conditioning, man learns to implement behaviors

299

of rationalization, suppression, intellectualization, denial, sublimation and repression to maintain illusions of personal self-worth,
and tends to resist notions that imply one is not as "evolved" as
one thought self to be. This attitude is quite human and a normal
part of Spiritual Evolution, as first man must accept and comprehend that which appears to be short-comings, imperfections and
frailties before one can learn to transcend the imposed boundaries
set by personal illusions. It is then that man truly embraces Divine
Patience as the fertile soil of Conscious Evolution from which the
Blossom of Divine Compassion soon grows.

WISDOM

Probably the most misunderstood Precept of Divine
Conscience is Wisdom. Divine Wisdom is far more than the acquisition of information or the accumulation of knowledge, as Divine
Wisdom is infused with Absolute Understanding of the conscionable application of information that does not compromise
Choice of Free Will or otherwise direct the course of natural order
in accordance with subjective reason or conclusion. Divine
Wisdom offers states of "Intuitive Knowingness" that transcend
reason or logic. Divine Wisdom offers the evolving conscience of
man a glimpse into "The Universal Mind," The Golden Mind of
Divine Being. Divine Wisdom is as the eternal flame that illuminates and warms the halls of The Temple of Liberation.

Through the application of Divine Wisdom, mortal man
allows self to effectively engage all life-situations with undaunted
Faith and Perseverance, knowing that all apparent problems in life
are merely situations whose time of resolution simply have not yet
come - but indeed will come, when it is good and right. This does
not mean that when Divine Wisdom is in operation that man can
arbitrarily determine when the time of resolution must or will be.

Rather, when Divine Wisdom is in operation, man is not concerned about the illusion of time, and applies The Divine Precepts of Patience and Compassion in embracing issues of relevance.

By contrast, typical notions of wisdom imply that great knowledge has been accumulated, and that one can "possess" wisdom. In the lower world of Third Dimension, wisdom, spelled with a lower case "w," is a glorified state of knowledge retention that affords man a path of rational, linear reality. As man engages the material world of Third Dimension, man tends not to venture beyond established limits of conventional wisdom, and therein lies the paradox. The more of Third Dimension reality man comprehends, the more man becomes aware that there is more to life than meets the eye. Man becomes aware of consciousness states beyond mortal comprehension, not through written descriptions, but through personal experiences that may be relegated to "unexplained experiences" until man can reason through the variety of phenomena that occur each day of incarnate life.

The integrity of conventional wisdom having been breached, man can no longer maintain that rational, empirical processes alone hold the answers to Universal Creation or Conscious Existence, even though many incarnate souls still refuse to relinquish the notion that science holds the keys to unlock the doors to Universal Conscience. Nonetheless, man will discover that only through the application of Divine Wisdom and by embracing the Intuitive Process can conscionable, lasting resolutions be effected - resolutions that positively impact upon The Greater Good of All Creation. Regardless of emotional input, limited resources of conscious information or relentless energies of discordance creating the illusion of insurmountable obstacles to states of resolution, The Grace of Divine Wisdom will forever lead the children of God through the fogs and mists of egocentric delusion into The Light of The One

Infinite Creator. For as Patience is the fertile soil from which the blossom of Compassion grows, so too must Wisdom be firmly rooted in the fertile soil of Patience in order to rise to embrace the blossom of Compassion and be as One with The Conscience of God.

MERCY

The Divine Precept of Mercy prescribes the conscionable allowance of Heart-centered Communion that through states of Enlightened Knowingness facilitates the Karmic Evolution of all things born of Universal Creation. The implementation of Divine Mercy is accomplished through the directives of an open, evolved Heart Chakra that allows conscionable, Divinely Inspired behaviors to be the expression of personal self. Further, through acts of Divine Mercy, mortal man is allowed to participate in the experience of Karmic Destiny without preoccupations or concerns about personal well-being or the linear practicality of assisting other children of God in need of Spiritual Upliftment. Through the application of Divine Mercy, mortal man comes to terms with the illusions of self-interest, and learns to freely, Selflessly give of self to any and all in need.

Unlike simple gestures of concern, kindness or consideration, Divine Mercy offers mortal man the opportunity to embrace every aspect of incarnate existence with the conscious intent of "Mindful Consideration," and the altruistic giving of self to conscionably impact upon The Greater Good of All Creation. Extending the true benevolence of Divine Mercy to the weary, abused, downtrodden, confused and afflicted is viewed by the awakened masses in much the same manner as breathing, eating or sleeping - as living in The Grace of Divine Mercy is as natural and as vital as any other life-sustaining process. To know Divine Mercy is to know The Kiss of God upon the battered body of Creation. To know Divine Mercy is to know the path that illuminates the shadows of chaos, disillusion and turmoil with The Light of The Living Spirit of God. To know Divine Mercy is to know and to share the reality of Evolved Self with all Creation in The Transcendent Bliss of Love Eternal.

SERENITY

The Teachings of Absolute Truth define the Precept of Divine Serenity as an evolved state of harmonious communion shared between elements of Universal Existence. Unlike the linear experience of peace, Divine Serenity occurs as a progression of Spiritual Unfoldment, and has no polarizing counterpart, as war, conflict or unrest would relate to peace. In effect, the Divine state of Contentment experienced in Divine Serenity is the outgrowth of the assimilation and application of Divine Patience, Divine Compassion, Divine Wisdom and Divine Mercy, for These are the basis that allow the experience of Divine Serenity to eventuate.

But the experience of Divine Serenity goes beyond the wonder and grace of harmonious communion, as the experience of Divine Serenity nurtures states of Transcendent Bliss and Divine Understanding in which perceptions of Truth exist in moments of Divine Illumination that facilitate unparalleled comprehension and the acceptance of all that is engaged in incarnate life. The reflection of Divine Serenity can be seen in the gentle, benevolent, knowing smile upon the lips of the Sage, or the enchanting experiences found in nature, when the mind of man surrenders to the majesty and awe inspired by the painted deserts, rolling landscapes and the fragrant aromas and sounds of life so abundant upon The Earth Mother, or in the mystical silence found in the depths of Meditation, when the soul of man knows The Blessed Countenance that fills The Conscience of God.

Though Divine Serenity can be experienced in fleeting moments, the children of God who have made ready for its acceptance quickly find that Divine Serenity becomes the order of each day instead of the unusual occurrence. As the children of God allow the surrender of more of the illusions related to personal self to The Omnipresent Will of The One Infinite Creator, too will it be discovered that the greater part of self is living in the essence of Divine Serenity - through the daily applications of Divine Patience, Divine Compassion, Divine Wisdom and Divine Mercy - and too will the children of God realize that the experience of Divine Serenity has always been a part of mankind's inherent Divine nature.

LOVE

The Precept of Divine Love is as unconditional and pervasive as The Light of The One Infinite Creator. Divine Love allows the behaviors of man to become the very expression of Evolved Self, as mortal man learns to actualize The Living God Spirit in every thought and action engaged in incarnate life. Divine Love is the Absolute, Selfless, Unconditional giving of self that facilitates The Greater Good of All Creation.

As man has addressed the concept of love within Third Dimension, emotional energies of personal desire, companionship, intimacy and co-dependent relationships have tended to be the range of behaviors and issues considered. Man's notions of love predominantly have been devoid of any sense of Divinity, as man's interests have been compelled by drives of ego that do not operate beyond the illusions of personal self. Such being the case, man's Third Dimensional world has offered little quarter for The Precept of Divine Love, yet man's world is truly incapable of destroying The Benevolence and Grace of Love Eternal.

As an Evolved State of Divine Conscience, Divine Love is realized through the cumulative applications of Divine Patience, Divine Compassion, Divine Wisdom, Divine Mercy, and Divine Serenity - all in the expression of Selfless devotion to the needs of Universal Creation. When mortal man evolves to embrace The Teachings of Divine Love, then man will have come to know the purpose of incarnate existence within The Light of The One Infinite Creator. When man has evolved through Karmic Resolution to comprehend The Lessons of Existence, man will have transcended the illusions of duality and consciously Ascended into The Infinite body of God. And too will man have completed the first evolutionary step on the road to The Temple of Liberation.

FAITH

In The Teachings of Absolute Truth, Divine Faith is identified as "The Knowingness of The Unknown," which translates to mean the steadfast guidance of the God-self. In the execution of Divine Faith, man just seems to "Know" that a given course is the appropriate course to engage, not due to the existence of any concrete reason, but through an inner sense of guidance that quietly stimulates a sense of well-being, even and especially when faced by chaotic circumstances that might tend to obscure possible choices. When mortal man displays Divine Faith, the material world can not influence the nature of decisions, or precipitate emotional responses to life-conditions.

In contrast to Intuitive Wisdom, Divine Faith does not offer solutions to problematic life-situations. Rather, it is Divine Faith that allows one "to Know The Way without knowing, to Trust the Unknown without validation, and to exist within Divinity by feeling The Presence of God." It is Divine Faith that frees mortal man from the linear contingent of proving that which is Interdimensional in nature actually exists in a world that primarily relies upon the rational senses to identify reality. It is Divine Faith that allows mortal man to discover the true reality of Evolved Self, as it is Faith that allows man to embrace The Infinite Body of God.

Unlike the Earth-bound systems of belief that require linear thought for implementation, Divine Faith requires neither thought nor promise of reward or any type of "future pay-off" to entice commitment or to be sustained. The linear thought process associated with man's belief systems or social processes invariably tend to incite emotional, reactionary behaviors that ultimately pit the egocentric designs of man's laws against The Universal Laws of God, albeit an unintended conflict of interests. Nonetheless, the thought processes and belief systems that man tends to engage contain elements of rationalization conceived to justify and/or over-rule any apparent conflict with that which might be considered to be Universal Interests. However, in cases that reflect the adverse impact capitalism and industrialization have had upon the very Life-Force of The Earth Mother, many children of God in positions of responsibility choose to address ecological issues with politically correct, or non-committal, or elusive responses, or respond by discussing the illusions of practical need and world-wide living standards that have improved despite the threats of deforestation, global warming and toxic damage incurred by the natural food chain. The difference between belief and Divine Faith is that belief requires linear support systems to sustain momentum and Divine Faith is Self-Sustained by The Presence of The Living God Spirit.

Divine Faith is as the wings of the hummingbird, moving faster than the eye can see, yet purposefully maintaining stability through the winds and rain of Third Dimension. Divine Faith is The Prayer of Acceptance that warms the hearts of the awakened children of God with The Wisdom of Allowance. Divine Faith is as the whisper that echoes throughout Eternity with The Benevolence and Grace of God's Infinite Love.

PERSEVERANCE

The discipline of Divine Perseverance is the effort of focused intent to transcend the obstacles encountered in the journey of Conscious Existence. As mortal man chooses to release self from the compelling emotions of ego, so too does mortal man discover more of self to commit to the active engagement of Conscious Evolution. It is the reality of Spiritual Unfoldment that allows man to realize the need for commitment of true self in the application and execution of Divine Perseverance, and as is the case for all Precepts of Divine Conscience, man reaches the time of readiness to implement the Divinity of Perseverance as a function of acceptance of personal self, The Omnipresent Grace of God and The Oneness of Universal Creation.

Without need or concern for personal interests, the avenue by which man utilizes the directives of Divine Perseverance lead man toward acts of conscionable service that attend the needs of The Greater Good of All Creation. By virtue of definition, if one has implemented Divine Perseverance, then one has focused all energies and aspects of self toward realities, concepts and acts that reflect an understanding of Higher Truth. In so doing, man embraces behaviors that demonstrate the emergence of the God-Self as man's expression of true, Evolved Self. Through Divine Perseverance, man learns that conflict is but an illusion, and that apparent obstacles to Conscious Evolution are simply opportunities for man to develop and sustain Conviction. As man assimilates more and more in learning The Lessons of Existence, man comes to know Divine Perseverance to be as gentle as the kiss of

Compassion, but as resilient and indomitable as the very fabric of Creation. By implementing Divine Perseverance, man comes to terms with the true purpose of incarnate existence, and learns to be an awakened child of God fully dedicated in mind, body and spirit to The Greater Good of All Universal Creation.

By contrast, the linear notion of perseverance implies an active attempt to overcome an object or force that hampers progress in attaining personal goals or accomplishments. The linear application of perseverance identifies opposing ideas, forces or realities that create a conflict that must be resolved. The conflict so identified is that between present life-conditions and the life-conditions man would wish to be in operation. Resolutions made through linear applications of perseverance define adversarial conditions and attempt to outline a course of action that will give man the outcome desired, which also identifies the presence of emotion in the linear application of perseverance.

Without the directives of Divine Perseverance, mortal man would be denied an effective, conscionable avenue by which the process of Transcendence could begin, for through Divine Perseverance does mortal man find Courage and Conviction to embrace the experience of incarnate existence. And through the realizations afforded mortal man by the implementation of Divine Perseverance, the obstacles to Conscious Existence once thought to be insurmountable become simple exercises in the applications of Love Eternal.

CONVICTION

The Teachings of Absolute Truth observe Divine Conviction to be the strength of God-Realization that lifts the veil of illusions of the importance of personal self from the evolving conscience of mortal man. When mankind has evolved to embrace The Presence of The One Infinite Creator as The Living Essence of Universal Creation, then too will mortal man have evolved to comprehend the significance of Third Dimensional existence and the greater importance of God-Conscious, Light-minded Behaviors. In effect, as mortal man learns to walk in "The Footsteps of God", man also learns that the presence of Truth and Love have always been a vital component of the collective soul of man. Man will have learned and will have come to demonstrate that The Precepts of Divine Conscience require neither validation through linear reasoning, nor systems of defense to protect its integrity from disbelievers. Man will have learned through the expressions of Evolved Self to remain undaunted, while offering Loving Kindness and Divine Compassion when confronted by hostility, discordance or blatant attack.

The application of Divine Conviction will have afforded mortal man the ability to withstand whatever threat or implied danger that the lower world of man might conceive to discredit, hamper or destroy The Path that leads to The Temple of Liberation. And therein lies The Grace of Divine Conviction - allowing mortal consciousness to traverse the illusions found within the world of self-indulgence, without reaction, harsh judgments or compelling drives to prove self-worth, thereby allowing mankind to become awakened, conscionable children of God in the engagement of all that is born of Universal Creation.

As a function of God-Realization, Divine Conviction is a gentle, nurturing sensation that fills mortal consciousness with a sense of purposeful well-being that defies comparison to any other physical sensation that man is capable of emulating or inducing. The feelings and behaviors stimulated by Divine Conviction are assertive but not aggressive, goal-directed but not accomplishment oriented, invigorating but not compelling, intuitive but not abstract and steadfast but not unrelenting or zealous.

The attitude of Divine Conviction is that of Selfless Devotion to The Wisdom of One in The Light of The One Infinite Creator, which affords mankind a clear, Heart-felt design by which to serve the needs of Universal Creation. And through the sense of Evolved Self instilled by the attitude of Divine Conviction, mankind need never again ponder the illusion of paradox presented by incarnate reality.

COURAGE

As man learns to embrace the obstacles found in the journey of Spiritual Evolution, man begins to commit more and more of self to the process that allows Spiritual Unfoldment to continue. It is not that man begins to feel a sense of accomplishment in having successfully negotiated an obstacle-laden path toward Divine Conscience, but that man will have come to allow more of total self to be committed to Spiritual Evolution simply because it feels "good and right." What this means is that man will have followed the "gentle voice of Intuition" that softly speaks from within to lead man in the engagement of all things born of Universal Creation, and in so doing, come to realize that the process of Spiritual Unfoldment is a self-affirming, self-sustaining process that becomes clearer and simpler with consistent engagement. In effect, man accepts reality by virtue of allowance and grows spiritually by virtue of nurturing the process of Spiritual Unfoldment.

Defined in The Teachings of Absolute Truth as the mental, emotional, physical and spiritual strength of commitment of self that fuels the diligence of Divine Perseverance, Divine Courage cannot be mistaken as an act of bravery or any other linear concept that implies conflict or aggression. The nature of Divine Courage is that of Allowance and Acceptance, instead of heroic notions of overcoming adversarial conflicts. And the function of Divine Courage is to further implement and/or sustain other Precepts of Divine Conscience. Through Divine Courage, mortal man finds a true, selfless companion in the journey toward The Temple of Liberation, as through the application of Divine Courage does mortal man discover yet another vehicle with which The Strength, Beauty and Grace of God-Conscious Reality can be expressed.

TRANSCENDENCE

Learning to move beyond the limits of linear consciousness can appear at times to be practically impossible, but to think self incapable of rising above restricting thought and behavior patterns is far more than mere illusion or self-doubt. For man to deny self the possibility of embracing The Greater Truth of Universal Creation is to deny self The Truth of Conscious Existence that lives in the heart of the Evolved Self, the God-Self that patiently awaits discovery within the consciousness of each incarnate being.

Transcendence is neither a mysterious process shrouded in mystical ritual, nor is it practiced and known only by Evolved Initiates of Obscure Spiritual Orders. Instead, Transcendence is a Divine Process accessible to all mankind. Transcendence is a simple, direct process that facilitates the release of judgmental, defensive, reactionary thoughts and behaviors that impede the revelation and practice of The Wisdom of One. Transcendence allows mortal consciousness to be released from conditioned, restricting, polarized patterns of rational existence to embrace the infinite realities of Universal Existence. Through Transcendence does mankind come to recognize the kinship existing between all things born of Universal Creation, as too does man shed the facades and pretenses of illusion to embrace The Revelation of Love Eternal.

To practice Transcendence, man should first be willing to see and resolve those aspects of self that are problematic, specifically those attitudes that tend to reflect hostility, resentment, frustration, anger, fear and similar energies of emotional discord. This is the moment in Conscious Evolution in which each soul incarnate being chooses to see self stripped bare of ego-facilitating devices, excuses, linear reasons and rationalizations to allow self to embrace the core motivations for behaviors. It is then that the soul incarnate fully enters The Divine Process of Transcendence by implementing four (4) principles: Acknowledgment, Forgiveness, Blessing and Release.

Acknowledgment is the simple identification and acceptance of attitudes and behaviors that are discovered to be in operation. There are no compelling drives or inclinations to justify that which is encountered. Rather, there is a genuine sense of receptiveness and willingness to embrace any and all emotions, delusions, fears or angers that form the matrix of discordant personality traits. Additionally, in Acknowledgment man does not indulge in self-pity, or place value judgments upon uncovered motivations, or consider issues of self-worth to be important. In effect, mortal man begins to operate outside of the influence of the ego-self through the process of Transcendence.

Second and of Universal Importance is the principle of Forgiveness. Forgiveness is vital in the acceptance of life-experiences and in understanding the reality of personal self. Without

Heart-felt Forgiveness, man cannot resolve dysfunctional emotional energies that impede the realization of God-Consciousness. Without True Forgiveness, man cannot evolve beyond the experience of discordance.

Forgiveness allows mankind to release self from performance anxieties and self-abasing tendencies. Through Forgiveness, all participants in discordant life-sequences are absolved of perceived "wrong-doing," for the indulgence of self-interest and human frailties are received with The Divine Precepts of Compassion and Mercy. Through Forgiveness, man learns that Liberation is a Divine State of Grace and Evolved Understanding in which perceptions and behaviors presuppose nothing, place demands of performance upon nothing and challenge or encroach upon the rights of nothing within the realm of Universal Creation.

The active engagement of Forgiveness leads man to the application of Selfless Blessing, which is the unconditional giving of Love to all experiences and conditions of life and self. Through Selfless Blessing, mortal man invokes The Presence of the Living God Spirit to fill and comfort the reality of each life-experience with Benevolence and Grace, and in so doing, man discovers the unilateral expression of Evolved Self to be The Loving Embrace of God.

And finally, the rendering of Selfless Blessing leads mortal consciousness to the moment of Release - letting go - allowing self to be free from encumbering emotions, guilts and misplaced feelings of responsibility. The act of Release is the culmination of the journey that transforms perceptions of Universal Reality from enigmatic, paradoxical equations into simple Absolute Truths of Serenity, Love, Benevolence and Grace. The act of Release clarifies man's understanding of that which is temporal as existing solely through egocentric design and that which is Eternal as born of

Love and God-Conscious Being. Release, letting go, is an act of Divine Conscience engaged by children of God who have come of age to experience The Liberation of Love as the moment of Conscious Ascension into The Transcendent Heart of God.

LIBERATION

As defined in The Teachings of Absolute Truth, The Divine Precept of Liberation is the all-encompassing, transcendent state of reality in which perceptions of Conscious Existence are made through The Conscience of God. In states of Liberation, human emotions are observed to be temporal necessities that when properly applied facilitate the release of Karmic Debt, and that ultimately facilitate conditions of Soul Evolution. From the vantage point of Liberation, mortal consciousness is elevated to the plane of Divine Reality in which personal need has neither meaning nor application. In Liberation, mortal man finds "Nirvana," yet chooses to be an active component in the evolution of the collective soul of man.

Unlike mythological conditions of after-life or "Heaven," Liberation is a Divine State of Being in which daily activities are conducted inter-dimensionally, thereby impacting upon The Greater Good of All Universal Creation. Through the eyes of "The Liberated," the only behaviors considered are those actions that will compliment "The Universal Community." Therefore, issues that affect only one group of incarnate souls, or one element of Creation, or have limited application tend not to be explored. But the foregoing is not to imply that issues that directly impact upon one specific element of Creation cannot or do not impact upon All Universal Creation as well. Rather that single-minded interests, personal preoccupations and issues compelled by egocentric drives are not the domain of The Liberated.

Liberation is a Divine State of Unconditional Love in which mortal consciousness is transformed to receive and apply The Conscience of God. Through Liberation does man fully embrace man's inherent, Divine Nature, and express the reality of Evolved Self in behaviors that exemplify the essence of Light-minded Being. As mortal man embraces The Path of Divine Conscience, too does man embark upon the journey that leads to The Temple of Liberation. And through the trials of Third Dimension, man learns to accept and apply The Lessons of Existence, and along the way comes to realize that the journey to reach The Temple of Liberation is simply the journey that leads back home - back to The Heart of God in the embrace of Love Eternal.

Upon initial examination, the foregoing Principles of Trans-Cultural Spirituality may appear to some to be demanding, or at best seem difficult to implement, but the practice of Trans-Cultural Spirituality is anything but an austere discipline, or a taxing, joyless approach to incarnate existence. Rather, Trans-Cultural Spirituality offers mortal man a system of Divine Tools by which the discovery of man's true Self can eventuate. Through Trans-Cultural Spirituality can mankind learn to release self from the compelling drives and cycles of egocentric desire, and return to behaviors that reflect a sense of reverence and respect for all that lives and breathes, all that swims and flies, all that grows and blossoms upon The Earth Mother. Through the practice of Trans-Cultural Spirituality can mortal man realize kinship with all that is born of Universal Creation, and become a responsible, awakened component part of The Infinite Body of God.

EPILOGUE

As the seeker of Spiritual Truth evolves and learns to actualize The Presence of The Living God Spirit in the experience of incarnate life, the awakened child of God emerges as The Beneficent Spirit of God alive in the fragile vessel of man. Each awakened child of God will have learned to transcend the notions of self-importance, as illusions of personal self will have been surrendered to The Greater Universal Will of The One Infinite Creator. And each child of God will have learned to follow the gentle voice of Truth that speaks from The Heart of God through the soul of man.

The Living Testament to Love Eternal demonstrated by man is embodied in the Selfless journey of the seeker of Spiritual Truth, as the seeker comes to realize that in the journey of Soul Evolution there is in Truth nothing to seek, rather everything to allow in the experience of Conscious Existence. The seeker learns that there is nothing of personal value to be demanded from the journey of Spiritual Unfoldment, rather is there everything to accept. The seeker learns that in the moment of experience does the conscience of man feel the Truth of Reality as The Knowingness of God, as there is nothing, no rewards or personal embellishments to be expected from engaging The Path of Spiritual Conscience - for by embracing The Path of Divine Conscience does man live in Peace in The Heart of Love Eternal.

As the seeker of Spiritual Truth wades through the seas of misinformation, half-truths, superstition, speculation and religious dogma, acknowledging the right for every child of God to believe as he/she sees fit, an overwhelming sense of sadness can easily overtake the seeker. And in the midst of discovery does the seek-

317

er acknowledge the degree to which Divine Truth has been distorted by institutions, individuals and groups to control the thoughts and behaviors of man.

"In the beginning was The Word and The Word was God," but man's interpretation of "The Word" is not the same as "The Word." Indeed, man's interpretation of "The Word" was and remains to be a tool used to control and manipulate the thoughts and behaviors of the masses. But the seeker of Spiritual Truth recognizes The Word of God not through an interpretation or opinion, as that which is God's Own Truth resonates throughout one's consciousness in a fashion decidedly unlike the drives, edicts and compulsions born of ego. That which is Truth is Divine, pure and uncompromised by convention, desire or the illusions of personal self.

As the seeker evolves and recognizes the hardships that lie ahead for those who cling to or are held captive by the illusions of ego and the importance of personal self, the sense of sadness experienced by the seeker arises from Heart-felt concern and empathy for the plight of so many children of God. And a similar sense of sadness is felt by the seeker when reflecting upon the many other children of God who consciously reject the reality of The Light of The One Infinite Creator.

But through the sadness the seeker may experience, a greater reality will unfold. In time, the seeker will embrace The Knowingness of Love Eternal that in unspoken resolution will offer the hand of Selflessness to facilitate the wounds of Creation. In time, the earnest seeker of Spiritual Truth will find self walking in the same footsteps of the Mystics, Prophets, Rishis and Sages since the beginning of Conscious Existence. And too shall the seeker come to know Serenity, as the seeker of Spiritual Truth will have learned to view the experience of incarnate life through evolved states of Liberation.

Through The Divine Silence of Evolved Consciousness, the awakened children of God will acknowledge The Sacred Covenant shared with The Spirit of Creation, as each conscious child of God will acknowledge the responsibility of sharing the essence of Divine Communion with all that is born of Universal Existence. Each evolved seeker, each awakened child of God, will know the inherent Oneness shared with The Universe, and demonstrate The Revelations of Divine Truth by walking softly upon The Earth Mother and respecting all that lives, breathes and exists upon Her.

The Path of Spiritual Conscience allows each child of God to discover his/her place in the continuum of Divine Order by facilitating unending awakenings to ever-unfolding higher, more refined levels of Absolute Truth. Each seeker will experience progressively more profound realizations about the nature of incarnate existence, the realities of The Wisdom of One and the very essence of Divine Thought engaged by The Conscience of The One Infinite Creator. Each earnest seeker will inevitably find self encompassed by The Living Ectoplasmic Presence of Divine Being and know The Face of God to be the same face seen each day smiling in the mirror of life. As time passes, the seeker of Spiritual Truth will discover that each day is a blessed event on the calendar of Eternity, as each day affords the consciousness of man yet another opportunity to know The Benevolent Grace of God alive in The Heart of Love Eternal.

Shalom, Adonai, Shalom

Appendix I

Aromatherapy Chart 1

1. Agarwood - clears hostile/discordant energy systems from environment
2. Amber - cleansing for internal organs; benevolent, calming and protecting
3. Cedar - purifying aroma that cleanses spiritual vibrations
4. Copal - resin used by Aztecs and Mayans to purify and to invoke energies in rituals and ceremonies
5. Frankincense - invokes strength of conviction while dispelling moods of depression, uncertainty and irrational behavior
6. Gardenia - sweet, uplifting, purifying aroma facilitates healing of heart chakra states
7. Gum Benzoin - resin used to cleanse and to invoke benevolent energies
8. Gum Mastic - resin used to intensify etheric consciousness
9. Henna - sweet-scented stimulant of dream states
10. Jasmine - invigorating, intoxicating aroma aids in lessening mental stress and depression
11. Juniper - cleansing, fresh-scented agent used to dispel discordant energies
12. Lavender - soothes and calms the nerves
13. Lotus - opens crown chakra and aids in awakening third eye perceptions; stimulates intuitive and conscious states of etheric presence
14. Musk - aids in developing personal will and conviction; helps to stimulate psychic energy
15. Myrrh - provides atmosphere that stimulates mental activity and heightens clarity of perception
16. Narcissus - offers transformational energy to soothe emotional energies
17. Rose - opens the heart chakra with sweet, purifying aroma
18. Sage - removes discordant vibrations from the environment
19. Sandalwood - provides calming vibrations and aromas conducive to Meditation and Spiritual Invocation
20. Sweet Grass - provides cleansing energy that invokes benevolent vibrations
21. Tuberose - sweet, benevolent scent that facilitates healing of heart chakra energies
22. Violet - softens charged emotions of aggression, hostility and discontent
23. Ylang-Ylang - calms emotions of anger and disappointment

Aromatherapy Chart 2

1. *Facilitates Healing and Opening of Heart Chakra:*
   - Gardenia
   - Rose
   - Lavender
   - Tuberose

2. *Calms, Soothes and Strengthens Mental and Emotional States:*
   - Amber (*internal organs*)
   - Frankincense
   - Jasmine
   - Lavender
   - Myrrh
   - Narcissus
   - Rose
   - Sandalwood

3. *Stimulates Crown, Third Eye and Etheric Consciousness:*
   - Gum Mastic
   - Henna
   - Jasmine
   - Lotus
   - Musk
   - Myrrh
   - Sandalwood

4. *Facilitates Evolution of Lower Chakra States:*
   - Agarwood
   - Amber
   - Jasmine
   - Rose

5. *Purifies and Cleanses Environment of Discordant Energies:*
   - Agarwood
   - Cedar
   - Copal
   - Gum Benzoin
   - Juniper
   - Sage
   - Sweet Grass

6. *Invokes Benevolent Energies and Spirit Presence:*
   - Amber
   - Copal
   - Gum Benzoin
   - Gum Mastic
   - Sandalwood
   - Sweet Grass

7. *Generates Atmosphere Conducive for Meditation:*
   - Frankincense
   - Gum Benzoin
   - Gum Mastic
   - Musk
   - Myrrh
   - Sandalwood
   - Sweet Grass

Appendix II

TRANS-CULTURAL SYMBOLS OF INTUITIVE WISDOM

I. COLORS
1. Purple - Strength, Knowingness, Power, Perception, Wisdom
2. Blue - Serenity, Understanding, Wisdom, Patience, Objectivity
3. Red - Intensity, Passion, Determination, Danger, Pain, Zeal
4. Yellow/Gold - Conviction, Perseverance, Divine Will
5. Green - Health, Life, Abundance, Prosperity
6. Black - Mystery, Danger, Emptiness, Loneliness, Discordance
7. White - Purity, Truth, Etheric Consciousness
8. Gray - Confusion, Indecision, Resistance, Lack of Clarity
9. Pink - Warmth, Comfort, Compassion, Mercy, Love
10. Lavender/Orchid - Tranquility, Spiritual Evolution, Intuition
11. Brown - Earthiness, Grounded Nature
12. Orange, - Personal Will, Emotional Strength, Conviction

II. GEOMETRIC SHAPES AND FORMS
13. Circle - Completion, Life Continuum
14. Triangle - Elements of Consciousness: Mind-Body-Spirit Complex
15. Square - Blessing of The Four Winds, Balance of Energies of The Four Cardinal Directions, The Four Primary Archangelic Energies, The Four Faces of God
16. Pyramid - Initiation into Aspects of Higher Truths, Etheric Communication
17. Ankh - Eternal Life of The Soul Essence
18. Cross - Christianity, Suffering-Atonement-Salvation, Unity Through The Acts of Benevolence, Love & Peace, Representation of The Human Form
19. Six-Pointed Star - Elements of Divine Truth & Universal Law: Patience, Compassion, Wisdom, Mercy, Serenity & Love
20. Five-Pointed Star - Doorway to Universal Expansion of Consciousness

III. TOOLS

21. Hammer - to build or repair various aspects of states of consciousness; to repair or replace walls of illusion of ego-facilitating facades

22. Key - to unlock mysteries of consciousness or to access hidden Truth; to release self from one state of consciousness and to proceed toward another, more viable state of being

23. Axe - to chop away or through counterproductive thought and/or behavior patterns; to chop through walls of illusion

24. Vise - to hold fast in resistance to or refusal of acknowledgement of change or need for change in thought or behavior patterns; to be trapped, held captive, in counterproductive thought and/or behavior patterns

25. Saw - to cut through or trim away unnecessary aspects of conditioned behaviors

26. Rope - to tie together various aspects of being; to restrict mobility or movement toward understanding or resolving discordance; to hold in bondage; to limit access to elements of Divine Truth

27. Clamp - to hold together, bond or integrate different elements or aspects of one's consciousness; to prevent growth or to retard development of Spiritual Consciousness

28. Scissors - to trim away rough edges of thought or behavior processes; to refine expressions of various aspects of consciousness

29. Knife - to pierce through layers of conditioned behaviors to access understanding of factors responsible for discordant episodes; common tool used to represent degrees of anger and rage

30. Fence/Wall - obstacle designed to impede The Unfoldment Process; barrier placed to protect self from invasion, exposure or emotional injury; barrier designed to shield self from True Reality of one's life condition; barrier designed to protect care-

fully constructed illusion of self; demarcation point between two mutually exclusive aspects of self or states of being

31. Needle & Thread - to repair minor damage or injury to emotional matrix
32. Shovel - to dig beneath the surface; to go beyond the apparent reality; to dig through layers of confusion or discordance to access core motivations for behaviors that facilitate the releasing of self from counterproductive life conditions
33. Rake, Hoe, Pick - to clear entanglements; to make ready for the seeding of elements of Higher Consciousness

IV. TREES & FLOWERS

34. Cedar - Purity, Spiritual Upliftment, Power, Prosperity, Longevity
35. Weeping Willow - Compassion, Grace, Sadness, Mercy
36. Oak - Majesty, Character, Strength, Dominance
37. Douglas Fir/Pine - Cleansing, Purification, Purging of Discordance
38. Redwood - Longevity, Wisdom, Perseverance
39. Rose - Beauty, Love, Devotion
40. Lotus Blossom - Enlightenment, Perfection, Spiritual Truth/Evolution, Crown Chakra Opening, Beauty
41. Corn/Rice - Sustenance, Basic Nourishment for Survival
42. Olive Branch - Peace

V. ACTIVITIES

43. Running - Escape, Fear of Confrontation
44. Flying - Freedom
45. Swimming - Bonding with the Element of Water, Engaging in Cleansing Ritual
46. Falling - Helplessness
47. Floating (in midair) - Release from Earthly Burdens, State of Bliss

VI. OBJECTS, PLACES & MODES OF TRANSPORTATION

48. Blanket - Warmth, Security, Dependency
49. Rocking Chair - Contentment, Contemplation
50. Bed - Rest, Sleep, Sexual Encounter
51. Hotel/Building Complex/Mall - Microcosm of Reality, Multiplicity of Reality Factors, Unknown Elements of Personal Reality Awaiting Discover
52. Escalator/Elevator/Stairway - Ascension, Movement from One State of Consciousness to Another
53. Car - Transition, Possibility of Change, Extension of Ego-Self
54. Castle - Intrigue, Chivalry, Romance, Adventure
55. Bridge - Transition From or Connection Between Two Aspects of Consciousness or Two States of Being or Two Elements of Reality
56. Tunnel - Uncertain Passageway, Transition Through Darkness
57. Train - Grounding of Earthly Consciousness, Transforming Perceptions of Reality
58. Ship/Boat - Lulling Discordance into States Conducive to Transmutation; Air of Freshness Infused into One's Perception of Reality; Transition through Cleansing/Release Process
59. Airplane - Rapid Transition through States of Etheric Consciousness; Understanding and Acceptance of States of Higher Consciousness Resultant from the Integration of Etheric and Mental Processes

VII. NATURAL SETTINGS/OCCURRENCES

60. Mountain - Serenity, Enlightenment, Solitude
61. Cave - Inner Self, Inner Sanctuary, Hidden Agenda
62. Rain/Drops of Water - Tears, Purging, Release or Expression of Pain, Sadness or Unhappiness
63. Rivers/Waterfalls (running water) - Cleansing of Discordance
64. Ocean Waves - Cleansing, Rebirthing
65. Lake - Reservoir of Life, Hope, Consciousness

66. Jungle/Tropical Rain Forest - Entanglements, Confusion, Abundance, Complexity
67. Mountain Valley - Security, Protection, Seclusion, Hope
68. Fire - Purification, Destruction, Passion
69. Volcanic Eruption - Explosive Discharge of Deep-Seated Emotions
70. Earthquake - Realignment of Energy States, Thought Patterns or Emotional Conditions
71. Sun - Giver of Life, Energizer, Masculine Presence, Stimulates Hope and Sense of Well Being
72. Moon - Feminine Cycle, Emotional Expressions

VIII. ANIMALS

73. Bald Eagle - Etheric Truth, Spiritual Freedom, Unfettered Flight, One's Reality of Truth, Supreme Knowledge
74. Golden Eagle - Spirit-Keeper, Transmutation of Discordant Energies
75. Hawk - Perception of True Reality, Bearer of Messages from The God Spirit
76. Owl - Illumination, Wisdom, Silence in Traversing Life's Obstacles
77. Snowy Owl - Supreme Protecting Spirit Presence for the Earthly Consciousness of Mortal Man
78. Crow - Seer of Two Worlds–the World of Spirit & the World of Man, Holds Key to The Duality of Truth Principle, Spirit-Keeper of The Sacred Laws of Existence
79. Dove - Purity, Peace, Harmony
80. Lion - Strength, Power, Independence, Aggression
81. Tiger - Fearlessness, Disciplined Awareness, Self-Containment
82. Leopard - Treachery, Cunning, Unpredictability
83. Cheetah - Speed, Concentration, Decisiveness
84. Mountain Lion - Strength, Independence, Conviction, Authority
85. Bear - Wisdom, Introspection, Loyalty, Strength of Conviction

86. Dog - Loyalty, Companionship
87. Cat (domestic) - Independence, Free-Spirited Life Condition, Awareness of All Aspects of Reality
88. Snake - Earth Energy of Protection Through The Release of Discordance, Grounding Vibration
89. Deer - Innocence, Gentleness, Frailty
90. Badger - Anger, Aggression, Assertiveness
91. Wolf - Knowledge, Devotion, Loyalty
92. Cobra - Protective Earth Spirit Presence
93. Horse - Strength, Power, Endurance
94. Rabbit - Fear, Impulsiveness, Nervousness
95. Fox - Cleverness, Stealth, Adaptability
96. Lamb - Purity, Gentleness, Innocence
97. Butterfly - Transformation
98. Turtle - Fortitude, Self-Sufficiency, Consciousness of Mother Earth
99. Lizard - Regeneration
100. Porcupine - Self-Assurance, Defense Without Aggression, Trust
101. Squirrel - Industriousness, Preparation
102. Bat - Spiritual Initiation, Rebirth
103. Vulture - Self-Centeredness, Opportunism
104. Buffalo - Honor, Humility Through Prayer, Gratitude, Abundant Life
105. Cow - Life-Giving Energy That Shows Respect for All Things
106. Scarab - Cycles of Life, Rebirth
107. Dragon - Earth Energy of Life & Knowledge, Energetic, Powerful & Unwavering
108. Spider - Creative Vibration, Weaver of Illusion, Demonstrates The Unlimited Patterns or Possibilities of Life
109. Sea Gull - Endurance, Perseverance
110. Baby (human) - Beginnings, Freshness, Innocence, Dependence, Responsibility, Fresh Start, Fledgling Idea, New Project

IX. NUMBERS

111. One - Unity, Force of Creation
112. Two - Duality, Polarity
113. Three - Trinity, Spiritual Completion
114. Four - Stability, Dependability, Purpose
115. Five - Change, Versatility
116. Six - Christ-Consciousness, Compassion, Balance, Intuition, Peace, Harmony
117. Seven - Perfect Order
118. Eight - Evolution, Regeneration, Balance
119. Nine - Truth, Completion, Initiation
120. Ten - Perfection, Unity, Completion of Project or Phase of Growth
121. Eleven - New Beginnings, Start of More Sophisticated Processes of Consciousness
122. Twelve - Spiritual Perfection, Completion, Cosmic Order

Appendix III

CRYSTALS AND MINERALS FOR LOVING TOUCH THERAPY™

Agate, Blue Lace - (5) - 18x13mm, (1) 25x18mm

Amethyst Quartz - (5) 16x12mm, (1) 18x13mm

Aventurine - (5) 18x13mm, (1) 25x18mm

Citrine Quartz - (6) 12x10mm

Emerald - (1) 7x5mm

Garnet - (4) 10mm round

Jade, Green - (5) 16x12mm, (1) 18x13mm

Jasper, Red - (5) 18x13mm, (1) 25x18mm

Lapis Lazuli - (5) 16x12mm, (1) 18x13mm

Malachite - (10) 10mm round

Moonstone - (1) Peach 12x10mm, (1) Silver 12x10mm

Obsidian, Mahogany - (5) 18x13mm, (5) 25x18mm, (1) 40x30mm

Obsidian, Rainbow - (2) free-form shapes 15-40gm each

Obsidian, Sheen - (2) polished eggs 175-300gm each

Obsidian, Snowflake - (5) 18x13mm, (5) 25x18mm, (1) 40x30mm

Peridot - (3) 7x5mm

Quartz Crystal Generator - (1) 35-125gm

Rhodocrosite - (2) 18x13mm

Rhodonite - (5) 18x13mm, (5) 25x18mm, (1) 40x30mm

Rose Quartz - (5) 25x18mm, (1) 40x30mm

Ruby - (1) 6x4mm

Tiger's Eye - (5) 18x13mm, (5) 25x18mm, (1) 40x30mm

Turquoise - (1) 18x13mm

Unakite - (5) 18x13mm, (5) 25x18mm, (1) 40x30mm

Appendix IV

CRYSTAL/MINERAL - CHAKRA ASSOCIATIONS

BASE CHAKRA - 1st

Apache Tears
Black Tourmaline *(Schorl)*
Fire Agate
Garnet
Hematite
Mahogany Obsidian
Neptunite

Plume Agate
Rainbow Obsidian
Rhodonite
Ruby
Snowflake Obsidian
Smoky Quartz
Tourmalated Quartz

NAVEL CHAKRA - 2nd

Amber
Barite
Bloodstone
Carnelian
Chrysotile
Citrine Quartz
Fire Agate
Mahogany
Moss Agate

Plume Agate
Pyrophyllite
Realgar
Rutilated Quartz
Tiger's Eye
Topaz *(Imperial, Golden)*
Vanadanite
Wulfenite

SOLAR PLEXUS CHAKRA - 3rd

Amber
Apatite *(Yellow)*
Chrysotile
Malachite
Pampa Onyx

Peridot
Rhodocrosite
Sulfur
Sunstone
Topaz *(Golden)*

HEART CHAKRA - 4th

Actinolite

Alunite

Atacamite

Aventurine *(Green)*

Chrysocolla

Chrysoprase

Chrysotile

Cuprite

Dioptase

Emerald

Green Tourmaline *(Elbaite)*

Jade

Kunzite *(Pink)*

Moonstone

Orthoclase

Pampa Onyx

Peridot

Pink Tourmaline

Rhodocrosite

Rose Quartz

Unakite

Variscite

Zoisite

THROAT CHAKRA - 5th

Amazonite

Apatite *(Blue)*

Aquamarine

Blue Lace Agate

Blue Tourmaline *(Indicolite)*

Kyanite *(Blue)*

Larimar

Turquoise

Youngite

THIRD EYE CHAKRA - 6th

Amethyst

Apophyllite

Azurite

Calcite

Chalcopyrite

Fluorite

Iolite

Labradorite

Lapis Lazuli

Lazulite

Moonstone

Pyrite

Smithsonite

Sodalite

Sugilite

Youngite

CROWN CHAKRA - 7th

Adamite

Apophyllite

Aragonite

Calcite

Celestite

Clear Quartz

Danberite

Diamond

Moonstone

Satin Kyanite

Selenite

Ulexite

ETHERIC SELF - 8TH *through* 12th

Adamite

Anhydrite

Apophyllite

Calcite *(Mango, Salmon)*

Onyx

Smithsonite

Stibnite

Zebrastone

Appendix V

LIST OF CHARTS, FIGURES, DIAGRAMS & ILLUSTRATIONS

In Acknowledgement Of

The Omnipresent Grace And Illumination

Granted By The One Infinite Creator,

Without Which This Text Could Not

Have Been Written -

Sri Akhenaton

ACKNOWLEDGEMENTS

Typesetting:
Janice Ellis

Book Design, Illustrations, Cover Design:
Marten Graphics
Columbia, Maryland

Proof Reading:
Marilyn Egbert
Ann Galiber
Nana Ewool-Robotham

Cover Concept:
Sri Akhenaton

Printer:
Thomson-Shore, Inc.
Dexter, Michigan

SPECIAL NOTES

The author and publisher welcome comments regarding the nature and content of this text. Sri Akhenaton will personally answer letters received by the publisher.

Please address comments to:

Sri Akhenaton
c/o THE PORTAL PRESS
P. O. Box 1449
Columbia, Maryland 21044

Additional copies of this text can be obtained from the publisher by sending $21.95 plus $3.85 for postage and handling (*Maryland residents, please include 5% sales tax*) to the address above.

On-Line Retailing
of Consecrated Spiritual Products

Portal Enterprises offers a unique collection of Consecrated Spiritual Products that have been cleansed, blessed and prepared by Sri Akhenaton. Through Sri Akhenaton, Oils, Incenses and Crystals are charged with Divine Light Vibrations to enhance the resonance pattern of each item. This additional preparation ensures that the Consecrated Spiritual Products prepared at Portal Enterprises will resonate with optimum efficiency and the highest intensity within The Spectrum of Divine Light.

To view our selection of Consecrated Oils, Incenses, Crystals, Spiritual Tools, Books and our extensive line of Nutritional Supplements, visit our Web Site at www.portal-found.com.

PORTAL ENTERPRISES
P. O. Box 1449
Columbia, Maryland 21044
or
call us at (301) 317-5873
Fax: (301) 317-9081
E-Mail: portal@portal-found.com

When in the Baltimore/Washington, D.C. metropolitan area, plan a visit to The Crystal Gallery at Portal Enterprises, where over 100 different varieties of Crystals & Minerals, Oils, Incenses and Spiritual Tools are displayed and offered for sale. Call or write in advance for Gallery hours and directions.

BOOKS by SRI AKHENATON

LOVING TOUCH: The Sacred Covenant of Divine Communion
ISBN 0-9621839-8-9 $21.95 + $3.85 postage & handling

THE DAWNING: Coming of Age
ISBN 0-9621839-7-0 $11.95 + $3.85 postage & handling

CRYSTAL COMMUNION: LoveLight Meditations
ISBN 0-9621839-4-6 $21.95 + $3.85 postage & handling

REFLECTIONS FROM THE GOLDEN MIND
ISBN 0-9621839-6-2 $12.95 + $3.85 postage & handling

**DISCUSSIONS OF SPIRITUAL ATTUNEMENT
& SOUL EVOLUTION, VOLUME II**
ISBN 0-9621839-5-4 $12.95 + $3.85 postage & handling

AUTHOR PROFILE

An evolved Mystic and an innovative Teacher of diverse Esoteric, Spiritual Philosophies, Sri Akhenaton serves the needs of Creation by offering inspired, Heart-centered principles of Divine Love and the profound simplicity of The Wisdom of One to seekers of Enlightenment to help comfort and explain the experience of mortal life. Through Spiritual, intuitive and practical guidance that ultimately leads aspirants to the unfoldment of God-Conscious Being, Sri Akhenaton touches the hearts and fills the souls of those he embraces with The Light of The Living God Spirit to assist each person in comprehending the nature of the Spiritual Path, the purpose of life on Earth and in rediscovering the true meaning of being "a child of God."

Sri Akhenaton is a beacon of Truth and Love illuminating the darkness of uncertainty, fear, anger, suffering and disbelief with The Divine Radiance of The Light and Conscience of One, thereby revealing The Universal Acknowledgement that all things born of Creation contain the same Light/Life Vibration of Divine Consciousness, and warrant the same care, consideration and Loving Kindness that man would deem appropriate for him/herself.

It is with the deepest Sincerity and Conviction that Sri Akhenaton offers his life and consciousness as tools to transmit The Divine Light Energy of The One Infinite Creator, and in so doing, assist in facilitating the evolutionary moment of awakening to God-Conscious Being for the collective soul of man. Through his teachings and practice of "Trans-Cultural" Spiritual Consciousness, Sri Akhenaton embraces the journey of life with Serenity, Patience, Compassion and joyful wonderment, taking "one day, one step at a time," in his giving of Self for The Greater Good of All Creation.

*Printed with Soy Ink
on Recycled Paper*